Fessenden Nott Otis

Illustrated History of the Panama Railroad

Fessenden Nott Otis

Illustrated History of the Panama Railroad

ISBN/EAN: 9783744696852

Printed in Europe, USA, Canada, Australia, Japan

Cover: Foto ©ninafisch / pixelio.de

More available books at www.hansebooks.com

ERRATA.

Page 56, line 2 from top, for Appendix C, p. 139, read *Appendix D, p. 145, et seq.*

Page 76, last line, for literal read *littoral.*

Page 179, under the cut, read Tower of San Jerome, *at Old Panama.*

Page 182, line 17 from top, for 45,000 read 4500.

Page 213, line 2 from bottom, for page 88, et seq., read page 141, et seq.

Page 214, line 18 from top, for Panama Mail Steamship Company read *Pacific Mail and Panama Railroad Steam-ship Companies.*

Page 231, line 2 from top, for copper, and barilla, read and copper barilla.

ILLUSTRATED HISTORY

OF

THE PANAMA RAILROAD;

TOGETHER WITH A

TRAVELER'S GUIDE AND BUSINESS MAN'S HANDBOOK FOR THE PANAMA RAILROAD AND ITS CONNECTIONS

WITH

EUROPE, THE UNITED STATES, THE NORTH AND SOUTH ATLANTIC AND PACIFIC COASTS, CHINA, AUSTRALIA, AND JAPAN, BY SAIL AND STEAM.

BY F. N. OTIS.

NEW YORK:
HARPER & BROTHERS, PUBLISHERS,
FRANKLIN SQUARE.
1861.

Entered, according to Act of Congress, in the year one thousand eight hundred and sixty-one, by

F. N. OTIS,

In the Clerk's Office of the District Court of the Southern District of New York.

PREFACE.

In preparing the "Hand-book of the Panama Railroad," the endeavor has been to present,

1. A full and reliable history of the road, from the inception of the original contract to the present day, and such an account of its present condition and business regulations as would be likely to interest and benefit the traveling and commercial public.

2. All necessary information for the shipper and the traveler concerning the various lines of steam and sail communication connecting with the road.

3. A brief account of the present condition, commercial and other resources, of the countries bordering the Pacific coast, and doing business with the United States and Europe over the Panama Railroad, with such information in regard to the expenses connected with commercial transactions in those countries as it has been thought would prove serviceable to the mercantile and shipping interests.

In preparing this work from the most recent authorities and reliable sources, the strictest accuracy has been the first consideration. The tariffs and commercial regulations have been taken from documents published by the United States government in 1858. To the following works (not credited in place) the Author is indebted for valuable statistics: *Harper's Cyclopædia of Commerce*, 1858; *Appleton's American Cyclopædia*, 1860–1861. To Mr. DAVID HOADLEY, President of the Panama Railroad, Mr. ALLAN M'LANE, President of the Pacific Mail Steam-ship Company, Mr. GEORGE M. TOTTEN, Chief Engineer, Mr. JOSEPH F. JOY, Secretary, and Mr. ALEXANDER J. CENTER, former Vice-president and Superintendent of the Panama Railroad, the Author is indebted for great and uniform kindness in affording facilities for procuring reliable data, and for much important information; also to Capt. J. M. Dow, of the steam-ship Guatemala (Central American Steam-ship Company), Mr. WM. NELSON, Commercial Agent of the Panama Railroad Company at Panama, Mr. CHARLES T. BIDWELL, Agent for the Pacific Steam Navigation Company at Panama, Mr. GEORGE PETRIE, General Manager of the Pacific Steam Navigation Company at Callao, Mr. J. W. HAWES, of Panama, and Capt. J. H. WINDLE, of Tarrytown, New York (formerly in the United States Mail Steam-ship Company's service), the Author is indebted for valuable favors.

F. N. OTIS.

New York, July 15, 1861.

CONTENTS.

HISTORY OF THE PANAMA RAILROAD.

Importance of the Panama Railroad, p.15. Geographical Position of the Isthmus, 15. Early Projects for Transit, 16. Messrs. Aspinwall and Law's Mail Contracts, 16. Mr. Aspinwall's ulterior Views, 17. Messrs. Chauncey and Stephens, 17. Mr. Baldwin's Exploration, 17. Contract with New Granada, 17. Company chartered, 18. Survey of the Line, 21. Difficulties of the Work, 22. Messrs. Totten and Trautwine's Contract, 22. Gorgona selected as the Atlantic Terminus, 22. Abandoned for Navy Bay, 25. Totten and Trautwine as Engineers, 25. Manzanilla Island, 26. Breaking Ground, 26. Arrival of Mr. Stephens, 27. Work in the Swamp, 27. The first Shanty, 31. Sickness of the Laborers, 31. Progress of the Work, 32. The first Train, 32. Aspinwall named, 33. Death of Mr. Stephens, 34. Contract with Mr. Story abandoned, 34. Mr. Hoadley elected President, 35. Mortality among the Laborers, 35. Work from the Panama Side, 36. The first through Train, 36. General Description of the Road, 36-39. Works at the Termini, 40. Permanent Works on the Line, 41. The Bridge at Barbacoas, 41. Table of Grades, 42. Operations at Aspinwall and Panama, 42, 45. Receipts and Expenses of the Road, 46. Health of the Isthmus, 46. Safety to Property, 49. Sources of the Business of the Road, 50. Ocean Connections with the Road, 51. Connections with the Pacific Coast, 52-55. Character of the Service performed, 56.

APPENDIX A.

Merchandise and Treasure passing over the Road in 1859-60, p. 57, 58.

APPENDIX B.

Financial Statements of the Road from 1852 to 1860, p. 61-69.

TRAVELER'S GUIDE.

Table of Distances, *via* Cape Horn and the Isthmus, p. 70. The City of Aspinwall, 73. The Wharf, 73. Shops and Hotels, 74. Telegraph, 75. The Freight Depôt, 76. The Mingillo, 76. San Blas Indians, 77. The Ice-house, 78. Public Buildings, 78, 79. The Paseo Coral, 79. Climate and Productions of the Isthmus, 80-83. Journey over the Road,

CONTENTS.

80–131. Mangrove Bushes, 84. Oysters, 84. Mount Hope, 87. Birds, 87. Vegetation, 88. Alligators, 89. The Mindee, 90. Palms, 90. Gatun Station, 93. Lion and Tiger Hills, 94. The Espiritu Santo, 95. Ahorca Lagarto, 96. Stephens's Tree, 96. The Forest, 101. Bujio Soldado, 101. Stephens's Cottage, 102. Bueno Vistita, 102. Aborigines, 102. Fruits, 105. Natives, 106. Frijoli Station, 106. The Machete, 106. Animal Life, 107. Barbacoas, 108. San Pablo Station, 113. Mamei, 113. Matachin, 113. Gorgona, 113. Obispo, 114. Empire Station, 119. Culebra, 119. The Summit, 119. The Descent, 119. Basaltic Cliffs, 120. Paraiso, 125. The Hill of the Buccaneers, 125. The Rio Grande, 125. Panama, 126. Situation, 126. History, 131. Antiquities, 131.

APPENDIX C.

Time-table of the Panama Railroad, p. 137. Steamer Trains, 137. Rates for Freight and Passage, 137–140. Classification of Freight, 138. Rates of Coinage received and paid out by the Panama Railroad, 140. Wharfage, Lighterage, and Harbor Regulations, 141–144. Regulations in regard to Freight, 141. Rates of Storage, 142. Rates of Wharfage and Light Money, 143. Harbor Regulations of the Port of Aspinwall, 143. Through Bills of Lading from Europe and the United States to Panama, San Francisco, Oregon, Washington Territory, etc., 144.

APPENDIX D.

Steam and Sail Lines connecting with the Panama Railroad, p. 145. Rates of Passage and Freight, 145. ATLANTIC AND PACIFIC STEAM-SHIP COMPANY—Rates of Passage and Freight, 145. PACIFIC MAIL STEAM-SHIP COMPANY—Rates of Passage and Freight, 146. OREGON AND CALIFORNIA STEAM-SHIP COMPANY—Rates of Passage and Freight, Ports, etc., 148, 149. CENTRAL AMERICAN STEAM-SHIP LINE—Ports, Time of Arrival and Departure, Prices of Passage and Freight, 149, 150. Rates of through Freight from Central America to Aspinwall and to South American Ports, 150. Rates of through Freight from New York, by sail vessels, etc., to Central American Ports, 151. Through Bills of Lading from Central American Ports to Liverpool, 151, 152. PACIFIC STEAM NAVIGATION COMPANY—Itinerary, Rates of Passage and Freight, through Bills of Lading, etc., 152–157. ROYAL MAIL STEAM PACKET COMPANY—Agencies, List of Ships, 158. Itinerary, 159. Prices of Passage, etc., 160–173. HOLT'S LIVERPOOL AND WEST INDIA SHIPS—Rates of Freight, under through Bills of Lading, to Central American Ports, 174. Panama Railroad Company's Sailing Vessels between New York and Aspinwall—through Bills of Lading to Ports of South America, 175, 176. Rates of Freight, etc., 176, 177.

OFFICERS AND DIRECTORS OF THE PANAMA RAILROAD, p. 178.

THE REPUBLICS OF CENTRAL AMERICA.

Ports of Entry for American Steamers, and Distances between each, p. 181. —*Costa Rica:* Statistics, 182. Climate, 183. Harbor Regulations, 185. Custom-house Regulations, 186. Exports, 187. Coins and Weights, 187. **Tariff,** 187. Rates of Wages, 188.—*Nicaragua:* Statistics, 188. Climate and Productions, 190.—*San Salvador:* Statistics, 193. Topography, 194. Tariff, 196. Harbors, 197. Commercial Regulations, 197.—*Guatemala:* Statistics, 198. Climate and Productions, 199. Political Divisions, 201. Inhabitants, 202. Ports, 202. Harbor Regulations, 204. **Tariff,** 205. Imports and Exports, 206. Wages, 206.

THE REPUBLICS OF SOUTH AMERICA.

New Granada: Climate, p. 207. Population, 208. Political Divisions, 209. Productions, 209. Education, 210. Bogotá, 210. Rivers, 211. Ports, 211. Aspinwall and Panama, 213. Tides, 214. Port Regulations, 216. Tariff, 216.—*Ecuador:* Statistics, 219. Productions, 220. Climate, 221. Population, 221. Quito, 222. Ports, 222. Exports and Imports, 223. Port Regulations, 223. Currency, 223. Tariff, 224.—*Peru:* Statistics, 225. Productions, 226. Political Divisions, 226. Population, 227. Education, 227. Lima, 227. Exports, 229. Ports, 229. Currency, 231. Tariff, 232.—*Bolivia:* Statistics, 234. Productions, 235. Tariff, 236.— *Chili:* Statistics, 237. Productions, 238. Exports, 239. Climate, 239. Inhabitants, 239. Santiago, 240. Valparaiso, 242. Ports, 241–245. Imports, 244. Tariff, 245. Port Charges, 246.

MEXICO.

Connections with the Panama Railroad Company, p. 247. Pacific Mail Company and Flint and Holliday's Steam Lines, 247. Acapulco, 247. Manzanilla, 248. Other Pacific Ports, 248. Trade with these Ports, 249. Passenger Regulations, 250. Mexican Currency, 251.

CALIFORNIA, OREGON, VANCOUVER, ETC.

California: San Francisco, p. 253. Exports of California, 254. Production of Gold from 1848 to 1860, 254. Shipments of Treasure in 1860, 255. Exports of Silver and Quicksilver, 255. Other Exports from California, 256. Imports, 256. Passengers to and from San Francisco, 257. —*Oregon, etc.:* Productions, 258. Sea-ports, 259. Express Business to the Pacific Coasts, 261. Wells, Fargo, and Company, 261. **Express Rates,** 263. Express Agencies and Offices, 263.

ILLUSTRATIONS.

ON THE ROAD	*Frontispiece.*
MAP—THE LINE OF THE PANAMA RAILROAD	Page 5
MAP—CONNECTIONS OF THE PANAMA RAILROAD	6
WESTERN SUBURB OF PANAMA	14
RUNNING THE LINES	20
PARAISO	23
THE FIRST SHANTY	30
ANCIENT BRIDGE, OLD PANAMA	37
THE CABILDO, PANAMA	43
VIEW FROM THE RAMPARTS, PANAMA	47
NORTHEASTERN RAMPART, PANAMA	53
SOUTHEASTERN RAMPART, PANAMA	59
VIEW OF ASPINWALL	72
DEPARTURE FOR PANAMA	81
MOUNT HOPE	86
GATUN STATION	92
STEPHENS'S TREE	97
BUJIO SOLDADO	100
STEPHENS'S COTTAGE	103
BREAD-FRUIT, STAR-APPLE, MANGO, AVOCADO PEAR	105
BARBACOAS BRIDGE	109
SAN PABLO STATION	112
NATIVE HUT AT MATACHIN	114
MAMEI STATION	115
MONUMENT HILL	117
BASALTIC CLIFF	121
PARAISO STATION	124
TERMINUS AT PANAMA	127
CITY OF PANAMA	130
CATHEDRAL AT PANAMA	133
RUINS OF CHURCH OF SAN DOMINGO	136
TOWER OF SAN JEROME	179
NATIVE BONGO, PANAMA	191

WESTERN SUBURB (SANTA ANA) OF PANAMA.

HAND-BOOK

OF

THE PANAMA RAILROAD.

In ancient or in modern times there has, perhaps, been no one work which in a few brief years has accomplished so much, and which promises for the future so great benefit to the commercial interests of the world, as the present railway thoroughfare between the Atlantic and Pacific Oceans at the Isthmus of Panama. A glance at its geographical position can not fail to discover to the most casual observer that, situated as it is midway between the northern and southern, and alike between the eastern and western hemispheres, it forms a natural culminating point for the great commercial travel of the globe. Wise men in every enlightened nation had seen this for centuries, and had urged the importance of free interoceanic communication at this point; but its lofty and rugged mountain ranges, its deep and pestiferous morasses, seemed almost equally to defy the skill of the engineer and the physical endurance of the laborer. Even the possibility of opening such a communication by the government exercising jurisdiction over that portion of the isthmus through which it should pass had never been seriously entertained; but New Granada had long and earnestly challenged the more powerful nations of the world to break down this barrier to commerce and civilization, and reap the richest benefits which might result therefrom. England had looked toward the project with longing eyes, but quailed before the magnitude of the labor. France had done more—surveyed and entered into a contract to establish it; but too many millions were found necessary for its completion, and it was lost by default.

Events at last occurred which turned the attention of the American people to this transit, viz., the settlement of the northwestern boundary, by which we came into possession of Oregon, and the war with Mexico, which added California to our possessions. But, while the accession of these territories was of the highest importance to us in a national point of view, their distance rendered them almost inaccessible to the class of emigrants who usually settle our new domains, as well as inconvenient to the proper administration of law and government. Still, urged on by that pioneering spirit which seems inherent in the blood of the American, and invited by the prolific soil and genial climate of these distant possessions, and a prospect of a new and enlarged field for commercial pursuits, large numbers of our people migrated thither around Cape Horn. Congress, however, in 1848, in order to render these countries more accessible, authorized contracts to be entered into for the establishment of two mail lines of steam-ships, the one from New York and New Orleans to Chagres, and the other to connect with this by the Isthmus of Panama, from Panama to California and Oregon. The inducements to invest in these projects were not sufficient to attract the favorable attention of capitalists, and the contracts were taken by parties without means, who offered them for sale, and for a long time without success.

Men were at last found bold enough to venture upon the enterprise. Mr. William H. Aspinwall secured the line on the Pacific side, and George Law that on the Atlantic. In the Atlantic contract there was comparatively little risk, and a promise of almost immediate remuneration, as it connected with the cities of Savannah and New Orleans, and terminated at the portals of the Pacific Ocean. But the

Pacific contract was looked upon by the generality of business men as a certain sequestration of a large amount of property for an indefinite time, with a faint prospect of profit; and the wonder seemed to be that so sound a man as Mr. Aspinwall should have engaged in it. But it soon became evident that he expected no great profit from the steam-ship line *per se;* but that, with those enlarged and far-reaching views for which he is so justly noted, this line was only a part of the great plan which he had conceived, the remainder being embraced in the bold design of a railroad across the Isthmus of Panama; and at this time he, with Mr. Henry Chauncey and Mr. John L. Stephens, entered into a contract with the government of New Granada for the construction of that work. Mr. Chauncey, like Mr. Aspinwall, was a large-minded and public-spirited capitalist, whose integrity and straightforwardness were undoubted. Mr. Stephens possessed an experience in the country through which the road was to pass, and a knowledge of its geography and its inhabitants, gained by practical study and observation. These three gentlemen were associated together for the prosecution of this great enterprise, and shortly after, Mr. Stephens, accompanied by Mr. J. L. Baldwin, a skillful and experienced engineer, made an exploration of the route, and decided upon its entire feasibility, dissipating the fears entertained by many that no line could be established without such heavy grades as would interfere materially with the paying character of the undertaking by the discovery of a summit gap no more than three hundred feet above the ocean level.

A formal contract was then entered into with the government of New Granada, on the most favorable terms, for the exclusive privilege of constructing a railroad across the Isthmus of Panama. Among the most important concessions by the terms of this contract was one guaranteeing that all public lands lying on the line of the road were to be used gratuitously by the **Company**; also a gift of 250,000 acres of land, to be selected by the grantees from any public lands on the Isthmus. Two ports, one on the Atlantic and the other on the Pacific (which were to be the termini of the road), were to be *free* ports; and the privilege was granted of establishing such tolls as the Company might think proper. The contract was to continue in force for forty-nine years, subject to the right of New Granada to take possession of the road at the expiration of twenty years after its completion, on payment of five millions of dollars; at the expiration of thirty years, on payment of four millions; and at the expiration of forty years, on payment of two millions. Three per cent. was to be paid to the New Granadian government upon all dividends declared. The entire work was to be completed within eight years, and a sum of one hundred and twenty thousand dollars was to be deposited at its commencement, as security for the fulfillment of the contract, but to be refunded, with interest, on the completion of the road within the given time.

Up to this period calculations for the ultimate success of the undertaking were based upon the advantages it would afford in shortening, by many thousand miles, not only the route to California and Oregon, but to China, Australia, and the East Indies, and in the development of the rich, but then almost inaccessible countries bordering the whole Pacific coast. At this time, however (the latter part of 1848), the discovery of gold in California, with its accompanying tide of emigration across the Isthmus of Panama, changed the prospects of this projected road; and, from an enterprise which looked far into the future for its rewards, it became one promising immediate returns from the capital and labor invested, and in which the people, as well as the government of the United States, must be immediately and deeply interested. A charter was now granted by the Legislature of the State of New York for the formation of a

RUNNING THE LINES.

stock company, under which one million dollars of stock was taken—the original grantees having previously transferred their contract into the hands of this company. A large and experienced party of engineers, under the command of Colonel G. W. Hughes, of the United States Topographical Corps, were sent down, in the early part of 1849, to survey and locate the line of the road. The result of their work not only confirmed the previous reconnoissance in regard to the entire practicability of the railroad, but another summit gap was discovered by Mr. J. L. Baldwin, thirty-seven feet lower than that previously established by him, and a line was run from ocean to ocean not exceeding fifty miles in length. The Pacific terminus of the road was located at the city of Panama, on Panama Bay, and the Atlantic terminus at Navy Bay, on the Atlantic shore.

The character and geographical position of the country through which the line of the road had been carried was such as might well have made the hardiest projectors shrink from attempting its construction. The first thirteen miles, beginning at Navy Bay, was through a deep morass, covered with the densest jungle, reeking with malaria, and abounding with almost every species of wild beasts, noxious reptiles, and venomous insects known in the tropics. Farther on, though some of the land was so fair and beautiful that the natives called it *Paraiso*, the greater part of the line was through a rugged country, along steep hill-sides, over wild chasms, spanning turbulent rivers and furious mountain torrents, until the summit-ridge was surmounted, when it descended abruptly to the shores of the Pacific Ocean.

Situated between the parallels of 8° and 9° north of the equator, a sultry tropical heat prevailed throughout the year, nearly half of which time the country was deluged with rains that, if they would not seriously damage the works, were certain to impede their progress, and add greatly to the arduous character of the undertaking. The whole isthmus, though covered with the most luxuriant vegetative growth, possessed little or no timber sufficiently durable to be of use in the construction of a permanent work. The native population, composed of a mongrel race of Spaniards, Indians, and Negroes, were too indolent and unaccustomed to labor to be depended on to any great extent. The resources of the country were entirely inadequate for the support of laborers. Men, materials, and provisions were to be transported thousands of miles. And yet, despite all these obstacles, the dim glimpses of which had, at a previous time, caused European capitalists to shrink back with fear, our bold operators at once, and earnestly, pushed forward this stupendous enterprise.

In the early part of 1849 a contract was entered into with Messrs. George M. Totten and John C. Trautwine for the construction of the road. The services of these gentlemen had been solicited by the Company, not only on account of their previously established reputation as skillful and successful engineers, but from having only a short time before been engaged upon a work of considerable magnitude in a neighboring province—the "Canal del Dique," connecting the Magdalena River with the Caribbean Sea at Carthagena: they had, consequently, a large experience in the character and resources of the country, and the conditions necessary to the success of such a project. The contractors at once proceeded to the Isthmus with a large force, and commenced the final location of the road.

Basing their operations upon the reconnoisance of Colonel Hughes and party, a native town called Gorgona, on the Chagres River, about thirty miles from the Atlantic, was selected as a point for the commencement of the work. This place was chosen on account of the facilities it afforded for communication with the Atlantic by the River Chagres (which was supposed to be navigable to this point for vessels of light draught), by which men, materials, and stores

PARAISO.

could be transported to a central point on the proposed road; and, on the completion of the Pacific section, traffic between the two oceans could at once be established, while the Atlantic section might be completed at the leisure or convenience of the Company. To this end, two steam-boats of very light draught were dispatched to Chagres for the navigation of the river. It was soon ascertained, however, that it was impossible to make use of these boats (drawing only from fourteen to eighteen inches of water), and that even the native bongoes and canoes were capable of the service only by great labor and exposure. In addition to this, the rush of California travel, which was then directed through this river as far as Gorgona, had so raised the hire of the native boatmen that the expense of river transportation was enormously increased. It was therefore determined to change the point of beginning to the Atlantic terminus of the road.

Mr. Trautwine, after a careful survey of the whole line of coast from the mouth of the Chagres to the harbor of Porto Bello, had located this terminus at the island of Manzanilla, on the eastern shore of the Bay of Limon, or Navy Bay, where the city of Aspinwall now stands. It was also found that, instead of a secluded and rarely-visited region, where laborers and materials such as the country afforded were comparatively inexpensive, as was the case when the contract was framed, and had been time out of mind, it was now swarming with emigrants from all parts of the globe *en route* for the land of gold. The conditions under which the contract was entered into were changed, the whole *morale* of the country had assumed an entirely different aspect, and it was evidently impossible to continue the work under the arrangement agreed upon. A fair representation of these things being made to the Company by Messrs. Totten and Trautwine, they were released from their obligations as contractors, and retained as engineers, the Com-

B

pany having determined to take charge of the construction themselves.

The plan of commencing at the Atlantic terminus being approved, Colonel Totten left for Carthagena to make arrangements for procuring an increased supply of laborers. Mr. Trautwine, in company with Mr. Baldwin, as chief assistant engineer, then proceeded to Manzanilla Island with a small party, and commenced clearing in the month of May, 1850. This island, cut off from the main land by a narrow frith, contained an area of a little more than one square mile. It was a virgin swamp, covered with a dense growth of the tortuous, water-loving mangrove, and interlaced with huge vines and thorny shrubs, defying entrance even to the wild beasts common to the country. In the black, slimy mud of its surface alligators and other reptiles abounded; while the air was laden with pestilential vapors, and swarming with sand-flies and musquitoes. These last proved so annoying to the laborers that, unless their faces were protected by gauze veils, no work could be done, even at midday. Residence on the island was impossible. The party had their quarters in an old brig which brought down materials for building, tools, provisions, etc., and was anchored in the bay.

Thus situated, with a mere handful of native assistants —most of the original forty or fifty having previously deserted on account of the higher wages and easier life promised them by the Transit—Messrs. Trautwine and Baldwin struck the first blow upon this great work. No imposing ceremony inaugurated the "breaking ground." Two American citizens, leaping, axe in hand, from a native canoe upon a wild and desolate island, their retinue consisting of half a dozen Indians, who clear the path with rude knives, strike their glittering axes into the nearest tree; the rapid blows reverberate from shore to shore, and the stately cocoa crashes upon the beach. Thus unostentatiously was announced the commencement of a railway, which, from the interests and difficulties involved, might well be looked upon as one of the grandest and boldest enterprises ever attempted.

Work upon the island was now fairly commenced. A portion was cleared, and a temporary store-house erected from the materials on board the brig. On the 1st of June Colonel Totten arrived from Carthagena with forty natives of that province as laborers for the work: these were descendants of the old Spanish slaves, a peaceable and industrious race, who, from having been employed on the works in Carthagena for several years, proved a valuable accession to their forces. Mr. T. was accompanied by Mr. John L. Stephens, the president of the Company, who was on his return from Bogotá, where he had been to obtain some important revisions in the contract. With their increased corps the clearing progressed rapidly; but the rainy season soon setting in, the discomforts to which they were subjected were very great. The island was still uninhabitable, and the whole party were forced to live on board the brig, which was crowded to its utmost capacity. Here they were by no means exempt from the causes which deterred them from living on shore, for below decks the vessel was alive with musquitoes and sand-flies, which were a source of such annoyance and suffering that almost all preferred to sleep upon the deck, exposed to the drenching rains, rather than endure their attacks. In addition to this, most of their number were kept nauseated by the ceaseless motion of the vessel. Labor and malarious influences during the day, exposure and unrest at night, soon told upon their health, and in a short time more than half the party were attacked with malarious fevers. Having neither a physician nor any comfortable place of rest, their sufferings were severe. At this time the hull of a condemned steam-boat—the Telegraph —lying at Chagres, was purchased, and sent down as a residence. This proved a vast improvement upon the accommodations afforded by the brig, but still annoyance from the insects was at times almost insupportable.

In the latter part of June Mr. Totten again left for Carthagena to procure more men, and Messrs. Stephens and Trautwine returned to New York to digest farther plans of procedure. The work was left in charge of Mr. Baldwin, who continued the clearing with his crippled forces until the latter part of the following month, when Mr. Totten returned with fifty more laborers. Surveys of the island and adjacent country were now pushed vigorously onward. It was in the depth of the rainy season, and the working parties, in addition to being constantly drenched from above, were forced to wade in from two to four feet of mud and water, over the mangrove stumps and tangled vines of the imperfect openings cut by the natives, who, with their *machetas*, preceded them to clear the way. Then, at night, saturated and exhausted, they dragged themselves back to their quarters in the Telegraph, to toss until morning among the pitiless insects. Numbers were daily taken down with fever; and, notwithstanding that the whole working party was changed weekly, large accessions were constantly needed to keep up the required force. The works were alternately in charge of Messrs. Totten and Baldwin, one attending to the duty while the other recuperated from his last attack of fever. In the month of July Mr. Trautwine returned with a surgeon—Dr. Totten, a brother of the colonel—and several assistant engineers. About fifty Irishmen also arrived soon after from New Orleans.

The line had already been located for two and a half miles, and decided upon for two miles farther. It was so laid out as to strike a range of small hills half a league from the terminus, when it again stretched into the deep morass. The distance now required to be traversed from the work to the terminus was so great, and attended with so much

THE FIRST SHANTY.

fatigue and loss of time, that it was determined to erect a shanty for Mr. Baldwin and party in the swamp. The lumber for this was dragged on the backs of the men for more than three miles. Here was erected the first dwelling-house, built of rude boards, high upon the stumps of trees, to raise it above the waters of the swamp; and in the heart of this dank, howling wilderness our hardy pioneers took up their abode.

Large parties of mechanics and laborers were now constantly arriving from Jamaica, Carthagena, and the United States, so that the quarters on board the hulk were no longer adequate to house them. The insects had greatly diminished in numbers as the clearing progressed, and shanties were erected on the high ground before alluded to for the accommodation of the laborers. In August, 1850, the work of construction was commenced at this place. Another station was also established eight miles distant, opposite to the native town of Gatun, on the bank of the Chagres River, which was navigable to this point; and two of the Company's vessels arriving, laden with machinery, building material, and stores, they were debarked here, and the work of piling and grading was carried on from this station toward the terminus. The number of men now employed on both stations was between three and four hundred, among whom were many mechanics. The construction and surveys for a time progressed with vigor, and comfortable dwellings and hospitals were erected; but sickness, caused by exposure to the incessant rains, working waist-deep in the water, and in an atmosphere saturated with malarious poison, soon made such sad inroads among them that, in a few weeks, more than half their number were on the hospital records, and, either frightened by the fevers or seduced by higher wages offered on the California Transit, so many of the remnant deserted that the work came to a pause. Here the bravest might well have faltered, and even turned back from so dark a prospect as was then presented to the leaders of this forlorn hope; but they were men whom personal perils and privations could not daunt, whose energy and determination toil and suffering could not vanquish. Even in this apparent cessation of labor they were not idle; but, pushing off into the neighboring islands and provinces, they collected recruits in such numbers that but a few weeks had passed before the work was again forced onward. Colonel Totten now assumed the direction of the work, and Mr. Center, the vice-president of the Company, repaired to the Isthmus to co-operate with him in the rapid advancement of the enterprise, so that by December over a thousand laborers were employed. With the commencement of the dry season the sickliness abated, the hospitals were soon cleared, and by April, 1851, a large portion of the road between the terminus and Gatun was completed. The line had been located to Barbacoas, sixteen miles farther on, while Mr. J. C. Campbell, chief assistant engineer, was actively employed in extending the location toward Panama, and work had been commenced at several intervening points.

Docks had been constructed at Navy Bay, and vessels were almost daily arriving from Jamaica and Carthagena with laborers, and from New York with stores, machinery, and materials for the road. On the first day of October, 1851, a train of working cars, drawn by a locomotive, passed over the road as far as Gatun. In the following month two large steam-ships, the Georgia and Philadelphia, arrived at the open roadstead of Chagres with passengers from the United States *en route* for California *via* the Chagres River Transit; but the weather was so tempestuous that, after several lives had been lost in attempting to effect a landing, they were forced to take refuge in the harbor of Navy Bay. It was then proposed that, instead of waiting for fair weather in order to return to Chagres, the passengers should be transported over the railroad to Gatun, from whence they could proceed up the river in bongoes as usual. There was not yet a single passenger car on the road: an accident like the present had never been included in the calculations of the Company. Every objection was, however, soon overruled by the anxious emigrants, over one thousand in number, who were then disembarked and safely transported on a train of working cars to the Rio Chagres at Gatun.

At about this time the affairs of the Company in New York looked very dark and unpromising. The first subscription of one million dollars of stock was expended, and the shares had gone down to a low figure. The directors were obliged to keep the work moving, at an enormous expense, on their own individual credit. Never since the commencement of the undertaking had its supporters been more disheartened; but on the return of the Georgia to New York, carrying news that the California passengers had landed at Navy Bay instead of Chagres, and had traveled over a portion of the Panama Railway, its friends were inspired with renewed hope, the value of its stock was enhanced, and the steadfast upholders of the work were relieved from the doubts and anxieties that had well-nigh overwhelmed them.

Up to this time the settlement around the terminus at Navy Bay had been without a distinctive name: it was now proposed by Mr. Stephens, the president of the Company, that it should commemorate the services of one of the originators and unswerving friends of the road. On the 2d of February, 1852, it was formally inaugurated as a city, and named ASPINWALL. The works during this season progressed with rapidity, for great numbers of laborers were constantly arriving, and the mail-steamers, which now came regularly to Navy Bay, as regularly, on their return, carried away the sick and disabled. By March the road was completed to a station on the Rio Chagres called Bujio Soldado, eight miles beyond Gatun, and passenger trains ran in connection with every steamer; by the 6th of July it was pushed on to Barbacoas, at which point the course of the road was intersected by the Chagres River, making a total distance from the city of Aspinwall of twenty-three miles.

Thus far the work had cost much more than was anticipated. In the hope of constructing the remainder more economically, it was decided by the Board of Directors to complete the road from Barbacoas to Panama by contract. Accordingly, an agreement was entered into with Minor C. Story, as principal, to complete the work. The death of the lamented president of the Company, Mr. John L. Stephens, took place at this time. From the very inception of the original contract he had devoted to the enterprise his active and intelligent mind with a zeal that knew no faltering. Much of his time had been spent amid the dangers and hardships of the wilderness through which it was projected, and his loss was deeply deplored by the Company. Mr. William C. Young was appointed his successor.

The work under the contract for construction had been commenced by the attempted erection of a bridge across the Chagres River at Barbacoas. The river at this point was about three hundred feet in width, flowing through a deep and rocky channel, and subject to sudden and resistless freshets, often rising forty feet in a single night: the bridge was nearly completed when one span was swept away. Work was again commenced upon it, as well as upon several sections of the road between this point and the Pacific terminus. At times there was a force of several hundred men employed; but they were mostly Irish, unable to endure the effects of the climate, and, being also badly cared for, their numbers were soon so thinned by sickness and death that the contractor found himself unable to accomplish any part of the contract for the price agreed upon. The work faltered, and at last stopped almost entirely; so that when a year had expired not only was the bridge still unfinished, but not a tenth part of the work under the contract was completed, and the Company were obliged again to take the enterprise into their own hands, and carry it on by the same system pursued before the unfortunate contract was entered into. Mr. Young now resigned the presidency, and Mr. David Hoadley (the present president) was appointed his successor—a gentleman who deservedly enjoys the respect and confidence not alone of the Company which he represents, but also of the entire commercial community.

Valuable time had been lost from the delay occasioned by the non-fulfillment of the late contract. Not disheartened, however, the Company now redoubled their exertions, determined, if possible, to retrieve the error. Their working force was increased as rapidly as possible, drawing laborers from almost every quarter of the globe. Irishmen were imported from Ireland, Coolies from Hindostan, Chinamen from China. English, French, Germans, and Austrians, amounting in all to more than seven thousand men, were thus gathered in, appropriately as it were, to construct this highway for all nations. It was now anticipated that, with the enormous forces employed, the time required for the completion of the entire work would be in a ratio proportionate to the numerical increase of laborers, all of whom were supposed to be hardy, able-bodied men. But it was soon found that many of these people, from their previous habits and modes of life, were little adapted to the work for which they were engaged. The Chinamen, one thousand in number, had been brought to the Isthmus by the Company, and every possible care taken which could conduce to their health and comfort. Their hill-rice, their tea, and opium, in sufficient quantity to last for several months, had been imported with them—they were carefully housed and attended to—and it was expected that they would prove efficient and valuable men. But they had been engaged upon the work scarcely a month before almost the entire body became affected with a melancholic, suicidal tendency, and scores of them ended their unhappy existence by their own hands. Disease broke out among them, and raged so fiercely that in a few weeks scarcely two hundred remained. The freshly-imported Irishmen and Frenchmen also suffered severely, and there was found no other resource but to reship them as soon as possible, and replenish from the neighboring provinces and Jamaica, the natives of which (with the exception of the Northmen of America) were found best able to resist the influences of the climate. Notwithstanding these discouragements, and many others too numerous to be narrated within the compass of this brief sketch, the work continued to advance, so that by January, 1854, the summit-ridge was reached, distant from the Atlantic terminus thirty-seven miles, and eleven miles from the city of Panama.

Simultaneously with the operations toward the Pacific, a large force was established at Panama, under the superintendence of Mr. J. Young, one of the Company's most efficient and energetic officers, and the road was pushed rapidly onward, over the plains of Panama, through the swamps of Corrisal and Correndeu, and up the valley of the Rio Grande, to meet the advancing work from the Atlantic side; and on the 27th day of January, 1855, at midnight, in darkness and rain, the last rail was laid, and on the following day a locomotive passed from ocean to ocean.

The entire length of the road was 47 miles 3.020 feet, with a maximum grade of sixty feet to the mile. The summit grade was $258\frac{64}{100}$ feet above the assumed grade at the Atlantic, and $242\frac{7}{10}$ above the assumed grade at the Pacific terminus, being $263\frac{9}{100}$ feet above the *mean* tide of the Atlantic Ocean, and the summit-ridge two hundred and eighty-seven feet above the same level. Commencing at the city

ANCIENT BRIDGE AT OLD PANAMA.

of Aspinwall, on Limon or **Navy Bay**, the Atlantic terminus of the road, latitude 9° 21′ 23″ N. and longitude 79° 53′ 52″ W., the road skirted the western shore of the island of Manzanilla for about three quarters of a mile, then bent to the east, and crossed the channel which separates the island from the main land at a point nearly central of the breadth of the island, thence around the southern and eastern shore of Navy Bay until it reached the small river Mindee, cutting off a bend of this river about one thousand feet from its mouth; then it stretched across the peninsula formed by this bay and the River Chagres up to the mouth of the River Obispo, one of its branches, seldom, however, following the tortuous course of that stream, but cutting across its bends, and touching it only at intervals of two or three miles. The line continued upon the right or easterly bank of the Chagres as far as Barbacoas (twenty-five miles from Aspinwall), where it crossed that river by a wooden bridge six hundred and twenty-five feet in length; from thence it followed the left bank of the Chagres to the mouth of the Obispo River, thirty-one miles from the Atlantic terminus, leaving the native town of Gorgona on the left. After striking the Obispo, the line followed the valley of this stream to its head in the summit-ridge, which it reached $37\frac{3}{8}$ miles from the Atlantic and $10\frac{1}{8}$ miles from the Pacific terminus. The lower part of the valley of the Obispo, being crooked and bound in by precipitous hills, compelled the line to cross the stream twice within the first mile, when it passed the summit-ridge by a cut one fourth of a mile in length and twenty-four feet in depth, and then struck the head waters of the Rio Grande, which flows into the Pacific Ocean. Following the left bank of this stream, and descending by a grade of sixty feet to the mile for the first four miles, the line crossed the rivers Pedro Miguel, Caimitillo, and Cardenas, near their entrance into the Rio Grande; thence it stretched across the savannas of Corrisal and the swamps of Correndeu, and cut through a spur of Mount Ancon, leaving the main elevation to the right, and reached the Pacific Ocean at Playa Prieta, the northern suburb of the city of Panama.

Four tracks were laid at the Atlantic and three at the Pacific terminus, and the line of the road was well supplied with sidings and machinery for reversing locomotives. A machine shop one hundred and fifty feet long by fifty wide, stocked with first class machinery, sufficient to do all the repairs required for the road, was in operation at Aspinwall; also a blacksmith's shop, containing six suitable forges, and a brass foundry, with a small cupola for iron castings. There was also a car-repair shop, one hundred feet long by eighty feet wide, a freight-house and passenger depôt at either terminus, and suitable buildings for the accommodation of the employes of the Company.

A pier of four hundred and fifty feet in length was constructed at the Panama terminus, which gave greatly increased facilities for embarking and landing passengers and freight, and a steam-tug was substituted for the lighters and small boats which had been previously used for transportation between ship and shore, a distance of two and a half miles. The Company owned, by purchase, fourteen acres of land, having a front of five hundred feet on the bay. The Company also obtained by purchase, in connection with the Pacific Mail Steam-ship Company, a group of four islands in the Bay of Panama, about two and a half miles from the city, affording good shelter and anchorage for vessels of the largest class, and well supplied with good springs of water.

But the road at this time, though in *working* order and performing a large and daily-increasing service, was by no means actually completed. Much of the work, especially on the Pacific division, was of a temporary character; streams were crossed on temporary trestles, many of them of timber procured from the adjoining woods, and which it was known would not last more than six or eight months; deep ravines, requiring embankments from twenty to eighty feet in height (which it was found, from the nature of the adjoining soil, as well as from the amount of work involved in filling them, would delay the laying of the track for many months), were crossed on temporary trestle-work, in order to obtain the advantage of immediate communication between the two oceans by rail, thereby saving the thousands of men, women, and children, who were then crossing the Isthmus every month, the thirteen miles of mule-ride over a dangerous path, as well as the almost incredible hardships and perils to which they were subjected.

The difficulty and expense of keeping the road open in this state was very great; but, while this was safely accomplished, the work, under the energetic and skillful management of Messrs. Totten and Center, rapidly assumed a permanent character; firm and thoroughly secured embankments took the place of the trestle-work; for the temporary bridges were substituted heavy iron substantial structures, with abutments of stone.

Some idea of the magnitude of the bridge and culvert work may be obtained when it is known that the water-ways on the route were no less than one hundred and seventy in number, viz., one hundred and thirty-four culverts, drains, and bridges ten feet and under, the remaining bridges ranging from twelve to six hundred and twenty-five feet in breadth.

The iron bridge across the Chagres at Barbacoas may be taken, for its great strength and durability, as the type of all like structures on the line of the road. This bridge was composed of six spans of over a hundred feet each, built of boiler iron, with a top and bottom chord two feet in breadth and one inch in thickness, and joined together by a web of boiler iron nine feet in height at the centre and seven feet at the ends. The track was laid on iron floor-girders three feet apart, and the whole structure supported by five piers and two abutments of hewn stone twenty-six feet wide and eight feet in thickness, increasing in the proportion of an inch to the foot down to their foundations, which were constructed of piles and concrete.

The ballasting, which was, however, previously well under way, was carried on and completed throughout the entire line of the road in the most substantial manner, and the rapidly decaying spruce, pine, and native wood ties were removed, and replaced with ties of lignum-vitæ, imported from the province of Carthagena. Additional buildings for the accommodation of freight and passengers were erected at the Pacific terminus, to meet the wants of a greatly increased business, and at the Atlantic terminus new and commodious wharves were built, besides a massive stone warehouse three hundred feet long by eighty wide, the stone taken from quarries along the line of the road. Large and commodious station-houses, for the use of the local superintendents, were erected at intervals of four miles along the entire line, and an electric telegraph was established between the termini for the use of the Company. These, besides many other improvements, in reducing grades* and straightening curves, were accomplished

* TABLE OF THE GRADES FROM ASPINWALL TO PANAMA.

Rate of grade per mile in feet.	Length of grade in feet.	Rate of grade per mile in feet.	Length of grade in feet.
Level.	123,539	24.82	418
2.64	1,000	26.40	13,600
5.28	1,900	30.00	8,868
7.92	1,500	30.25	1,936
8.45	2,500	31.68	1,100
9.24	3,100	34.15	1,400
10.56	13,313	36.00	2,200
12.14	2,600	36.96	2,396
12.41	4,300	37.49	1,916
13.20	6,500	38.54	1,707
15.10	2,100	46.20	3,430
15.84	3,700	47.30	3,250
17.42	200	52.80	6,300
19.01	1,400	58.87	3,355
20.60	4,900	60.00	20,107
21.12	4,595		71,983
23.25	2,052		179,199
	179,199		251,182

THE CABILDO AT PANAMA.

during the two years following the opening of the road in 1855, involving an additional expenditure of nearly two millions of dollars. This great expenditure was not, however, incurred without satisfactory proof that the enterprise would equal, in its pecuniary advantages, all the calculations which had been made in regard to its increase of revenue. Up to the opening of the road in 1855, that is to say, from the running of the first passenger train in 1852, the amount received for the transportation of passengers and freight was $2,125,232 31. See Appendix B, p. 61, et seq.

From 1857 the Company were actively engaged in establishing every needful arrangement and improvement which was found necessary to facilitate the perfect working of the road. Side tracks at either terminus were added to meet its increased requirements; the wharves at Aspinwall were improved and covered, and substantial bulk-heads were erected over a considerable portion of the frontage of the port. Much of the low ground on the island was filled in and laid out into streets, and many buildings erected. In addition to this, an immense reservoir was in process of construction on the site of a natural basin some two miles distant, from which water was to be conveyed in iron pipes to Aspinwall for the use of the town and shipping; and a substantial iron light-house, sixty feet in height, and furnished with a Fresnel light, was substituted for the wooden structure at the western side of the entrance to the port. At Panama the wooden pier was replaced by one of iron four hundred and fifty feet in length, and steam-tugs for towage, and several iron launches, each of one hundred tons burthen, were added to the facilities for the transhipment of goods between ship and shore. These were the principal works and improvements up to January, 1859, when the construction account of the road was closed, showing its entire cost up to that date to have been eight millions of dollars.

The *gross earnings* of the road up to that time amounted

to eight millions one hundred and forty-six thousand six hundred and five dollars.

The running expenses, together with depreciation in iron, ties, buildings, etc., amounted to $2,174,876 51, leaving a balance of $5,971,728 66 as the legitimate returns for the money invested in the road in a period of seven years, during the first of which but twelve miles were in operation, the second twenty-three, the third thirty-one: only for the last four years was the road in use throughout its entire extent.

Out of these receipts, the directors of the Company, having paid the regular interest on all mortgage and other bonds, a ten per cent. dividend to stockholders in 1852, one of seven per cent. in each of the years 1853 and '54, and one of twelve per cent. for every succeeding year, showed a balance of $529,041 50, besides a sinking fund of $153,395 83, and no floating debt.

The increase in the receipts from the commencement of the road was as follows:

From December, 1852, 12 miles open, } $73,266 32.
To " 1853, 23 " "
From 1853 to 1854, 31 miles open, $131,143 91.
From 1854 to 1855, opening of the entire road, $645,497 29.
From 1855 to 1858 showed an increase of $416,006 84; and
From 1858 to 1859, an increase above that of $419,477 93.

(For a particular statement of items of expenditure and income, see Appendix B, page 61, et seq.)

HEALTH OF THE ISTHMUS.

It may interest the general reader to know that more than 196,000 passengers have been transported over the road during the five years ending in December, 1859, and it is not known that a single case of sickness has occurred during or in consequence of the transit since the entire opening of the road in 1855. The diseases contracted by persons in transit previous to that time were of a purely ma-

VIEW FROM THE RAMPARTS, LOOKING TOWARD THE SITE OF THE ANCIENT CITY.

larious character, and identical with the intermittent (fever and ague) and bilious fevers of the Western States, always found resulting from great exposure and fatigue, so often unavoidable while the transit was performed upon mules and in open boats, occupying from two to five days, the traveler frequently obliged to live upon the vilest food, and sleep upon the wet ground or in the but little less comfortless huts of the natives; the comfortable railway carriage, and the passage from ocean to ocean reduced to *three hours*, having fully demonstrated a *perfect* immunity to the traveler from all those varieties of sickness long popularly recognized under the head of *Panama Fever*. The sanitary condition not only of Aspinwall, but of the country along the entire line of the road, has also been improved by the filling in and draining of the swamp and low land to such a degree that the congestive forms of fever among the laborers and residents which, during the earlier days of the road, were the chief causes of mortality, are now rarely met with, and the whole line of the transit will, in point of healthiness, compare favorably with many of the equally recent settlements in the Western States.

SAFETY TO PROPERTY.

The amount of specie conveyed over the road from 1855 to 1860 was over three hundred millions of dollars, *without the loss of a single dollar;* and during the same period there were sent over the road nearly 100,000 bags of mail matter (the greater part of which consisted of mails between the Atlantic States and California), not one of which was lost. And of the many thousands of tons of freight which have been transported over the Panama Railroad since it was first opened, the losses by damage and otherwise do not exceed five thousand dollars.

SOURCES OF BUSINESS.

Erroneous impressions in regard to the sources from whence the business of the Panama Railroad is derived prevail extensively even among intelligent business men and members of our national councils, many regarding it as entirely dependent upon our trade with California. The fact seems to be overlooked that while California has a population estimated at only 500,000, the population of Central America is over 2,000,000; and that that portion of South America, whose only means of communicating with the Atlantic is either by the Isthmus of Panama or around Cape Horn, contains nearly 8,000,000, and that regular and direct steam marine communication exists between those countries and the Panama Railroad.

The fact that up to the establishment of the Isthmus Railroad the trade of South and Central America had been carried on almost exclusively with Europe (that between the United States and those countries being estimated at less than ten per cent. of the whole) has prevented its magnitude and importance from being fully appreciated by the American people.

Careful estimates, however, show that the value of the trade of these countries to and from the Atlantic exceeds $60,000,000 per annum. The managers of the Panama Railroad Company, from its earliest existence, were aware of that important circumstance, and looked confidently to the business of those regions already existing, and that which would undoubtedly be developed by the facilities afforded by the railroad, as one of the surest elements in its ultimate and permanent success.

It was not lost sight of that the European trade (as far as European influence extended) would cling tenaciously to its circuitous track around Cape Horn, fully aware that, when the business was turned into the direct route across the Isthmus, a large portion of the trade would be inevitably directed to the nearer markets of the United States; notwithstanding this, the Company rested in the conviction that the shortening of the distance from three thousand to more than four thousand miles for the South American markets, and more than five thousand for the Pacific Central American, besides the avoidance of the well-known perils of Cape Horn, must bring much of the most valuable merchandise across their road so soon as those countries were able to avail themselves of its advantages. The South American states, Chili, Peru, Bolivia, and Ecuador, were put in immediate connection with the road by a British line of steam-ships, which was organized some time previous to the opening of the road, and which, up to that time, had been mainly dependent upon the coastwise trade. The business resulting fully justified the expectations of the Company (see Appendix A, page 57, et seq.); but the Central American states had at that time no means of connection with the road. Their Pacific ports had been so long shut out from remunerative commercial relations that they could not at once realize the advantages the Isthmus railroad offered over the tedious and expensive land-route to the Atlantic; they required to be lifted from the ruts along which they had been creeping and groaning for ages, and placed upon this great commercial highway.

This was accomplished in 1856 by the Panama Railroad Company, who at that time organized a line of steam communication with all their ports from Panama to San Jose de Guatemala.

This departure from the legitimate business of the road was not made until the directors had vainly exhausted every available means in their power for the establishment of an independent company. But the development of the Central American trade was so manifestly for the interest of the Isthmus transit, and so certain to follow the establishment of such a line, that they finally decided to identify its interests with those of the road. In the latter part of 1856 the first vessel was dispatched under the command of Capt. J. M. Dow. The returns from the monthly voyages of the "Columbus" soon proved the wisdom of the measure, for in less than two years the cargoes of merchandise brought from those states for transportation over the road often exceeded half a million of dollars, while a large amount of foreign merchandise found its way to those countries by the same channel.

In 1858, the business over the road from the South and Central American states exceeded in value *nine times* the freighting business of California *via* the Isthmus, and by 1860 less than *one fifteenth* of the freighting business of the road was due to the California trade, the remaining fourteen fifteenths consisting mainly of shipments from the United States, British manufactures and other goods shipped direct from England for South and Central America, and the produce of those countries in return, such as indigo, cochineal, India-rubber, coffee, cocoa, deer-skins and goat-skins, besides orchilla, pearl-shells, tobacco, balsams, Peruvian bark, ores, straw hats, etc., etc.

When it comes to be considered that in the California trade large amounts of goods and merchandise for Oregon and Washington Territory and the British Possessions are included, likewise occasional shipments from China and the Sandwich Islands, and that it is still in its infancy, the importance of the South and Central American trade to the Panama Railroad may be in a measure appreciated. The conveyances by which the business of the Pacific coast finds its way to and from the road are,

1st. By the Pacific Mail Steam-ship Company, plying trimonthly between California, Mexico, and Panama, with a fleet of twelve large steam-ships.

2d. The Oregon and California Steam-ship Company,

RAMPARTS ON THE NORTHEASTERN BEACH OF PANAMA.

running between California, Oregon, and Washington Territory, with a branch line to the Mexican coast, and connecting with the Pacific Mail Steam-ship Company tri-monthly, with a fleet of five steam-ships.

3d. The Pacific Steam Navigation Company, plying semi-monthly between Chili, Bolivia, Peru, Ecuador, New Granada, and Panama, with a fleet of nine large steamers for the main service, and three smaller steam-ships performing a coasting service, and connecting with the main line.

4th. The Central American Steam-ship Company, running semi-monthly between Guatemala, Salvador, Costa Rica, Nicaragua, and Panama, with two large steam-ships and one steam-tug.

Besides these are numerous sailing vessels with freight from different ports for transportation over the road.

On the Atlantic side are,

1st. The Atlantic and Pacific Steam-ship Company, plying tri-monthly between New York and Aspinwall.

2d. The Royal Mail Steam Packet Company, running semi-monthly between England, the West Indies, the eastern coast of South and Central America, and Aspinwall, with a fleet of twenty-three large steam-ships.

3d. Holt's line of screw steamers between Liverpool and Aspinwall, monthly—two steamers.

Besides the steam lines are,

1st. The Bremen and Aspinwall line of sailing vessels, monthly.

2d. The Bordeaux and Aspinwall line of sailing vessels, quarterly.

3d. The Panama Railroad Company's line of sailing vessels between Liverpool and Aspinwall, monthly.

4th. The Panama Railroad Company's line of sailing vessels from New York to Aspinwall—seven vessels: three barks and four brigs.

5th. Five ships a year from Boston to Aspinwall. For

particular information in regard to these lines, see Appendix C, p. 139, et seq.

CHARACTER OF THE SERVICE PERFORMED ON THE ROAD.

As early as the year 1855 daily trains were established each way over the road, requiring in its then imperfect state from five to six hours for the transit. As the character of the road improved, a corresponding improvement took place in the time-table, and for the past three years the passage has been uniformly and safely accomplished in three hours, or even less, when the exigency of the case required it. The rolling stock of the road has always been most ample. Fifteen hundred passengers, with the United States mails, and the freight of three steam-ships, have not unfrequently been transported over the road during a single half day. The engines, some eleven in number, are of the first class, averaging twenty tons burden; the passenger-cars are large and commodious, and built for convenience and comfort, especially with reference to the climate; the cars for the transportation of the mails and treasure are entirely of iron. The usual freight-cars are built to carry not only the ordinary freight, but the heaviest and coarsest materials—large quantities of gold and silver ore, timber, anchors, and chains of the largest size, cannon shot and shells, iron-work in pieces of twenty-five tons, heavy machinery, guano, whale-oil, etc., more or less of which are daily passing over the road. The arrangements for the loading and unloading of cargoes are unusually perfect; double tracks run from the main road down the different wharves to the very ship's side, and the lading process is so effectively managed that frequently less than two hours pass between the *arrival of the largest ships,* laden with from two to three hundred tons of merchandise, besides the baggage of from four to eight hundred passengers, and the *departure of the trains* for Panama bearing the entire freight.

APPENDIX A.

Statement of Merchandise, destined for San Francisco, transported over the Panama Railroad during the two Years ending respectively July 31st, 1859 and 1860.

Years.	Tons measurement.	Tons weight.	No. of packages.	Total tons.
1859	$5626\frac{33}{40}$	$381\frac{754}{2000}$	24,482	$5665\frac{3}{5}$
1860	$6911\frac{36}{40}$	$755\frac{542}{2000}$	46,061	$7667\frac{1}{6}$

Statement of Merchandise from San Francisco transported over the Panama Railroad for the two Years above named.

Years.	No. of packages.	Tons measurement.	Tons weight.	Total tons.
1859	259	$321\frac{18}{40}$		$321\frac{8}{20}$
1860	525	$61\frac{12}{40}$	$12\frac{1052}{2000}$	$73\frac{3}{4}$

Statement of Treasure from San Francisco transported over the Panama Railroad for the two Years above named.

Years.	Number of packages.	Amount.
1859	2399	$37,173,187 25
1860	2476	38,247,613 62

Statement of Merchandise, destined for Central American Ports, transported over the Panama Railroad for the Years 1859 and 1860.

Years.	No. of packages.	Tons measurement.	Tons weight.	Total tons.
1859	11,319	$1644\frac{31}{40}$	$11\frac{1217}{2000}$	$1655\frac{3}{5}$
1860	23,257	$3064\frac{32}{40}$	$219\frac{729}{2000}$	$3284\frac{1}{6}$

Statement of Merchandise from Central American Ports transported over the Panama Railroad for the two Years ending respectively July 31, 1859 and 1860.

Years	No. of Hides.	Coffee.	Skins.	Indigo.	Cochineal.	India-rubber.	Bark.	Balsam.	Cocoa.	Ores.	Copper.	Cigars.	Amalgama.	Sundries.	Tobacco.	Dye-wood.	Total.
1859	26,892	5717	468	6910	3633	63	1	327	2	16	16	—	—	48	14	1408	45,575
1860	65,899	8270	745	5420	6239	777	4	286	5	359	—7	8	124	—	—		88,143

Statement of Merchandise, destined for the West Coast of South America, transported over the Panama Railroad for the two Years above named.

Years.	Number of packages.	Jewelry, etc. Value of.	Tons measurement.	Tons weight.	Total tons.
1859	1063	$90,342	$199\frac{31}{40}$	$1\frac{139}{2000}$	$198\frac{1}{2}$
1860	8413	1,809,000	$1099\frac{37}{40}$	$30\frac{725}{2000}$	$1130\frac{1}{4}$

Statement of Merchandise from the West Coast of South America transported over the Panama Railroad for the two Years ending respectively July 31st, 1859 and 1860.

Years.	No. of Hides.	Number of packages of									Total.
		Skins.	India-rubber.	Bark.	Cocoa.	Tobacco.	Orchilla.	Sundries.	Copper.	
1859	147		2			25				174
1860	2017	979	188	571	1706	93	32	20	6243	11,850
			Treasure ....$							

The above comprises only the merchandise brought under *through bills of lading*; all other is included in the following table.

Statement of Merchandise from Panama, N. G., transported over the Panama Railroad for the two Years ending respectively July 31st, 1859 and 1860, not under through Bills of Lading.

Years.	No. of Hides.	Number of packages of														Total.
		Skins.	Bark.	Indigo.	India-rubber.	Cocoa.	Orchilla.	Dye-wood.	Coffee.	Copper.	Sundries.	Pearl-shells.	Sarsaparilla.	Hats.	Cigars.	Tobacco.	Sperm oil.	
1859	35,721	166	6628	42	2	1572	25	14	1	52	46	851	93	—	1	78	—	45,292
1860	29,869	220	5453	95	45	2413	164	1000	220	38	35	525	19	8	5	25	98	40,832

SPECIE.

Year.	Number of packages.	Amount.
1860	28	$100,342 00

SOUTHEASTERN RAMPART.

APPENDIX B.

PANAMA RAILROAD COMPANY.

Financial Statement for the Year ending December 31st, 1852.

Gross receipts to December 31st, 1852		$250,161 81
Amount credited Construction Account for proportion of running expenses	$ 65,000 00	
Sundry expenses, mule hire for troops, etc.	8,999 32	
Dividend No. 1, 10 per cent. on $1,467,720	146,772 00	
New Granadian government proportion of dividend	4,403 16	225,174 48
Balance to credit of Income Account		$24,987 33

Statement for the Year ending December 31st, 1853.

Balance to credit of Income Account, December 31st, 1852		$ 24,987 33
Gross receipts to December 31st, 1853		322,428 13
		$347,415 46
Amount charged for running expenses	$113,949 99	
Dividend No. 2, 5 per cent. on $2,194,062	109,703 10	
New Granadian government proportion of dividend	3,291 09	226,944 18
Balance to Income Account, December 31st, 1853		$120,471 28
Dividend No. 3, 3½ per cent. on $2,716,572	$95,080 02	
New Granadian government proportion of dividend	2,852 40	97,932 42
Balance to credit of Income Account		$22,538 86

Statement for the Year ending December 31st, 1854.

Balance to credit of Income Account, December 31st, 1853			$22,538 86
Gross receipts to December 31st, 1854			453,572 04
			$476,110 90
Amount charged for running expenses	$116,542 37		
Dividend No. 4, July, 3½ per cent. on $2,832,000	99,120 00		
Interest on bonds, due July 1st, on $2,168,000, at 3½ per cent.	75,880 00		
" on bonds, due January 1st, on $2,125,000, at 3½ per cent.	74,375 00		
New Granadian government proportion of dividend	2,543 63		368,461 00
Balance to Income Account, December 31st, 1854			$107,649 90
Dividend No. 5, January, 3½ per cent. on $2,875,000	$100,625 00		
New Granadian government proportion of dividend	3,018 75		103,643 75
Balance to credit of Income Account			$4,006 15

Statement for the Year ending December 31st, 1855.

Balance to credit of Income Account, December 31st, 1854			$4,006 15
Gross receipts to December 31st, 1855			1,099,069 33
			$1,103,075 48
Amount charged for running expenses	$284,156 00		
Dividend No. 6, July, 6 per cent. on $3,743,000	224,580 00		
New Granadian government proportion of dividend	6,737 40		
Interest on bonds due July 1st, $1,257,000, at 3½ per cent.	43,995 00		
" on sterling mortgage bonds, with commission and exchange	53,466 78		
" on bonds due January 1st, $468,000, at 3½ per cent.	16,380 00		
" on sterling mortgage bonds, with commission and exchange	77,770 00		
Office expenses to January 1st	8,918 00		
Interest on bonds converted	8,210 00		724,213 18
Balance to Income Account, December 31st, 1855			$378,862 30
Dividend No. 7, January, 6 per cent. on $4,532,000	$271,920 00		
New Granadian government proportion of dividend	8,157 60		280,077 60
Balance to credit of Income Account			$98,784 70

PANAMA RAILROAD.

Statement for the Year ending December 31st, 1856.

Balance to credit of Income Account, December 31st, 1855			$98,784
Amount of earnings received to credit same, to December 31st, 1856			1,284,639
United States Post-office Department—mail-service for quarter ending December 30			42,204
Earnings in December, for which returns have not been received, and uncollected freight on the Isthmus			27,500
Royal Mail Steam Packet Company—freight on foreign treasure not yet adjusted			6,398
			$1,459,525
Deduct interest on sterling bonds (£450,000), including exchange and commission		$9,905	
" " on convertible bonds, 1st July, $283,000—3½ per cent.		8,750	
" " " " 1st Jan., 250,000 " "			$155,540
			18,655
Running expenses, per returns of chief engineer and superintendent			323,788
Office expenses			22,266
New Granadian government proportion of mail receipts			10,000
			$530,249
Dividend No. 8, paid July 1st	$283,020		
New Granadian government proportion, 3 per cent	8,490	291,510	
			821,759
Balance to credit of Income Account, December 31st, 1856			$637,766
Dividend No. 9, declared January 5th, on $4,750,000, at 6 per cent.	$285,000		
New Granadian government proportion, 3 per cent	8,550		293,550
Balance to credit of Income Account after dividends			$344,216

Statement for the Year ending December 31st, 1857.

Balance to credit of Income Account, after dividend, January 5, 1857				$378,394 42
Receipts from December 31st, 1856, to December 31st, 1857, viz.:				
From passengers		$698,250 18		
" freight		354,437 78		
" do.—treasure		122,076 60		
" mails		112,058 12		
" baggage		16,591 03		
" miscellaneous		2,405 89	$1,305,819 60	
				$1,684,214 02
Deduct interest on first mortgage sterling bonds (£450,000), with exchange and commission		$155,540 00		
" second " " (£56,250), for 6 mos. "		9,720 00		
" convertible bonds, 1st July ... $223,000, at 3½ per cent. $7,805				
" " " 1st Jan. ... $160,000, " " " 5,500		13,405 00		
Running expenses		348,387 00		
Estimated depreciation in iron, ties, etc.		40,000 00		
Loss on steamers Columbus and Panama		50,000 00		
Office expenses		22,250 00		
New Granadian government proportion of mail receipts		10,000 00	$649,302 00	
				$944,520 60
Dividend No. 10, July 6th, on $4,770,000, 6 per cent.	$286,620 00			
New Granadian government proportion do., 3 per cent.	8,596 60		295,218 60	
Balance to credit of Income Account, December 31st, 1857				$739,693 42
Dividend No. 11, January 4th, on $4,840,000, 6 per cent.	$290,400			
New Granadian government proportion do., 3 per cent.	8,712		$299,112	
Amount appropriated to Sinking Fund			50,000	349,112 00
Balance to credit of Income Account after dividends				$390,581 42

PANAMA RAILROAD. 65

Statement for the Year ending December 31st, 1858.

Balance to credit of Income Account, after dividend, January 4th, 1858			$392,855 91
Receipts from December 31st, 1857, to December 31st, 1858:			
From passengers	$743,573 27		
" freight—merchandise	432,455 73		
" " treasure	147,853 78		
" mail transportation	100,000 00		
" baggage	18,509 76		
" miscellaneous, wharfage, light money, etc.	3,683 73		
Earnings in December, for which returns have not been received, estimated	60,000 00	$1,506,076 27	
			$1,898,932 18
Deduct interest on first mortgage bonds (£450,000), with exchange and commission	$153,860 88		
" second " " (£129,375), " " " "	28,470 28		
" convertible bonds, July 1st, $77,000, at 3½ per cent	$2,695 } 3,850 00		
" " " Jan. 1st, $33,000, " " "	1,155 }		
Running expenses	386,234 39		
Equipment Account	13,523 13		
Depreciation in iron, ties, etc.	40,000 00		
Office expenses	22,750 00		
New Granadian government proportion of mail receipts	10,000 00		
	$658,688 68		
Dividend No. 12, June 30th, on $4,923,000, at 6 per cent	$295,380 00		
New Granadian government proportion, 3 per cent	8,861 40		
Appropriated to Sinking Fund, June 30th	50,000 00	354,241 40	
Balance to credit of Income Account, December 31st, 1858			$886,002 10
Dividend No. 13, Jan. 3d, 1859, on $4,967,000, at 6 per cent	$298,020 00		
New Granadian government proportion, 3 per cent	8,940 60		
Appropriated to Sinking Fund, Jan. 3d, 1859	50,000 00		$356,960 60
Balance to credit of Income Account after dividends			$529,041 50

Statement for the Year ending December 31st, 1858—continued.

The Construction Account, now closed, amounts to $8,000,000 00
Which is represented by
  Capital stock $4,967,000 00
  Convertible bonds 33,000 00
  First mortgage sterling bonds, due Dec. 1st, 1859 ... $ 750,000 }
    "   "   "   "   " April 10th, 1865 ...   1,250,000 } 2,000,000 00
  Second mortgage sterling bonds, due Feb. 20th, 1872 .... 1,000,000 00
                                                                          ─────────────
                                                                          $8,000,000 00

Of the latter, 425 bonds, equal at par to $425,000, are still in the hands of the Company unissued. The Sinking Fund invested now amounts to $153,395 83. The Company has no floating debt.

Statement for the Year ending December 31st, 1859.

Balance to credit of Income Account, after dividend, January 6th, 1859, per statement $529,041 50
Add excess of receipts over estimate for portion of December, 1858 ....   6,068 13
                                                                                            ───────────
                                                                                            $535,109 63
Receipts from December 31st, 1858, to December 31st, 1859:
  For passengers $1,068,832 17
   " freight—merchandise 537,689 01
   "   "   treasure 153,876 98
   " mail transportation 100,000 00
   " baggage 18,951 65
   " miscellaneous, wharfage, light money, etc. 6,094 76
  Earnings for the latter part of December, not yet received, estimated at   40,000 00
                                                                           ──────────────
                                                                                          1,925,444 57
                                                                                          ─────────────
                                                                                          $2,460,554 20
Deduct interest on first mortgage bonds (£150,000), with exchange and commission $150,694 37
   "   "   " second   "   "   (£225,000),   "   "   " 77,770 00
   "   "   " convertible bonds, July 1st, $33,000, at 3½ per cent ... $1,155 00 }
   "   "   "   "   "   Jan. 1st, $27,000, " "   "   ...   945 00 } 2,100 00
  Running expenses 416,818 76
  Premium of exchange on remittances to meet bonds, paid in London, December 1st .   73,157 78
  Office expenses 25,207 43

PANAMA RAILROAD.

Appropriated to cover depreciation in iron, ties, buildings, etc.		40,000 00	
New Granadian government proportion of mail receipts		10,000 00	795,748 84
			$1,664,805 86
Dividend No. 14, paid July 1st, on $4,967,000, 6 per cent	$298,020 00		
" 15, payable January 3d, 1860, on $4,973,000, 6 per cent	298,380 00		
New Granadian government proportion, 3 per cent, on ditto	17,892 00		
Appropriated to Sinking Fund	100,000 00	714,292 00	
Surplus income after dividend, January 3d, 1860			$950,513 86

Balance as above		$950,513 86
Sinking Fund and accumulations		260,962 21
		$1,211,476 07

Out of which the Company have paid during 1859,		
For stock in North Atlantic Steam-ship Company	$500,000 00	
" steamer Guatemala	150,000 00	
On account of bonds, due December 1st	550,000 00	
	$1,200,000 00	

All the Company's interest in steamers is covered by marine insurance excepting the Columbus, valued at $25,000.

The cost of the road, per Construction Account, closed January, 1859, is $8,000,000 00
Against which there are,

Capital stock	$4,973,000 00	
Convertible bonds	27,000 00	
Sterling bonds, due 1865	1,250,000 00	
" " 1872	1,150,000 00	
	$7,400,000 00	

Statement for the Year ending December 31st, 1860.

Balance to credit of Income Account, after dividend, January 3d, 1860, per statement			$950,513 86
Add excess of receipts over estimate for portion of December			10,227 55
			$960,741 41
Deduct payment for portion of sterling bonds retired in December, 1859, the balance having been paid from the Sinking Fund			442,830 13
			$517,911 28
Receipts from December 31st, 1859, to December 31st, 1860:			
For passengers		$686,378 74	
" freight, merchandise (including baggage)		618,578 04	
" treasure		128,946 38	
" mail transportation		50,000 00	
" miscellaneous, wharfage, light money, interest, etc.		14,972 66	
" earnings uncollected, or for which returns have not been received, estimated		50,000 00	$1,550,875 82
			$2,068,792 10

Surplus after dividends of 1859

Deduct interest on sterling bonds (£540,000), with exchange and commission		$186,468 45	
" convertible bonds, $24,000, at 7 per cent.		1,680 00	
Running expenses, including materials, repairs, subsistences, labor, etc.		406,050 55	
Equipment Account, new cars, etc.		$17,019 32	
Permanent improvements (paid for out of Income Account, Construction being closed):			
New wharves	20,072 13		
Water-works	15,204 16		
Dredging machine	18,489 96		
Stone-breakers and engines	5,000 00	75,785 57	
Office expenses		22,904 73	
New Granadian government proportion of mail receipts		10,000 00	$702,889 30
			$1,365,897 80
Dividend No. 16, paid July 2d, 1860, on $4,976,000, 6 per cent.		$298,560 00	
" 17, payable January 2d, 1861, on $4,976,000, 6 per cent.		298,560 00	
New Granadian government proportion of do., 3 per cent.		17,973 60	

PANAMA RAILROAD.

Paid trustees of Sinking Fund, July, 1860.................... 50,000 00 } 100,000 00
Appropriated to   "   December, 1860......................... 50,000 00 }
Surplus after dividends of 1860.. $650,804 20

                                                                              $715,093 60

GENERAL STATEMENT.

Assets: Construction Account $8,000,000 00
        Cash in bank 204,920 52
        Loans on demand 127,455 75
        Amounts due from agents and others.. 93,088 52
        Cavan Brothers & Co., London 49,557 31
        Sinking Fund 50,369 06
        Real estate on the Isthmus and islands in the Bay of Panama................... 69,431 97
        Stock in North Atlantic Steam-ship Co... 500,000 00
        Steamer Guatemala (cost $155,000), valued at.................................. 130,000 00
           "   Columbus (cost $50,500),   " 25,000 00
        Steam-tugs and launches in the Bay of Panama (cost $50,500), valued at........ 25,000 00
        Interest in sailing vessels (cost $41,000), valued at......................... 28,000 00

                                                                                      $9,302,823 13

Liabilities: Capital stock... $4,976,000 00
             Sterling bonds, with exchange 2,466,237 78
             Convertible bonds..   24,000 00
             Book accounts..   44,900 60
             Dividend declared and payable Jan. 2d, with New Granadian government proportion. 307,546 80
             Trustees of Sinking Fund, appropriation not invested......................   50,000 00
             Undivided earnings from road... $650,804 20
               "   of steamers, sailing vessels, tugs, and launches (after
                      deducting depreciation).............................. 183,333 75
               "   bonds redeemed.. 600,000 00—1,434,142 95

                                                                                      $9,302,823 13

Jos. F. Joy, *Secretary.*

The early history and present condition of the road, at least so much of it as has been thought would prove interesting and serviceable to the general reader, has been presented. The sources of its present business have been shown, and some idea of its probable increase from these; but a large and important field within the legitimate scope of the enterprise demands a little attention from its bearings on the future business of the road. A glance at the geographical situation of the Isthmus of Panama, in its relation with Australia, China, Japan, and the Sandwich Islands, will discover the capacity of the transit to shorten the distances from those countries to the markets of the United States by so many thousands of miles as must make it an eventual necessity for the trade, at least a large portion of it, to seek this, the only direct route between the Atlantic and Pacific Oceans.*

TRAVELER'S GUIDE.

As the traveler enters the harbor of Navy Bay he can not fail to observe the beauty of the scene spread out before him. On the right and in front of the harbor, which sweeps around a semicircle of some three miles in extent, the primeval forest of the tropics, with its dense vinous un-

---

* The distance from N. York to Sydney, Australia, *via* Cape Horn, is 12,870
  "   "   "   "   *via* Panama....... 9,950
       In favor of Panama.................................. 2,720
The distance from N. York to Honolulu, S'dwich Isl., *via* Cape Horn 13,560
  "   "   "   "   *via* Panama... 6,800
       In favor of Panama.................................. 6,760
The distance from New York to Hong Kong, *via* Cape Horn 17,420
  "   "   "   " *via* Panama........... 11,850
       In favor of Panama.................................. 5,570
The distance from New York to Jeddo, Japan, *via* Cape Horn...... 16,710
  "   "   "   " *via* Panama.......... 10,220
       In favor of Panama.................................. 6,490
Distance from England to Sydney, Australia, *via* Cape of G. Hope 12,828
  "   "   "   " *via* Panama 12,730
       In favor of Panama.................................. 98

dergrowth and its towering cocoa and palm trees, meets his view; on the left, from the iron light-house on the extreme seaward point, the brightly-painted Americo-Spanish town of Aspinwall extends, its long covered wharves filled with the shipping of many nations. A verandaed street skirts the shore, and a dense equatorial forest rising up behind is relieved by the faint and misty mountain range, which forms the *back-bone* of the Isthmus, and connects the great *Cordillera* of the northern and southern continents—the Rocky Mountains and the Andes. This harbor (said to have been discovered by Columbus during his third voyage, and by him named "Navy Bay") is three miles in length by two in breadth, with an average depth of seven fathoms, affording good anchorage ground in every part. Since the establishment of the Panama Railroad it has been a rendezvous for the United States Atlantic squadron, and one or more frigates of the first class may usually be seen at anchor; also a United States store-ship, which has its permanent station here.

The city of Aspinwall, which has grown up from the necessity of its position as the Atlantic terminus of the railroad, while answering its purpose as a receiving and transhipping depôt, has but little, architecturally, to recommend it to notice, the dwellings, some two hundred in number, being of wood, and built in a style midway between the New England house and the verandaed structures usual in the tropics. They are built on land leased from the Company by private individuals.

The voyager coming to Aspinwall by the United States mail steam-ships will be landed at the end of an immense wharf belonging to the Company, and will find it worth his while to take a walk about the town ere making the transit of the Isthmus. First, it may not be amiss to notice the wharf itself, which extends from the shore out upon a coral reef, nearly a thousand feet, to where a depth of wa ter exists sufficient to float the largest ships. It is forty feet in breadth, and covered by a lofty metallic roof; the piles upon which it stands are coppered to protect them from the *teredo*, a boring worm which infests these waters, and rapidly destroys every kind of timber unless thus protected. At the upper end of the wharf a grove of cocoanut-trees shoots up through the flooring, and at any and every season of the year the cocoanut, in the bud, the blossom, and full grown, may here be seen. Several large iron tanks are situated at the head of the wharf, each of a capacity of several thousand gallons. The whole island of Manzanilla, upon which Aspinwall is situated, a mile in length by three quarters in width, being a low coral foundation, has no springs of water, and that obtained by digging is so brackish that rain-water is used instead; these tanks, filled by the rains which prevail for more than half the year, before the establishment of the great reservoir, furnished the supply of water for the shipping during the dry season. At the head of the wharf you reach the quadruple track of the railway. Proceeding toward its Atlantic terminus, you pass, on your left, the line of stores, shops, and hotels which were visible from the entrance of the harbor. The shops, perhaps half a dozen in number, usually display a very respectable assortment of goods, principally ready-made clothing, fancy articles, and groceries. Among them are several quite extensive importing houses of French, English, and American merchandise, and Havana cigars for the South American market and the shipping visiting the port.

The hotels,* of which there are, great and small, at least a dozen, have, for this country, very fair accommodation for all classes of travelers, at from one to four dollars per day;

---

* Probably the best accommodation will be found at the Howard, City, and Aspinwall Hotels. Usual charge for first class passengers $3 per day. Second class passengers are accommodated at the other houses at considerably lower rates. It is well to have the terms well understood beforehand.

but little business, however, is done among them except on the arrival of the passenger steamers of the California line. In 1852, when these hotels were erected, travelers were often detained here for several days, when the landlords drove a brisk trade; but now the ship-loads of passengers are seldom detained here more than two or three hours, and, although a brisk business is done for the time, the publican finds his opportunity too brief to realize much profit.

At the end of the row stands the Panama Railroad Company's office, a respectable fire-proof two-story brick building, into the upper windows of which the wires of the Isthmus Telegraph converge. The poles, or, more properly, the pillars, which serve to support the wires of this telegraph line, from their symmetry, strength, and novel construction, are worthy of particular notice. They are apparently of *hewn stone*. Some two years since, after much trouble and expense had resulted in consequence of the rapid decay of the wooden poles formerly used, Colonel Totten conceived the idea of moulding a support of concrete. A small straight stick of the necessary height was placed upright, and surrounded by a jointed wooden mould, fifteen inches in diameter at the base, tapering to about eight inches at the top, and sunk into the earth sufficiently for firm support; this was filled with *concrete*, and allowed to stand for several days. When the mould was removed, it was found firm and strong, and apparently every way adapted to the purpose. This fact once settled, the entire line was supplied with these quasi stone columns, but little exceeding the unsightly wooden poles in expense, and perfectly weather and insect proof. It is now nearly two years since their establishment, and they bid fair, extraordinary occurrences excepted, to last for a century.

Farther along the track, on your right, you pass the main railroad wharf, at which any day in the year several vessels, sail or steam, may be seen actively discharging cargoes for shipment across the road. A couple of hundred yards brings you to a massive stone structure three hundred feet long by eighty wide, through whose broad-arched entrances a triple track is laid. This is the freight depôt of the Panama Railroad Company, and the following description by a recent visitor will give the traveler an idea of its usual internal appearance:

"Bales of quina bark from the interior were piled many tiers deep, and reached to the iron triangular-braced roof of the edifice. Ceroons of indigo and cochineal from San Salvador and Guatemala; coffee from Costa Rica, and cacao from Ecuador; sarsaparilla from Nicaragua, and ivory-nuts from Porto Bello; copper ore from Bolivia; silver bars from Chili; boxes of hard dollars from Mexico, and gold ore from California; hides from the whole range of the North and South Pacific coast; hundreds of bushels of glistening pearl-oyster shells from the fisheries of Panama lay heaped along the floor, flanked by no end of North American beef, pork, flour, bread, and cheese, for the provisioning of the Pacific coast, and English and French goods for the same markets; while in a train of cattle-cars that stood on one of the tracks were huddled about a hundred meek-looking lamas from Peru, on their way to the island of Cuba, among whose mountains they are used for beasts of burden as well as for their wool."

Its situation is on the direct line of the road, its seaward side opening by great doors out upon the waters of the bay, so as to allow vessels of light tonnage to discharge cargo directly into the depôt, while for the heavier a covered wharf extends from the centre into six fathom water. On emerging from the farther extremity of the freight-house, a hundred paces brings you to the *Mingillo*, or native market-place. A few lusty half-naked negroes, descended from the African slaves of the old Spanish dominion (who form a large proportion of the literal population of the Isthmus) are generally seen supplying their customers with fish, cassava, bananas, plantains, and many other fruits and vegetables of the country, from out the bongoes which lay alongside the wharf, or, grouped on the shore over smoking kettles of *sancoche*, ladling out this favorite compound to their native patrons. Large quantities of the vegetable ivory-nut are also brought here by the natives for barter and sale. Sometimes a few aboriginal Indians from the region of San Blas (some sixty miles down the coast) may be seen here. Rather under the medium stature, they are broad-shouldered and muscular, with the straight black hair and high cheek-bones of the North American tribes. They have a peculiar interest from the fact that they belong to a tribe never subjugated by the *Conquistadores*, but who have maintained an unwavering hostility to the Spaniard since the first discovery of the country, and have cherished such a jealousy of their independence that, to the present day, no white man has been permitted to land upon their shores. Their usual dress consists of a simple fold of cloth tied about the loins, though they are not unfrequently seen clad after the manner of the Spanish natives, in a loose shirt and loose cotton or hempen trowsers. Though apparently apathetic and uncommunicative, there is a considerable degree of intelligence in their expression, and a conscious independence in their bearing, that gives one a fair idea of the races which Columbus and his followers found here in the days of old. They have recently allowed one or two small trading schooners twice or thrice a year to anchor near their shores and traffic with them, receiving calicoes, beads, and other ornaments, machetas, etc., in exchange for tortoise-shell, ivory-nuts, and gold dust; but every attempt to explore their country has been uniformly resisted. Their chief weapon is the bow and arrow (the arrow armed with fishbones), in the use of which they are said to be very skillful, and to be in the habit of using it effectively not only upon land, but in their waters; with barbed palm-wood arrows some four feet in length, they have the reputation of being able to transfix large fish at a distance of two or three feet beneath the surface.

Along the opposite side of the railway from the *Mingillo* lies a broad lagoon covering a couple of acres, and connected with the waters of the harbor by a narrow opening under the road. This lagoon is crossed at about the centre by a recently-made street, and will soon be still farther reduced in extent by others. A line of low tenements, principally occupied by the native population, a few stores, and a large hotel, the Aspinwall House, bound its opposite shore, beyond which a dense swamp-forest shuts off the view. Proceeding a little farther, you pass "Johnson's Ice-house," or, rather, if you have an eye to creature comfort, you will not pass it, for it is a depôt for ice and such things for the inner man as may be preserved in it of northern product. Five ships a year come consigned to this establishment from the Boston Ice Company, and Johnson, "the Ice-man of the Isthmus," is decidedly a man whose acquaintance is worth cultivating in this climate. Turning now to the left, toward the sea-beach, which forms a semicircle around this end of the island, the driving surf of centuries has washed up along its whole extent a wide barrier of shells and coral. Upon this you will first observe the hospitals of the Railroad Company, a couple of large, airy buildings, surrounded by generous tiers of piazzas, about which a general air of tidiness and comfort prevails. Although built for the exclusive use of the Company, strangers requiring medical aid are permitted to avail themselves of their advantages. A little to the left is a long wooden building, which contains the lecture-room, library, and club-room of the employés of the Company. A well-selected library of several hundred volumes, and the standard periodicals and journals, may be seen here; there are also materials for a snug game of billiards, backgammon, or chess. Three or four neat little cottages come next along the line of the beach, the residences of the principal officers of the Company, with little garden-plats in the rear, and an occasional cocoa-tree throwing pleasant shadows over them. A little farther on is a fine corrugated iron dwelling, the residence of the Royal Mail Steam Packet Company's agent; next to this is seen the general domestic rendezvous of the Railroad Company's officials (usually known as the "Mess-house"), imbedded in a grove of cocoa and banana trees. Within fifty yards of the rolling surf, the sea-breeze ever playing through its surrounding foliage, it would be difficult to find a more desirable tropical residence.

Still farther on to the right are the buildings of the terminus, car repositories, etc., and machine-shops, whose tall chimneys send up steady columns of smoke, while the ring of many hammers breaks cheerily upon the ear. Along the beach a nicely-graded road has been constructed, which extends the entire circumference of the island, and for more than two thirds of its course it passes along or through the dense and luxuriant tropical forest with which nearly one half the island is still covered. The "Paseo Coral," as this beautiful walk or drive is called, was built by the citizens of Aspinwall, every facility and aid being rendered by the Railroad Company; and morning and evening, especially on Sundays and holidays, it is a favorite resort of the inhabitants of all classes, a few on horseback or in light wagons, but the great majority on foot. Any lover of the beautiful in nature will find it worth his while to make a tour of this "Paseo;" on one side charming glimpses of the ocean and of the "Archipelago" (which cuts off the island of Manzanilla from the main land) meet the eye at every turn, and at almost any point the conchologist may step out upon the coral reef and find sea-shells, fans, and coral to an indefinite extent; on the other, a great variety of tropical vegetation invites the lover of botany to cull from its varied and luxuriant growth; here and there narrow paths lead from it to little native plantations of banana, papaya, and yam, imbedded in which the native hut, with its severely simple furnishing, may be seen, and will convey to the traveler an idea of the habits and character of the native inhabitant of this country. The land in and about Aspinwall, though highly productive, has not yet been brought under proper cultivation to any extent, though several promising plantations have been recently established by foreign residents; fowls, yams, and tropical fruits are, however, found in plenty, and native beef is abundant; the harbor also abounds in excellent fish, and the neighboring islands afford an unlimited supply of the finest green turtle, the usual market-price of which is five cents per pound. Aspinwall, though belonging to New Granada, has a separate civic government, the control of which is possessed chiefly by residents from the United States, most of whom are connected with the Panama Railroad Company.

JOURNEY OVER THE ROAD.

While the principal portion of the route of the Panama Railroad affords to the traveler but little of historic interest apart from its own construction, passing as it does through the heart of a primeval tropical forest for many miles of its extent, and among the wildest and most picturesque mountain scenery, along beautiful rivers, fertile plains, and luxuriant lowlands, for the remainder it affords the observant traveler an opportunity of an easy enjoyment and acquaintance with intertropical nature unsurpassed in any part of the world. Though in point of climate a perpetual summer reigns, the summer and winter are represented by the dry and wet seasons, which produce in the appearance of the vegetation a constant succession of changes in color and form ever new and beautiful. From May until October

DEPARTURE FOR PANAMA.

the rains fall almost daily for several hours; there are usually also several hours each day of bright sunshine. Occasionally throughout the wet season the rain falls for several days without cessation, and in violence and amount seldom if ever seen in northern latitudes. During this season the forests are clothed in brilliant and varied greens, and many of the large forest-trees are covered with blossoms of white, scarlet, or yellow, which, together with the myriads of parasites, epiphytes, and flowering vines, often produce the most gorgeous effects. During the dry season, which occupies the rest of the year, while showers are not uncommon, it is usual to see two, and even three months pass without rain, and the vegetation is scarcely less beautiful than in the wet, though toward the latter part many of the larger trees are destitute of foliage, and the browns and yellows of dying leaves are seen on every side; yet the rich greens still preponderate sufficiently to give a decided summer character to the whole; and the evergreen palms, from which hang numberless clusters of ripe palm-nuts of the richest scarlet; the lowland trees, that blossom at every season; and the passifloras, and many other beautiful flowers, that develop only in the dry season, make it difficult to say which of the two seasons will afford the rarest botanical and floral treat to the traveler; at any and every season the vegetation is varied, luxuriant, and gorgeous beyond comparison. There are, besides, at almost every step, objects novel and interesting among the riches of the animal kingdom, and also in the varied geological formations displayed along the line of the road; in fact, few locations in the world present a more promising field of research for the botanist, the geologist, or the student of natural history. Eminent scientific men from the United States, England, and Germany have already spent considerable time and labor in explorations here, but the results of their researches have not as yet been given to the public. As, however, few travelers over the road have any opportunity other than that afforded by the rapid railway transit to examine the objects of interest on its course, a brief account of the more prominent and readily recognized will perhaps be deemed sufficient for the general reader.

In making the journey over the railroad to the Pacific terminus, starting at the depôt at Aspinwall, a third of a mile brings you to that part of the island shore where the railway leaves it, and crosses over the frith to the swamps of the main land. At this point, which is crossed by an artificial isthmus (built originally of piles and crib-work, but since replaced by solid stone and earth), the channel is about two hundred yards in width, broadening rapidly to the eastward into a miniature archipelago, with a dozen little islands overgrown with mangrove bushes, and lying upon its glassy surface like emeralds upon a mirror. To the westward it again expands into a wide, placid basin, only separated by a narrow belt of foliage from the waters of the bay. The shores on every hand are skirted with a dense growth of mangrove bushes, which droop deep into the water, while directly in front, through the vista opened by the railway, an apparently interminable forest meets the eye. These waters abound in the beautiful varieties of fish known among the natives as "flores del mar," or "the flowers of the sea:" in shape and size they resemble the sun-fish of our Northern lakes, and are remarkable for their varied and brilliant colors.

The mangrove bushes are not unlike the banyan-tree in the manner of their growth. Their branches, shooting downward, frequently enter the soil, take root, and, interlacing again and again, form a barrier requiring a stout hatchet or machete to overcome. Many of the branches which dip into the water are loaded with a variety of the Crustaceæ, almost, if not quite, identical with our Northern oysters, varying in size from a dime to a dollar: several pounds often

MOUNT HOPE.

depend from a single bough. Submerged by every tide, they are well nourished and exceedingly palatable, and, although so small, well worth the trouble of opening. English snipe, plover, teal, heron, and pelican are abundant about here at certain seasons.

About a mile farther on, to the left of a spur of high land, through which the railway passes by a deep long cut, is seen the tall forest of Mount Hope, upon which is located the general cemetery of Aspinwall. A pleasant winding path through the thick undergrowth soon brings you upon the spot. Dense foliage surrounds it on every side. This place was selected for a burial-ground shortly after the commencement of the road, and many victims to the hardships of the work and the virulence of the climate were then buried here; but those days of trial have passed, and the long grass waving over their graves tells of the years since then. A few are recent, and marked by simple monuments; among them will be noticed several of the officers of the United States Home Squadron. The lamented Strain (whose suffering and heroism as the leader of the ill-fated Darien expedition are still fresh in the memory of his countrymen) lies buried here. The surrounding woods, especially toward evening and in the early morning, are vocal with the notes of numerous birds. The sweet and sonorous whistle of the *turpiale* and the cooing of the turtle-dove mingle with the harsh cries of the parrot tribe and the still harsher note of the toucan. Frequent opportunities occur of procuring these different varieties of birds from the natives, as they are more or less numerous along the entire line of the road, and become domesticated with little trouble. The turpiale, which is about the size of a robin, with deep black and bright yellow plumage, is quite equal to the magpie in intelligence and cunning, and is one of the finest whistlers known. The toucan, a dark scarlet-breasted bird, about the size of a pigeon, with a heavy serrated bill six or seven inches in length, is one of the ornithological curiosities of this region; picking up its food on the point of its huge beak, by a sudden jerk it tosses it up half a yard, and as it falls catches it deep in its throat; it also makes extraordinary motions over the water when attempting to drink. The habits of the toucan in this respect were noticed by the early Spanish-American priests, who, averring that this bird, in drinking, made the sign of the cross over the water, called it "Dios te de" (God gives it thee). Considerable land in the vicinity of Mount Hope has been cleared, and cultivated with success and profit. Proceeding along the track beyond Mount Hope, you begin to bring more fully into view the wondrous wealth of the Isthmian forest. For a space of fifty feet on either side of the solid track embankment the original growth has been swept away and replaced by a rich display of aquatic plants, through whose broad shining leaves myriads of callas and long, slim-petaled pond-lilies struggle out to fill the air with their delicious perfume. This low and recent vegetation is walled in by a primeval growth of a variety and luxuriance that almost defies description. Palm-trees, slender and tall, from under whose crowns hang long scarlet and yellow tassels; palms, low and huge, with trunks scarce lifted above the slimy ooze, sending out graceful pinnate leaves half a dozen yards in length; great cedro and espabe trees, towering up like giants for a hundred feet, then sending out strong arms that almost clasp each other across the clearing, their trunks covered with thick vines and parasites. These and many other varieties are so closely set and interwoven together that the eye fails to penetrate into the depths of the forest. The great number and variety of parasitic growths can not fail to attract constant attention. Almost every tree and shrub supports more or less of these treacherous leeches, in form and size ranging from the simple tuft of grass to the enormous growths whose branches equal in magnitude those of the largest trees, and frequently exceed those of the poor victim from which their strength is drawn. Some are seen which had originally taken root upon the trunks of large and thrifty trees, which, under their exhausting demands and vice-like embrace, have died and rotted out, leaving the well-conditioned leech, though a mere shell, upright, and so like the original tree that, except for occasional apertures which discloses the hollowness within, their villainy might at a little distance escape detection. Many bear beautiful and fragrant flowers. A curious and exceedingly common variety springs from seeds deposited in the ordure of birds upon the highest trees, sending long fibrous tendrils, without a single branching twig, down to the earth, when it again takes root, and increases in size until it frequently attains a diameter of five or six inches. Often trees, so decayed that otherwise they must have fallen, are by these supports retained in their upright position for many years. The smaller ones, combining pliability with great strength, are much used as cordage by the natives. Trailing vines and blossoming creepers are on every side in great profusion and luxuriance, enwrapping the trees and hanging in variegated festoons from the branches. As you proceed, every moment new, and, if possible, richer varieties of vegetation pass in quick review, until you are almost lost in wonder and admiration. At about three miles from the terminus a bend is cut off in the small sluggish stream, called the Mindee, whose waters are half concealed by the overhanging verdure; along its banks the tall and graceful bamboo, that giant of the grasses, adds a new beauty to the scene. The waters of the Mindee, which empties into Navy Bay about a mile and a half from Aspinwall, abound with alligators, often of great size, which afford plenty of exciting sport to parties from the city, who make occasional incursions upon them, and to the natives, who value them greatly for their oil, which is used for medication, and their teeth, which are worn as potent charms. Not unfrequently these ugly beasts crawl out into the pools along the railway track, where they may be seen basking in the sun, scarcely deigning to lift their unwieldy heads as the train thunders by.

In the immediate vicinity of the Mindee some of the lands are dry enough to be susceptible of tillage. Native huts may here and there be seen near the road surrounded by patches of plantains, bananas, Indian-corn, and sugar-cane. Beyond this the forest vegetation is varied and enriched by a species of the palm, from the fruit of which the palm-oil of commerce is extracted. It differs little in form from the tasseled variety which has been previously noticed, except that it attains a greater size, and, instead of the gaudy tassel, bears immense clusters of scarlet nuts about as large as a lime; the clusters, shooting out from the trunk of the tree just underneath its foliage, hang by a single stem, and are often two or three feet in length, contrasting vividly with the surrounding verdure. The palm-tree, that prince of the vegetable kingdom, which is so characteristic of tropical vegetation, is nowhere more abundant in variety and beauty than upon the Isthmus, no less than twenty-one varieties having already been found and classified here. Conspicuous among them for their practical use to the natives of the country are the "wine palm," from the sap of which is distilled a sweet and intoxicating beverage; the "motombo," or sago palm, which furnishes the sago; the "ivory palm," producing the vegetable ivory-nut of commerce; the "glove palm," which furnishes, by the covering of its spatha, ready-made bags, capable of holding grain, etc., to the amount of nearly half a bushel; the "cabbage palm," the tender shoots upon the summit of which resemble in appearance and nutritiousness the ordinary cabbage; others also there are from which they manufacture flax, sugar, various domestic utensils, weapons, and

GATUN STATION.

food; besides this, the habitations of the people are framed of their trunks and roofed with their leaves.

Passing the seventh mile-post, you emerge from the swamp, and come to the Gatun Station, located upon the eastern bank of the Rio Chagres, which is at this point about fifty yards in width, and here makes a great bend, opening beautiful vistas through the dense forests up and down its course. This bank of the river is formed by a ridge of low hills, across the foot of which the railway runs. A few yards from the road, on the high ground to the left, are the buildings of the station. A large, two-story framed building, about forty feet in length by thirty in breadth, surrounded by piazzas and balustrades, is the residence of the local superintendent and the foreign workmen employed on this section. Suitable out-buildings are situated in the rear, and a little garden in front, where the roses and peonies, the pinks and pansies of our northern clime, challenge comparison with the orchids, fuchsias, and passifloras of the tropics; and there are radishes, cucumbers, and lettuce contrasting curiously with the native products of the place. With a few unimportant exceptions, this establishment is similar to that of all the stations, which are situated about four miles distant from each other along the entire length of the road. The duty of the local superintendent is not only to keep the track along his section in perfect repair, but to give his personal attention to all matters which can in any way impede the safety or dispatch of the regular trains; and to this ample service, in a great measure, is due the immunity from accident which has characterized the running of the Panama Railroad from its first establishment to the present day. On the opposite shore of the river stands the ancient native town of *Gatun*, which is composed of forty or fifty huts of cane and palm, and situated on the edge of a broad savanna that extends back to a range of hills a mile or two distant. This place is worthy of mention as a point where, in the days by-gone, the bongo-loads of California travelers used to stop for refreshment on their way up the river; where "eggs were then sold four for a dollar, and the rent for a hammock was two dollars a night."

From Gatun the course of the road lies along the base of an irregular line of high lands that rise up from the eastern side of the valley of the Rio Chagres, and a few hundred yards brings you to the Rio Gatun, a tributary of the Chagres, which is crossed by an iron truss-girder bridge of ninety-seven feet span. The dense swamp-growth looms up on either side like a wall, while rising out of it, close on the left, are two fine conical peaks, called "Lion" and "Tiger" hills, which attract attention by the regularity of their outlines and the dense and gorgeous forests with which they are covered. These hills received their titles from the immense numbers of howling monkeys which inhabited this district previous to and during the construction of the road, and whose frequent roaring made the night hideous, and were often mistaken by the uninitiated for the formidable animals which their cries closely resembled. These, as well as several smaller varieties, still abound in the neighborhood, and their howlings at nightfall are frequently heard, but the progress of improvement has driven them from the immediate vicinity of the road.

Passing the Lion Hill Station, which has a fine cultivated clearing on the high ground behind it, the vegetation becomes less dense, and more decidedly aquatic in its character; large patches of cane-brake, huge tree-ferns, low palms in great variety, and scrubby mangroves, rise out of the dark pools in the swamps by the road-side. Along this section is found that rare variety of the orchid family known as the "Espiritu Santo." Its blossom, which is of an alabaster whiteness, approaches the tulip in form, and gives forth a powerful perfume not unlike that of the magnolia; but it is neither for its beauty of shape, its purity of color, nor its fragrance that it is chiefly esteemed. Resting within the cup of the flower, so marvelously formed that no human skill, be it never so cunning, could excel the resemblance, lies the prone image of *a dove*. Its exquisitely moulded pinions hang lifeless from its sides, the head bends gently forward, the tiny bill, tipped with a delicate carmine, almost touches its snow-white breast, while the expression of the entire image (and it requires no stretch of the imagination to *see* the expression) seems the very incarnation of meekness and ethereal innocence. No one who has seen it can wonder that the early Spanish Catholic, ever on the alert for some phenomenon upon which to fasten the idea of a miraculous origin, should have bowed down before this matchless flower, and named it "Flor del Espiritu Santo," or "the Flower of the Holy Ghost," nor that the still more superstitious Indian should have accepted the imposing title, and ever after have gazed upon it with awe and devotional reverence, ascribing a peculiar sanctity even to the ground upon which it blossoms, and to the very air which it ladens with its delicious fragrance. It is found most frequently in low and marshy grounds, springing from decayed logs and crevices in the rocks. Some of the most vigorous plants attain a height of six or seven feet; the leaf-stalks are jointed, and throw out broad lanceolate leaves by pairs; the flower-stalks spring from the bulb, and are wholly destitute of leaves, often bearing a cluster of not less than a dozen or fifteen flowers. It is an annual, blooming in July, August, and September, and has in several instances been successfully cultivated in the conservatories of foreign lands. In former times bulbs of the plant could rarely be obtained, and then only with much labor and difficulty; but since their localities have become familiar to the less reverential Anglo-Saxon, great numbers have been gathered and distributed throughout different parts of the world, though their habits and necessities have been so little appreciated that efforts to bring them to flower usually prove ineffectual; if, however, they are procured in May or June, *after the flower-stalk has started*, when sufficient appropriate nutriment resides in the bulb to develop the perfect flowers, they can be safely transplanted, and will flower under the ordinary treatment adapted to the bulbous plants of colder climates. The bulbs, dried or growing, may be procured either at Aspinwall or Panama at from two to five dollars per dozen.

The next station is called "Ahorca Lagarto," "to hang the lizard," deriving its name from a landing-place on the Chagres near by; this, again, named from having, years back, been pitched upon as an encampment by a body of government troops, who suspended from a tree their banner, on which was a lizard, the insignia of the Order of Santiago. The land around this station, though low and level, is covered with a noble forest-growth, among which is found the huge cedro-tree, from which the native hollows out his canoe, sometimes of fifteen or twenty tons burthen; its broad, plane-shaped roots extend out on every side like buttresses, and its trunk towers up, without a branch, for a hundred feet, supporting a canopy of foliage often fifty yards in diameter. A short distance from the station, close to the left side of the track, is one called "Stephens's Tree," not less than five or six yards in diameter at its base. A luxuriant growth of vines decorates its trunk, and, winding out upon its branches, hangs down like a thickly-woven curtain to the lesser growth beneath. Its trunk is studded with parasites, and usually fine specimens of the Orchidaceæ may be seen blooming among its foliage. Several varieties of mahogany are also found here, and occasionally the lignum-vitæ-tree; the most of the trees, however, are only known by local names, which can convey

STEPHENS'S TREE.

BUJIO SOLDADO.

to the traveler but little idea of their character. Along the track may be seen the sensitive plant, with its feathery pink blossoms growing in wild profusion. The *Agave Americana*, or wild pine-apple, is also abundant. This plant is similar in form and growth to the cultivated pine-apple, except that the leaves are often eight or ten feet in length, and afford a vegetable fibre which makes excellent cloth; the fruit, which is edible and not unpleasant, is of the most brilliant scarlet, and forms a beautiful contrast with the surrounding foliage. A mile or so farther on the forest becomes less lofty, and the traveler soon passes what may easily be mistaken for the overgrown ruins of some ancient city: walls, watch-towers, tall columns, and Gothic arches are on either hand, and it will be difficult to realize that Nature alone, with a lavish and fantastic hand, has shaped this curious scene out of myriads of *convolvuli;* whole clumps of trees are covered in by them, so that they appear like the remains of huge fortifications; tall stumps of palm look like broken columns overgrown with verdure; and when they lean together, as in several instances is the case, great Gothic arches are formed. So dense is this en-shrouding web of creepers that scarce a tree or branch can be recognized through it over a space of several acres, and the whole of this wondrous display is, at certain seasons, decorated with bright blue trumpet-shaped flowers.

Leaving behind this city of verdure, a chain of high and densely-wooded hills on the left is brought into view, and, winding along its base, another station, called "Bujio Soldado," or "Buyo Soldado" ("*the Soldier's Home*"), is passed. Here opens, on the right, a fine view up the Rio Chagres. A mile farther on is an excellent quarry of freestone alongside the track, from which large quantities of building and ballasting material have been quarried by the Company. A little farther on, upon the edge of the steep river bank, is the site of a cottage, notable as having been the favorite residence of the late J. L. Stephens, the celebrated author and traveler, who spent much of his later life in developing this great railway enterprise; but little now remains except its ruins, and the stately palm that long ago threw its shadow over his once beautiful garden. From this point beautiful views up and down the river are visible, while across, the high opposing bank stretches back in a broad plateau, covered with low foliage, from among which occasional tall trees shoot up, until it meets a range of distant hills. Continuing your course, with an occasional view of the river, which winds like a great serpent along this tortuous valley, you soon come to the native town of "Bueno Vistita" ("beautiful little view"). This is a collection of thirty or forty rude palm huts, skirting the track, and occupied by the families of native laborers along the road. A few native women, bareheaded, in long, heavily-flounced muslin dresses, off at the shoulder, and usually a naked "picaninny" astride the hip, forms the chief feature of the population, while the balance is made up of dogs, pigs, chickens, and children, in a charming state of affiliation. Very few of the aborigines of the country are found on this portion of the Isthmus, the inhabitants being, for the most part, a mixture of Spaniard and Indian. There are, however, many Africans and half-breeds, descended from the old Spanish slaves of this province, or imported from Carthagena and Jamaica. The former, usually peaceable and industrious, cultivate little patches of land, and occasionally raise a few cattle; but the latter are a restless, turbulent set, requiring a strong hand to keep them in subjection; being, however, hardy and athletic, they have been much employed as laborers on the road. A glance into the huts of these people and at their surroundings will give an idea of the manner of living of the greatest portion of the native inhabitants of the country. The body of the dwelling is composed of bamboo; the roof is thatched with leaves of the

STEPHENS'S COTTAGE.

palm; the floor is the bare earth; occasionally there is a loft, which is reached by an upright post, with deep notches cut on either side answering for stairs. Hammocks of vegetable fibre or cotton cloth are the usual beds, which also constitute the favorite lounging-place during the day. Besides these, a rude bench or two, a kettle, half a dozen earthen platters and water-jars, and a few gourds for water, complete the furniture of the native hut. Sun-dried and fresh beef, and pork, eggs, and fowls, are cheap and plenty. Their food, however, is mostly vegetable, the yam and plantain holding the chief place. The *bread-fruit* is plentiful, and grows spontaneously. Rice is raised, and consumed to a considerable extent; and a large variety of tropical fruits

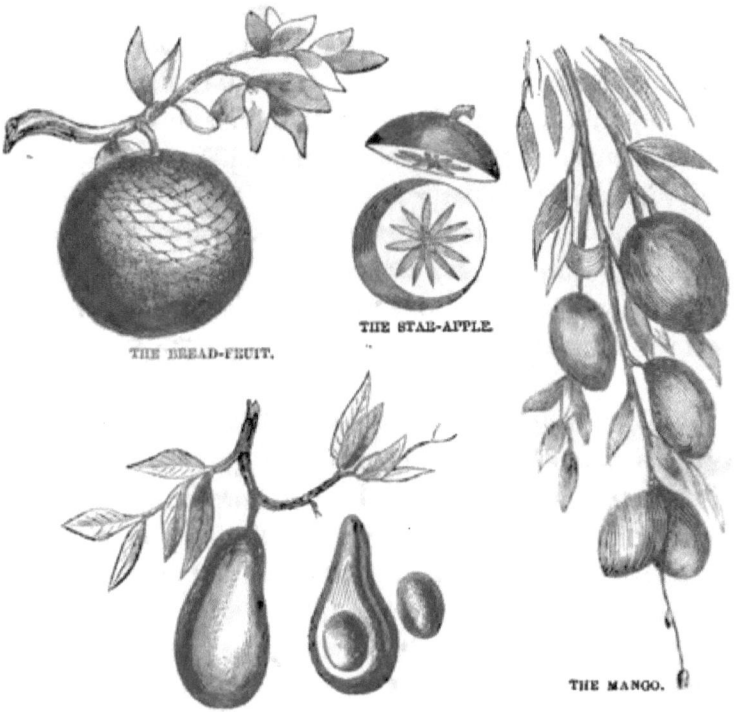

THE BREAD-FRUIT.   THE STAR-APPLE.   THE MANGO.
THE AVOCADO PEAR.

are abundant. Besides the pine-apple, orange, lemon, lime, and banana, which arrive at great perfection here, there are many kinds of fruit seldom seen out of the tropics, which are delicious and wholesome; the bread-fruit, the avocado or alligator pear, the papaya, the Mamei and star-apples, the chirimoya, the mango, the zapote, the granadilla (fruit of the passion-vine), and many others, growing spontaneously or with the most careless cultivation.

The Spanish language is universally spoken by the natives, greatly corrupted, however, by provincialisms. In disposition the native is usually peaceable and inoffensive. The Roman Catholic religion is universally professed, but their ideas of it, beyond a superstitious appreciation of the power and influence of the priests, and the efficacy of holy relics and tokens, are exceedingly limited.

Squatter sovereignty obtains here on a very liberal scale, each citizen being entitled to claim, occupy, and hold "all that lot, piece, or parcel of land" that can be distinctly seen from any given point thereon, of the unoccupied lands of the government. The Spaniard and half-breed frequently avail themselves of this privilege, carrying on cattle-raising to a considerable extent, besides occasionally producing a little sugar, rice, etc., for market. The general class of natives, however, are gregariously inclined, and seldom covet more than enough for a little hut and garden-patch which supplies the necessities of life.

Passing a couple of miles more of forest, intersected by one or two small tributaries of the Chagres River, you arrive at the Frijoli Station; here, during the dry season, may be seen the gorgeous scarlet passion-flower, as well as the purple variety, in great abundance. Occasionally small gangs of natives are seen engaged in clearing away the recent growths along the track with their machetas. The machete is a sort of hiltless broadsword, from two to three feet in length, heavy, straight, and pointed, with a handle of wood or bone, and is the universal companion of the native of this country; with it he cuts his path through the tangled forest, clears his little plantation, builds his hut; with it, too, he plants his crops and reaps them; it is usually his only weapon of offense and defense; and from the half-grown boy to the gray-headed patriarch, you seldom find one, waking or sleeping, without his cherished machete. This section is rich in its variety of the birds, beasts, reptiles, and insects peculiar to intertropical America. Here are found frequent colonies of the oriole, or hanging-bird, whose beautifully-woven nests, often two or three feet long, may be seen depending by scores from the trees. Several richly-colored varieties of parrots and toucans, trogons, tangers, humming-birds, etc., abound. Grouse and the crested wild turkey are found on the higher grounds of the interior. The tapir is occasionally found in the river and marshy grounds adjoining. Monkeys in variety, the opossum, the ant-eater, the peccary, or wild hog, the sloth, the deer, bear, cougar, and two or three varieties of the tiger-cat, are native here. Among the many varieties of the lizard tribe which abound is the iguana, which grows to a large size, viz., from three to six feet in length, and is eagerly sought for by the natives for its flesh, which is tender and delicate as a chicken, and also for its eggs. Females of this species are sometimes captured, cut open, the eggs removed, the animal permitted to escape, and the natives aver that after this barbarous proceeding they uniformly recover. The eggs are about the size of a marble, yellow and shriveled, and may be seen hanging in bunches for sale in any native market, and are by no means unpalatable. Land-crabs abound in great numbers, and are esteemed a delicate article of food. The most common variety is of a pale blue color, and as large as half a cocoanut. Stories are told of their rapacity and carnivorous tastes that almost surpass belief. It is said that the largest animals, dead or wounded past resistance, are frequently reduced by them to whitened skeletons in a single night. There are several other smaller varieties, some of which are beautifully colored. Among the venomous insects, the tarantula, the centipede, and the scorpion are frequently met. Among the troublesome insects are white, red, and black ants, musquitoes, sand-flies, fleas, garapatos, or wood-ticks, and the chigoe, or jigger, which last not only bites, but burrows under the skin, and there deposits its eggs, which, if not speedily removed, will hatch out a troublesome nest of minute worms, producing great inflammatory disturbance in the part. As, however, they are at first very superficial, and inclosed in a little membranous sac, this is easily removed entire with a needle, and no farther trouble ensues; they are fortunately not common here, and seldom annoy any but the barefooted native. Venomous snakes, though occasionally seen, are not common. The boa constrictor is native here, and sometimes is found from twelve to eighteen feet in length; it is, however, exceedingly rare to hear of any serious injury having been done by any of them. The alligator, which is found more or less plentifully in all parts of the Chagres and its tributaries, and the adjacent streams and swamps, frequently attacks and destroys dogs and cattle, and occasional instances have occurred where the natives, imprudently venturing into the waters infested with them, have fallen a prey to their rapacity.

Leaving Frijoli, fine fields of Indian-corn may be seen here and there nestled under the hills; dense groves of palms and superb displays of convolvuli are also found along this section for a couple of miles, when you approach the lofty banks of the Chagres at Barbacoas, and cross the river by a huge wrought-iron bridge six hundred and twenty-five feet in length, eighteen in breadth, and standing forty feet above the surface of the water, and said to be one of the longest and finest iron bridges in the world. After crossing the Chagres at this point, instead of low grounds and virgin forests, a beautiful stretch of meadow-

BRIDGE ACROSS THE RIVER CHAGRES AT BARBACOAS.

SAN PABLO STATION.

lands, bounded by high precipitous hills, meets the view; while the river, broad and swift, curves around like a horseshoe through its deep channel on the left and behind, displaying along its banks groups of a gigantic species of caoutchouc-tree, that breaks the outline of dense palm and cocoa groves.

The cultivation of the lands at this point is said to date back for more than two centuries, and to have been worked originally by the Jesuits. At about half a mile from the bridge the San Pablo Station is passed, and a little farther on a fine quarry of recent volcanic rock; from thence, through occasional cleared and cultivated lands, you pass to the station at Mamei and the native town of Gorgona, noted in the earlier days of Chagres River travel as a place where the wet and jaded traveler was accustomed to worry out the night on a raw hide, exposed to the insects and the rain, and in the morning, if he was fortunate, regale himself on jerked beef and plantains. The road now, leaving the course of the river, passes on through deep clay banks and rocky cuts, presenting little novelty beyond the magnitude of the labor expended upon them in establishing the railway, until, sweeping around a hill, the beautiful meadow-lands of Matachin open to the view. Here, rising in their stateliness, the classic sheaves of the royal palm shed an air of Eastern beauty over the landscape. A native village dots the foreground; on the left the waters of the Chagres, broadened at this point by the Rio Obispo (its greatest tributary), is seen through the ceiba groves that skirt its banks, while on the right and in front the scene is bounded by a group of conical hills covered with short grass and studded with palms. The completion of the Panama Railroad in 1855 was here celebrated with great ceremony and rejoicing, and the corner-stone of a monument to its originators and constructors was erected upon the crest of the highest and most beautiful of these hills.

The railway has several side branches at Matachin, and is the usual point of meeting for the trains from either terminus. As there is usually a little delay on such occasions, the natives take advantage of it to traffic with the passengers. Almost every hut displays something for sale:

NATIVE HUT AT MATACHIN.

cakes, "dulces," or native candy, and the various fruits of the region. Here the oranges are unusually fine. There is also a saloon, kept by a native, where very good English beer, French claret, crackers and cheese, etc., may be obtained. From Matachin, passing along the base of "*Monument Hill*," the narrow valley of the Rio Obispo is entered, and its waters are crossed by stout iron bridges twice within the distance of a mile; then you pass the Obispo Station, and continue along the course of the Obispo River, over a fine rolling and luxuriant woodland, where the delicious wild mango, the zapote, the nispero, and the guava are fre-

MAMEI STATION.

MONUMENT HILL—YAZAGHIN.

quently seen; also occasional native huts, surrounded by cultivated fields. From the station at Obispo the grade is ascending, with a maximum of sixty feet to the mile. Continuing to rise for about three miles, you pass the "Empire Station," and reach the "Summit," or highest elevation of the railway above the mean level of the Atlantic and Pacific Oceans. Here is a little native settlement called "Culebra" ("the Snake"), noted as having been the terminus of the road in 1854. Then, passengers arriving at this place by the cars from the Atlantic shore were compelled to mount upon mules, and flounder on through heavy sloughs and rapid streams, along the borders of deep ravines and over precipitous mountains, exposed to drenching rains in the wet season, and a broiling sun in the dry, not unfrequently attacked and plundered by banditti, with which the road was then infested, until, after a whole day's labor and peril, they arrived at Panama, only twelve miles distant. "Culebra" at that time was a thrifty place, boasting of two or three hotels, imported ready-made from the United States, into which often more than a thousand men, women, and children were promiscuously stowed for a night. There were also twenty or thirty native huts, about twelve feet square, each of which was considered of ample dimensions to house a dozen wayworn travelers, only too thankful to find a spot of dry ground upon which to spread their blankets; but its glory has departed, and scarce a vestige remains to tell of its former estate. From Culebra the road passes through a deep clay cutting from twenty to forty feet in depth, and nearly a third of a mile in length. At this point commences the Pacific slope of the road, with a descending grade of sixty feet to the mile.

The surrounding scenery now becomes bold and picturesque in the highest degree. Lofty conical mountains rise on every side from among the irregular ridges that form the upper boundaries of the Rio Grande. The course of the road now lies across steep rocky spurs and deep ravines between them and along their precipitous sides. High embankments and heavy cuttings are frequent. Here, also, the vegetation is profuse and gorgeous; tall forests cover the whole landscape as far as the eye can reach. At about a mile from the summit the road passes along the side of a huge basaltic cliff, whose great crystals, nearly a foot in diameter, and from eight to twelve feet in length, lie at an angle of about forty degrees. In the earlier days of the road this cliff presented a lofty, broken, and jagged appearance, that seemed almost to overhang and threaten the safety of those passing along the track below. These great crystals of basalt, firm and compact, but easily dislodged, have been so extensively used in the ballasting of the road, etc., along this section, that the once grand and picturesque appearance of the cliff is almost entirely destroyed; enough, however, remains to strike the beholder with admiring wonder, on contemplating this curious formation, at the still visible regularity and beauty of its crystallization, and with awe when he reflects upon the gigantic internal forces that have resulted in its upheaval. It is one of the few known examples in the world where the natural perpendicular which basaltic formations always assume (so beautifully seen in the Fingal's Cave at Staffa, and along the "Palisades" of the Hudson) has been so rent and displaced. But this whole region gives unmistakable evidence that great and comparatively recent volcanic forces have been instrumental in its formation. There is no continuity of the mountain ranges; conical peaks rise up on every side; perfect marine shells and coral are found on their very summits, and the strata of the rocks exposed by the cuttings of the railroad are all volcanic. The Rio Grande at this point is a narrow and noisy torrent, winding along through the dense forests far below the track; the caoba, the cedro, and the malvicino trees rise up like lords of the land over the end-

BASALTIC CLIFF.

F

PARAISO STATION.

less growths of palm and the innumerable varieties of other tropical woods that interweave below them. After nearly three miles of this, the beautiful undulating valley of "Paraiso," or "Paradise," is reached, surrounded by high conical hills, where Nature, in wild profusion, seems to have expended her choicest wealth. From Paraiso the road continues on over ravines, and curves around the base of frequent conical mountains, gradually descending until the low lands and swamps of the valley of the Rio Grande are passed, when looming up in the distance is seen the high, bald head of Mount Ancon, whose southern foot is washed by the waters of the Pacific Ocean. On the left rises "*Cerro de los Buccaneros*" ("the Hill of the Buccaneers"), from whose summit the pirate Morgan, on his marauding march across the Isthmus in 1670, had his first view of ancient Panama, and where he encamped on the night previous to his attack and pillage of that renowned city. Crossing by bridges of iron the San Pedro Miguel and the Caimitillo (narrow tide-water tributaries of the Rio Grande), the Rio Grande Station is passed. From thence, through alternate swamp and cultivated savanna, the muddy bed of the Rio Cardenas is crossed; when, leaving the Rio Grande to the eastward, a fine stretch of undulating country around the base of Mount Ancon is brought into view, enlivened by native huts and cultivated fields. About a mile farther on may be seen the long metallic roofs of the railroad buildings of the Pacific terminus peeping out from a grove of cocoa-trees, and a little beyond them, and to the right, the Cathedral towers, the high-tiled roofs and dilapidated fortifications of the city of Panama, while through the intervening foliage occasional glimpses of the "ever peaceful ocean" assure the traveler that the transit of the Isthmus is nearly accomplished, and a few minutes more brings him safely into the spacious passenger depôt of the Railroad Company at Panama.

Passing through the depôt, and from thence directly onward to the sandy beach of the Bay of Panama, about fifty yards distant, a beautiful panorama opens upon the view. On the left are the commodious warehouses and the long, covered, iron-piled wharf of the Railroad Company, alongside of which the small steamers and tugs lie to take on or discharge passengers and freight for the larger vessels anchored in the bay. Beyond the wharf a white sandy beach sweeps around a quarter circle of a couple of miles, skirted by tangled masses of foliage interspersed with groups of cocoa-trees. A ridge of high and broken, but heavily wooded land rises up behind, sloping down to the eastward toward the peaceful ocean, that stretches out to the horizon before you. On the right, the city, high-walled and turreted, stands boldly out into the ocean, like Balboa of old, as if still claiming dominion over the limitless expanse; no longer bristling with defiant cannon or decked with the flaunting colors of the Conquistador, but deserted, crumbling, and grass-grown, "mellowed into harmony by time." Within the walls a mass of high-tiled roofs, with here and there a dilapidated tower or pearl-shelled spire, combine to present a scene more beautiful than is often beheld. The city of Panama is peculiarly rich in historical associations connected with the early days of the Spanish rule in this country, and is full of the decayed monuments of its ancient splendor.

Panama is situated in lat. 8° 56′ N., and long. 79° 31′ 2″ W., upon a rocky peninsula that stretches out from the base of the high volcanic hill *Ancon*, and projects a quarter of a mile into the sea. It has at present a population of about 10,000 souls. Its roadstead is one of the finest in the world. At about two and a half miles northwest of the city are situated the beautiful islands of Perico, Flamenco, and Islñao, the joint property of the Panama Railroad and the Pacific Mail Steam-ship Companies, and are occu-

TERMINUS AT PANAMA.

CITY OF PANAMA.

pied by them as the rendezvous of the California and Central American lines of steam-ships. These islands are well wooded, and abound in fine springs of water. Flamenco, the largest of the three (about half a mile in length by a third in breadth), has on its southern side a fine beach, which, as the tides here rise and fall from twelve to twenty-one feet, gives admirable facilities for the repairs of the shipping. Excellent and capacious anchorage exists here. The city of Panama previously to 1744 (when the trade between Europe and Western America first began to be carried on around Cape Horn) was the principal entrepôt of trade on the Pacific coast. From that period, however, with the decline in the Spanish possessions in America, it became reduced in commercial importance almost to a nonentity, and so remained until the past few years. The establishment of the South Coast, the California, the Central American steam-ship lines, and that by which all the business of these lines is carried on, the Panama Railroad, have combined to render it again a place of considerable importance. At Panama there is a first-rate hotel, the Aspinwall House, probably the best on the Isthmus—charge three dollars per day.

The site of the "City of Panama the Ancient" (which was destroyed by the buccaneer Sir Henry Morgan in 1661) is located about six miles southeast of the present city, and is easily reached by water or land. If time permits, the traveler should by all means visit this spot. The ruins of its ancient fortifications, towers, churches, and public buildings are worthy of the attention of all interested in the early history of Central America, and will amply repay the antiquarian or the lover of the picturesque and beautiful the trouble of a visit to this most interesting of all the remains of Spanish greatness in this region. In the Appendices following will be found, first, all information appertaining to the regulations of the trains on the Panama Railroad, the rates of passage and of the transportation of every kind of freight, and all general information in regard to the regulations of the road which will be likely to be of service to the traveler or the man of business. Also an account of all its connections by sail and steam in the Atlantic and Pacific Oceans, their business regulations, and such information in regard to them and the countries and the places they connect with the road, as shall furnish a reliable source of reference to all interested, displaying, as far as is practicable in a small compass, the resources of each country and place, and affording a means of ascertaining the expenses attendant upon either a visit to those regions, or of doing business with them in the most economical and intelligent manner.

THE CATHEDRAL AT PANAMA.

RUINS OF CHURCH OF SAN DOMINGO, PANAMA.

APPENDIX C.

REGULATIONS OF THE PANAMA RAILROAD.

The regular trains are dispatched daily, Sundays excepted, from Aspinwall to Panama and from Panama to Aspinwall, as per time-table annexed:

TO PANAMA.			STATIONS.		TO ASPINWALL.	
Passenger.	Freight.	Miles.		Miles.	Passenger.	Freight.
Leave.	Leave.				Arrive.	Arrive.
8.15 A.M.	2.00 P.M.	....	Aspinwall	47½	1.00 P.M.	5.30 P.M.
8.50 "	2.35 "	7½	Gatun......	40½	12.25 "	4.55 "
9.38 "	3.20 "	16	Bujio	31½	11.45 "	4.15 "
10.00 "	3.45 "	22½	Barbacoas	25	11.15 A.M.	3.45 "
10.40 "	4.25 "	30	Matachin .	17½	10.40 "	3.10 "
11.20 "	5.05 "	37	Summit ...	10½	10.00 "	2.30 "
Arrive.	Arrive.				Leave.	Leave.
12.15 P.M.	6.00 "	47½	Panama...	....	9.00 "	1.30 "

Besides these regular trains, special trains are always employed whenever the service can not be adequately performed by the regular trains. There are often as many as five and six in number daily for weeks together.

Steamer Trains.—On the arrival of passenger steam-ships at Aspinwall, special trains are dispatched at any hour, so soon as the passengers are landed, provided that the state of the tide at Panama is such that they can be embarked for the connecting steam-ship immediately on the arrival of the trains. This arrangement has been made solely with a view of affording to the passenger the greatest degree of comfort and convenience consistent with dispatch. To those unacquainted with the cause, it may sometimes appear that time is unnecessarily lost: the Company only consults the interest of the passenger in this respect, and no detention is allowed beyond what is absolutely necessary. On the arrival of passenger steam-ships at Panama, the trains are dispatched for Aspinwall immediately on the landing of the passengers, who here step from the steamer directly into the cars without detention.

TARIFF OF RATES FOR PASSAGE AND FREIGHT.

Price of passage through, $25. Children under 12 years, half price; under 6 years, quarter do.

Special Rates of Freight.

Acids—Muriatic, Sulphuric, and Nitric..................................5 cts. per lb.
Baggage—passengers' (50 lbs. free)......................................10 cts. per lb.
Carriages..20 cts. per cubic foot.
Cartridges, with balls..5 cts. per lb.
Cattle, at owners' risk, ordinary trains, over eight..............$5 each.
   "   "   "   "   under eight....................$7 each.
   "   steamer trains, owners' risk, special agreement...............$25 each.
Coal ....$5 per ton of 2240 lbs.
Cocoanuts..$1 per hundred.
Coke..$7 per ton of 2240 lbs.
Copper Ore in bags ....⅜ths of one cent. per lb.
Demijohns (empty)..50 cts. each.
Dye-woods ....$7 per ton of 2240 lbs.

Express freight, by steamer trains..........................$1 80 per cubic foot.
Furniture, such as tables, chairs, bureaus, bedsteads, etc...25 cts. per cubic foot.
Gold, in dust, coined, or manufactured......................¼ per cent. on value.
Gunpowder, separate cars...................................5 cts. per lb.
Hides..15 cts. each.
Horses, at owners' risk, special agreement.................$40 each.
Jewelry..¼ per cent. on value.
Lumber—White Pine..$10 per M.
    "   Yellow Pine...$12 per M.
    "   Oak...$15 per M.
    "   Cedar and Mahogany..................................$15 per M.
Mules, at owners' risk, special agreement..................$20 each.
Oil, Whale and Palm, toward the Atlantic...................4 cts. per gallon.
Patent Fuel..$5 per ton of 2240 lbs.
Pitch..$1 per barrel.
Platina..¾ per cent. on value.
Poultry—Chickens, 75 cts. per dozen; Turkeys, $1 50 per dozen.
Precious Stones..¾ per cent. on value.
Rosin..$1 per barrel.
Sheep, at owners' risk, by passenger trains................$12½.
Shingles...$3 per M.
Silver, in bars, coined or manufactured....................¾ per cent. on value.
Silver Ore...½ per cent. on value.
Swine, at owners' risk.....................................$2 each.
Tar..$1 per barrel.
Tin Ores...⅜ of one cent per lb.
Quicksilver..50 cts. per iron flask.

Classification of Freight.

First class freight, comprising merchandise, in boxes
   and bales, not otherwise enumerated....................50 cts. per cubic foot.
Second class freight, as per description annexed...........1½ cts. per lb.
Third " " " " "..............................1 ct. per lb.
Fourth " " " " "..............................¾ of a ct. per lb.
Fifth " " " " "..............................½ a ct. per lb.
Sixth " " " " "..............................¼ of a ct. per lb.

All articles not specially named to be assimilated.

FIRST CLASS—50 CENTS PER CUBIC FOOT.

Bonnets, Books, Boots.
Caps, Cards (playing), Cassia lignea, Cigars, Cinnamon, Clothing.
Drugs, Dry Goods, not elsewhere enumerated.
Eau de Cologne, Essences, Essential Oils.
Feathers, Fire-works, Flannel; Furs, not otherwise enumerated.
Glass Shades and Looking-glasses, at owners' risk; Glassware, fine, stained, and plate, at owners' risk; Gloves.
Harness; Hats, fur or felt, and of Guayaquil or Panama straw; Hosiery.
Light goods, not elsewhere specified.
Matches, Medicines, Millinery, Musical Instruments.
Oil-cloth, Organs.
Paintings and Engravings, Paper Hangings, Paper, writing and printing; Peltry, not elsewhere specified; Percussion Caps, Perfumery, Pianos, Porcelain and China-ware, fine.
Saddlery, Shoes, Silks, Stationery; Statuary, at owners' risk.
Toys and Fancy Goods.

SECOND CLASS—1½ CENTS PER POUND.

Alcohol, Almonds, Anchovies, Aniseed.
Balsams, Baskets, Beeswax, Brandy, Britannia-ware.
Carpeting; Chandeliers, at owners' risk; Chocolate, Clocks, Cochineal, Confectionery, Cordials, Corks and Corkwood.
Eggs.
Fire-arms, Fruits (dried).
German Silver-ware, Gin, Groceries, not elsewhere specified.
Indigo.
Lamps (ornamental), Liquors of all kinds.
Mattresses.
Nuts, not elsewhere specified.
Picture-frames, Plated Goods, Platform Scales, Preserved Meats and Fruits.
Rum.
Sardines, Soap (fancy), Straw for manufacturing.
Tea, Tobacco (manufactured), Tortoise-shell, Treenails, Trees and Plants in mats.
Varnish in tins; Veneers.
Wooden-ware.

THIRD CLASS—1 CENT PER POUND.

Bagging, Balsam of Copaivi, Bark, Blankets, Brooms, Brushes, Burlaps.
Candles, Cutlery.
Domestics, unbleached, of cotton, in bales.
Gravestones.
Hay in compressed bales; Hemp, manufactures of, such as Canvas, Dowlas, and Osnaburgs.
Leather, dressed.
Nails, copper and brass.
Oil (toward Pacific), Ornaments of Stone, Clay, Marble, Alabaster.
Paints, dry and in oil.
Sarsaparilla, Spirits of Turpentine.
Tacks, Tin-ware; Tobacco, manufactured; Tubing, copper and brass; Type.
Whalebone, Wines; Wire, copper and brass; Wool of alpaca or vicuna.

FOURTH CLASS—¾ CENT PER POUND.

Agricultural Implements, Ale.
Bacon in casks; Beef, Blacking, Borax, Bottles (empty), Bread, Butter.
Castings of copper, brass, or bronze; Cheese, Cider, Copper Sheathing and Spikes, Copperas; Cotton in compressed bales; Cotton Waste, Crackers; Crockery, not elsewhere specified.
Deer-skins in bales.
Earthen-ware in casks or crates.
Felt (for sheathing), Fish, Flour.
Grindstones, Glassware (coarse), Window-glass, etc.; Goat-skins in bales.
Hams in casks; Hardware; Hats, coarse country straw or palm leaf; Hemp, unmanufactured; Herrings, Hollow-ware (iron), Hoops of wood or iron.
India-rubber.
Lard.
Machetas, Machinery, Mats, Matting, Meal, Millstones, Molasses.
Oakum, Oats, Orchilla Weed.
Pickles, Pork (salt), Porter, Potatoes.
Rice, Rope.
Safes (iron), Sago, Salt, Screws, Seeds, Sheep-skins in bales, Shot (in bags), Shovels, Sirups, Soap (common), Soda-water, Spades, Steel in bars and bundles, Stoves, Sugar, Sugar-mills, -moulds, and -pans.

Tallow; Tea (toward Atlantic); Tool-handles, Twine.
Vegetables, Vices (iron), Vinegar.
Window Glass, Wire (brass and copper), Wool of sheep.
Yarn (of cotton).
Zinc in sheets.

FIFTH CLASS—½ CENT PER POUND.

Anchors, Anvils.
Bananas, Beans.
Cables (iron), Cannon, Cannon Balls and Shot (iron), Cocoa, Coffee, Copper in bars, Corn (Indian), Crowbars.
Fruits of the Isthmus not otherwise enumerated.
Hollow Shot, Hoop Iron.
Ice, in quantity; Iron (old), Iron Bars and Pipes, Iron Boiler-plates, Iron Cables, Iron Castings (not machinery), Iron Tubing, Iron in bars.
Lead in pigs, sheet, and pipes, Lemons, Limes.
Nails (iron).
Old Junk (rope), Oranges.
Pearl-shells in sacks; Peas, Plantains.
Sheet Iron, Spikes (iron).
Zinc, ingots.

SIXTH CLASS—¼ CENT PER POUND.

Borate of Lime, Brick. Cement.
Guano in bags. Iron in pigs. Lime.
Marble for building purposes, including flooring tiles and paving.
Nitrate of Soda in bags.
Stone for building purposes, including paving-stones.

Special Conditions.

Freight to be charged on the gross weight of packages, and to be paid in advance or before delivery of goods.

All claims for loss or damage to be presented within five days, otherwise they will not be paid.

The Company will not be responsible for articles of extra value, beyond $100 per package, unless declared and way-billed accordingly.

No package, however small, will be transported for less than one dollar.

The Company will not be responsible for the breakage or loss of contents of any demijohn or jug.

Storage will be charged on all goods remaining in the Company's store-houses, after twenty-four hours, unless by special agreement.

JOSEPH F. JOY, Secretary.

N.B.—Goods shipped for California under through bills of lading must be corded and sealed at the New York Custom-house, or they will be liable to the payment of duties in San Francisco.

RATES OF COINAGE TO BE RECEIVED AND PAID OUT BY THE PANAMA RAILROAD COMPANY.

Gold Coin.

Spanish doubloons	$16 00	Mexican doubloons	$15 50
Peruvian "	15 50	Ecuadorian "	15 50
Bolivian "	15 50	New Granadian doubloons,	
Chilian "	15 50	new coinage	14 00
New Granadian ditto. (old)	15 50	Costa Rican and Central Amer-	
Columbian doubloons	15 50	ican doubloons	13 60

Fractional parts in proportion.

Gold 20 franc pieces	$3 80	Ten-guilder pieces	$3 80
Gold 10 franc pieces	1 90	Condors, New Granadian	8 50
English sovereigns	4 85	Condors, Chilian	8 00
English half sovereigns	2 42½		

Fractional parts in proportion.

United States gold and silver at par.

Silver Coin.

Spanish dollars, $1 00; half dollars, 40 cents; quarter dollars, 20 cents.
Mexican dollars, $1 00; half dollars, 40 cents; quarter dollars, 20 cents.

Fractional parts in proportion.

New Granadian dollars of 5 franc value $0 95
French 5 franc pieces 0 95

Fractional parts as heretofore.

Peruvian and Chilian dollars (new coinage) 0 90
Bolivian dollars (old coinage) 1 00
Bolivian half dollars and quarters not received.

N.B.—Smooth coin not received.

WHARFAGE, LIGHTERAGE, AND HARBOR REGULATIONS.

A pier, 450 feet in length, has been built in the Bay of Panama, to the end of which freight cars are run, to receive cargoes from lighters or vessels lying alongside, and deliver the same on board of vessels at Aspinwall. Vessels of from 200 to 300 tons can lie alongside the pier with safety, grounding in the mud at low water.

Iron launches of the capacity of 100 tons each have been built by the Company to load and discharge vessels whose draught of water prevents them from coming to the pier. These launches are towed to and from the pier by a powerful steam-tug. *The charge for lighterage is one and a half dollars per ton.*

At Aspinwall vessels load and discharge at the wharves. A fire-proof stone warehouse, 300 feet long by 85 feet wide, has been built for the use of the Company.

Regulations in regard to Freight.

1. All freight intended for the morning train must be delivered at the freight-houses of the Company before 5 P.M. on the day previous. The hours for receiving and delivering freight are from 7 to 9 A.M., from 10 A.M. until 2 P.M., and from 3 until 5 P.M.

2. No article will be transported over the road unless it is legibly and properly directed. Packages in bad order may be declined by the freight agent until properly repaired; or, if received in bad order, it will be so noted on the receipt given by the freight agent.

3. Goods will not be received for transportation without a freighting order from the shipper unless by special agreement. Shippers will deliver with their goods a bill of items, signed by themselves or agents, forms for which can be obtained on application to the freight agents. The freighting orders will be compared with the goods by the freight agent, and if found correct, a receipt will be given by him for the same, subject to the rules of the Company.

4. Freight deposited outside, or under the Company's sheds, remains at owners' risk until delivered into cars or freight-house, unless otherwise expressly agreed to; and freight agents will not receipt for goods unless so delivered.

5. Goods for transportation over the road will be received in their turn,

according to priority of delivery, and will remain at owners' risk until examined, compared, and receipted for. Goods for the Company's vessels will also be shipped in order of priority, heavy goods excepted, a sufficient quantity of which may first be put on board to make proper stowage.

6. No article will be delivered from the Company's freight-houses without a receipt or order from the consignee or owner. Draymen and porters calling for goods must be furnished with an order by the consignee, upon whom their receipts will be binding.

7. The Company will not be responsible for articles of extra value beyond $100 per package, unless declared and way-billed accordingly.

8. Freight will be charged on the gross weight of packages; and no package, however small, will be transported over the road for less than one dollar.

9. The Company will not be responsible for breakage or leakage of any description, the decay of any fruits or vegetables, the wastage of ice, or death of poultry or animals, from delay or detention on the road.

10. All payments for transportation will be made at the freight offices in United States currency or its equivalent, at the rates established by the Company (see pages 140, 141).

11. The terms for transportation over the road are prepayment, or cash on delivery of the goods, which may be detained by the freight agent until payment is made.

12. Storage will be charged on all goods remaining in the Company's store-houses for a longer period than twenty-four hours, except under special arrangements, or when they are under through bills of lading authorized by the Company.

Rates of Storage.

The following are the rates of storage per week:

Barrels	10 cts. each.	Boxes	10 cts. per bbl. bulk.
Half do	5 " "	Hides	1 ct. each.
Tobacco	10 " per bale.	Corn	5 cts. per sack.
Hats	20 " " "	Demijohns	20 " each.

All articles not above enumerated to be assimilated and charged in proportion.

13. Claims for loss or damage must be made within five days thereafter, and will be settled by the superintendent on application to him through the freight agents. A bill of the cost of articles lost will be required.

14. When goods are forwarded from Panama to Aspinwall for shipment in other than the lines of vessels above named, the service of the Railroad Company ceases with their delivery at the freight-house in Aspinwall, as in the case of local traffic.

The same principles apply also to the shipment of goods to ports on the Pacific, passing over the road from Aspinwall to Panama.

15. When goods are forwarded from Pacific ports for shipment at Aspinwall by vessels not running in connection with the road, it is necessary for shippers to make arrangements for the payment of freight, transportation, and shipping expenses.

16. Cargo arriving by the Central American steamers, unless under *through bills of lading,* must be received by the consignees on the wharf immediately after arrival; otherwise it will be left there at owners' risk; or, if deposited in the Company's store-houses, it will be at their risk and expense. Cargo for the Central American steamers must be delivered at the freight-house for shipment, otherwise the Company will not be responsible for damage from rain or other cause.

17. Consignees of goods at Aspinwall by the Company's line of sailing vessels will please attend and receive them when discharged, with as little de-

lay as possible, the Company not being liable for any loss or damage after delivery from ship's tackles.

18. When the goods of residents or agents at Panama arrive at Aspinwall from abroad for transportation over the road, and are consigned to them at Aspinwall, they must be delivered to the Company at their freight-house in the same manner and form as is usual with local traffic. This also applies to goods consigned to the Railroad Company at Aspinwall not shipped under through bills of lading.

RATES OF WHARFAGE AND LIGHT MONEY.

Wharfage.

Vessels under 50 tons		$0 75	per day.
" over 50 " and under 100		1 50	"
" " 100 " " 150		2 25	"
" " 150 " " 200		2 50	"
" " 200 " " 250		3 00	"
" " 250 " " 300		3 25	"
" " 300 " " 350		3 50	"
" " 350 " " 400		3 75	"

And 25 cents per day for each additional 50 tons.

Light Money.

Vessels under 100 tons	$1	each.
" over 100 " and under 200	3	"
" " 200 " " 300	5	"
" " 300 "	7	"

The above rates are calculated upon tonnage by American measurement, and payable in American currency or its equivalent.

HARBOR REGULATIONS OF THE PORT OF ASPINWALL, N. G., ESTABLISHED BY THE PANAMA RAILROAD COMPANY.

1. All vessels entering the harbor of Aspinwall will be charged light fees, and all vessels coming to wharf will be charged wharfage, in proportion to tonnage, as per printed rates of the Panama Railroad Company annexed.

2. Vessels using the donkey engines or mules of the Company (which can be had when not otherwise employed) will be charged as follows:

Use of engine for cargo, per day	$10 00
" " " coal, " ton	15
" mule " " " "	15

3. No vessel will be allowed to hang at the outer buoys, as they are to be used solely for convenience in hauling in and out and making sail.

4. Vessels entering the harbor will anchor outside of the line of buoys, where they will be visited by the harbor-master, who will assign them their berths. Regular lines of steamers or sailing vessels which have specified berths are exempt from the above rule. All vessels, after discharging, will also anchor outside the buoys.

5. No iron chains are allowed to be used in making fast to the wharves, unless by express permission from the harbor-master, and vessels will be held liable for any damage done to the wharves by unnecessary chafing, neglect, etc.

6. No coal-ashes, offal, or rubbish are to be thrown overboard by vessels at anchor in the harbor or at the wharves.

7. Masters of vessels will be governed by the directions of the harbor-master in changing berths, hauling to buoys, anchoring in any part of the harbor, etc., and are requested to notify him when wishing to haul, and also to give him at least six hours' notice before leaving port.

GEO. M. TOTTEN, *Chief Engineer.*

Through bills of lading are issued for merchandise from Europe and the Atlantic United States to Panama, San Francisco, Oregon, Washington Territory, etc., and also to the principal ports of South and Central America.

Parties in Europe desiring to ship goods to Panama or ports on the Pacific, under through bills of lading, will please apply to John Hamilton, at No. 6 Castle Street, Liverpool; in the United States to Mr. Joseph F. Joy, office of the Panama Railroad, 88 Wall Street, New York.

All freight to be prepaid.

No bill of lading signed for less than five dollars.

A Commercial and Shipping Agency has been established by the Company at Panama, under the management of Mr. Wm. Nelson, who will receive and forward merchandise or produce consigned to the Company for transportation over the road and shipment at Aspinwall or Panama, in accordance with shippers' instructions, for which services no commissions will be charged, and only such expenses as may actually be paid, thus obviating the necessity of appointing agents on the Isthmus.

Merchandise and produce consigned to the Company for transportation and shipment should be addressed to the superintendent of the road, or to the commercial agent of the Company at Panama, Mr. William Nelson. Goods so consigned will be promptly dispatched.

The average freight from New York to Liverpool by sailing vessels is twenty-five shillings sterling per ton; the average passage about twenty days. By screw steamers the freight is higher, but the passage only fifteen days.

Besides the steamers of the Royal Mail Steam Packet Company, which make regular semi-monthly trips between Southampton and Aspinwall, a screw steam-ship line has commenced running between the latter port and Liverpool. Lines of sailing vessels have also been established to run from London, Liverpool and Bordeaux to Aspinwall. These several lines furnish frequent and reliable opportunities to the merchants of the Southwest coast and Central America to obtain their supplies of European manufactured and other goods.

Goods sent by the Company's line of sailing vessels, and consigned to the secretary in New York for reshipment to Europe or elsewhere, will be forwarded free of commissions or other charges than those actually paid.

Farther information in regard to the number and character of the vessels of the various lines connecting with the Panama Railroad, agencies, ports of entry, prices of passage and freight, dates of sailing, etc., etc., will be found in the following Appendix.

APPENDIX D.

STEAM-SHIP LINES CONNECTING WITH THE PANAMA RAILROAD.

1st. The Atlantic and Pacific Steam-ship Company, running between New York and Aspinwall (below).

2d. The Pacific Mail Steam-ship Company, running between Panama and San Francisco (page 146).

3d. The Oregon and California Steam-ship Company, plying between California, Oregon, and Washington Territory (page 148).

4th. The Panama Railroad Company's Central American Line, running between Panama, Nicaragua, Costa Rica, Salvador and Guatemala (p. 149).

5th. The British Pacific Steam Navigation Company, running between Panama and the ports of New Granada, Ecuador, Peru, Bolivia, and Chili (page 152).

6th. The Royal Mail Steam Packet Company, running between the West Indies, the western coast of South and Central America, and Aspinwall (page 158).

7th. Holt's Screw Steam-ship Freight Line, running between Liverpool and Aspinwall (page 174).

LINES OF SAILING VESSELS.

1st. The Bremen and Aspinwall Line, between Bremen and Aspinwall.

2d. The Bordeaux and Aspinwall Line, between Bordeaux and Aspinwall.

3d. The Panama Railroad Company's Line between Liverpool and Aspinwall.

4th. The Panama Railroad Company's Line between New York and Aspinwall.

1st. THE ATLANTIC AND PACIFIC STEAM-SHIP COMPANY, RUNNING BETWEEN NEW YORK AND ASPINWALL DIRECT, CONNECTING AT PANAMA, BY THE PANAMA RAILROAD, WITH THE PACIFIC MAIL STEAM-SHIP COMPANY'S STEAMERS FOR CALIFORNIA.

The steamers of this line are the North Star, 1867 tons, the Northern Light, 1747 tons, and the Ariel, 1600 tons, one of which is dispatched on the 1st, 11th, and 21st day of every month, from the foot of Warren Street, North River, New York, at 12 o'clock, noon, precisely. When these dates fall on Sunday, the day of departure is on the Monday following.

Rates of Passage.—To Aspinwall.

In deck state-room	$70 00
" first cabin	60 00
" second cabin	50 00
" steerage	40 00

Freight.—To Aspinwall.

On merchandise, 50 cents per cubic foot (under 45 lbs.); heavy goods, 1 cent per pound; specie, 1 per cent. on value. No primage charged.

THROUGH PASSAGE AND FREIGHT.

By an arrangement with the Pacific Mail Steam-ship Company and the Panama Railroad Company, through passage tickets to San Francisco, California, are furnished at the office of this Company; also *through bills of lading* for freight, at the following **rates**:

Through Passage to San Francisco, California.

First cabin (including board)	$200 00
Second " " "	150 00
Steerage " "	100 00

Children under **6 years, quarter price**; over 6 and under 12, half price.

Baggage.—Fifty pounds of baggage is allowed to every adult passenger without charge. On all over this quantity ten cents per pound is required.

Through Freight.

To Panama—$1 per cubic foot (under 45 lbs. to the foot); heavy goods, 1¾ cents per pound (over 45 lbs. to the foot); specie, 1 per cent. on value.

To San Francisco—$1 75 per cubic foot (under 45 lbs.); heavy goods, 4 cents per pound; butter, sugar, and coffee, etc., 3½ cents per pound; specie, 1 per cent. on value. No primage charged.

No bill of lading signed for Aspinwall freight for less than $3, for Panama freight for less than $4, nor for San Francisco freight for less than $15.

No freight received on the day of sailing.

Bills of lading of the only form used are furnished to shippers on application at the office of the Company, No. 177 West Street, corner of Warren, New York City.   D. B. ALLEN, *Agent.*

The usual passage of these steamers between New York and Aspinwall is from eight to nine days.

2d. THE PACIFIC MAIL STEAM-SHIP COMPANY, RUNNING BETWEEN PANAMA AND SAN FRANCISCO, CALIFORNIA, TOUCHING AT MANZANILLA AND ACAPULCO, MEXICO.

The steamers of this Company are, the Golden Age, 2280 tons; the Golden Gate, 2067 tons; the Sonora, 1616 tons; the St. Louis, 1621 tons; the Uncle Sam, 1433 tons; the Washington, 1640 tons; the Orizaba, 1450 tons; the Fremont, 559 tons; the California, 1085 tons; the Toboga (tug), 189 tons. A magnificent steamer of 3000 tons burden is now on the stocks, and nearly completed, for the Panama and San Francisco service, and a second of similar character is projected.

The Golden Age, the Golden Gate, the St. Louis, and the Sonora perform the regular service between Panama and San Francisco. These steamers are dispatched alternately for San Francisco three times a month, on the arrival of the passengers from the Atlantic and Pacific Steam-ship Company's steamer at Panama. The dates usually fall on the 10th, 20th, and 30th of each month. The sailing dates from San Francisco fall upon the 1st, 11th, and 21st of each month.

Through Rates from San Francisco to New York, via Panama Railroad and Atlantic and Pacific Mail Steam-ship Company (including Isthmus).

Passage—deck state-rooms, $225; first cabin, $200; second cabin, $150; steerage, $100. Children between 6 and 12 years, half price; under 6 years, quarter price.

Through freight—"fast" (by connecting steamers), $3 50 per foot; "slow" (stopping over one steamer on the Isthmus), $1 75 per foot.

The rates for passage and freight from Panama to San Francisco, and the ports intermediate, are as follows, viz.:

Passage from Panama to San Francisco—first cabin, $175; second cabin, $125; steerage, $75. Passage from Panama to Acapulco, one half the above rates, and from Panama to Manzanilla, two thirds of the above rates.

The rates of freight from Panama to San Francisco: Havana cigars, English merchandise, and other freight of the same class, $50 per ton; freight originating in Panama also $50 per ton.

Freight from Panama to Acapulco: merchandise, $30 per ton; groceries, wines, and liquors, $25 per ton; tobacco and cocoa, 4 cents per lb.

Central American freight, with through bills of lading, from the Panama Railroad Company's steamers:

Coffee, 20 tons or under......... 2 cents per lb. and 5 per cent. primage.
  "   "   " over........... 1½ "   "   "   5   "   "
Sugar............................ 1¼ "   "   "   5   "   "

Consignees pay light-house fees, port charges, and primage.

Treasure from San Francisco to New York—$30,000 or over, 1½ per cent.; under $30,000, 2 per cent.

From San Francisco and Manzanilla to Panama—1½ per cent.; from Acapulco to Panama, 1½ per cent.

There is always at Panama an extra steamer in readiness for immediate use should occasion require. The ships of this company at this end of their route lie at their anchorage-ground between the Bay Islands, 2½ miles from the railroad terminus, where the depôt of the Company is located. Passengers are transported between ship and shore by the Company's steamer Toboga, which is of sufficiently light draught to lay alongside the railroad wharf at the terminus.

At Benicia, 30 miles from San Francisco, in the Straits of Cardenas, is located the depôt for the Company's steamers. At that place the Company have established commodious wharves, and a large foundry and machine-shop, where repairs are readily and efficiently executed for machinery of the largest class.

The general office of the Pacific Mail Steam-ship Company is at New York, No. 88 Wall Street.

Officers of the Pacific Mail Steam-ship Company.

President, Allan M'Lane.

Directors: William H. Aspinwall, Howard Potter, Samuel W. Comstock, Francis Skiddy, Frederick H. Wolcott, J. T. Soutter, Charles A. Davis, D. B. Allen.

Agents.

At Panama,	David M. Corwin.
" Acapulco,	D. B. Van Brunt.
" San Francisco,	Forbes and Babcock.
In Oregon,	J. M. Bruck.

The origin of the Pacific Mail Steam-ship Company dates back as far as the year 1847, when the Congress of the United States empowered the Secretary of the Navy to contract with Mr. Arnold Harris for the transportation of mails in steam-ships from Panama to Oregon, once a month each way, for a term of ten years, at an annual compensation of $199,000, the contract subject to the action of Congress at its next session of 1847–8. The treaty with Great Britain, which had previously adjusted the vexed question of the boundary-line of Oregon, had turned public attention to her rich valleys, and thousands of settlers were seeking a permanent home in Oregon by the wild paths to the Pacific across the Plains. The object of Congress in making an appropriation for steamer service on the Pacific was not only to facilitate the intercourse between the Atlantic States and the United States possessions on the Pacific, substituting a mode of travel which would bring settlers within thirty days' journey of the Atlantic States, thereby dispensing with the long and perilous journey overland, or the more tedious voyage around Cape Horn, but to have steamers on the Pacific easily convertible into war-steamers for the protection of actual settlers in that isolated land should occasion call for such service.

On the 20th of November, 1847, Mr. William H. Aspinwall became the assignee of Mr. Harris's contract, and about twenty-five sagacious and enterprising men of New York joined him in the effort to carry out the undertaking it involved. Contracts for the building of suitable vessels were made, and their construction pushed vigorously onward.

On the 2d of February, 1848, the treaty of Guadalupe Hidalgo was signed; in the following May ratifications were exchanged, and in July it was proclaimed, and California became the property of the United States, thus greatly increasing the immediate necessity of improved communication with the Pacific coast. The pioneer steam-ship, the California, was launched on the 19th of May, 1848, the Panama soon after, and the Oregon on the 5th of August of the same year.

On the 3d of August, 1848, the United States Congress granted to the Pacific Mail Steam-ship Company $199,000, being an advance of one year's pay, provided their steamers should touch at certain ports in California on their voyages.

On the 30th of September, 1848, the Company was formally organized, $400,000 of stock having been paid in according to the terms of their charter.

On the 5th of October, 1848, the California went to sea. Her consorts followed at short intervals. The discovery of the gold mines of California took place while the steamers were on their route to the Pacific; and the California, touching at the port of Panama, found there a multitude of anxious gold-seekers from the United States, who had crossed the Isthmus, via Chagres, to meet her for the voyage from thence to California. Each succeeding steamer found similar crowds awaiting its arrival, and the organization of the route, which at once took place, has continued in regular operation up to the present day, with such additions to their number and increased tonnage as the rapidly growing traffic required.

The Pacific Mail Steam-ship Company has always been characterized by the great and judicious liberality of its management.

No expense has been spared since the first formation of the Company to carry on their business with the greatest possible safety and dispatch, both for passengers and freight; and the comforts and general requirements of passengers have been so efficiently secured by able and courteous officers that it may be truthfully referred to as one of the most universally popular steam-ship lines in the world.

3d. THE OREGON AND CALIFORNIA STEAM-SHIP COMPANY, RUNNING BETWEEN SAN FRANCISCO AND THE PORTS OF OREGON, WASHINGTON TERRITORY, AND VANCOUVER'S ISLAND, TRI-MONTHLY, WITH A SOUTHERN BRANCH, MONTHLY SERVICE, BETWEEN SAN FRANCISCO AND THE MEXICAN PACIFIC COAST.

This line was established early in the present year (1861) by Messrs. Holliday & Flint, of San Francisco, who purchased the steam-ships Panama, of 1087 tons, Cortez, 1117, Republic, 850, Columbia, 777, and Sierra Nevada, 1247 tons, from the Pacific Mail Steam-ship Company, and took charge of the San Francisco, Oregon, Washington Territory, and Vancouver route, heretofore managed by the Pacific Mail Steam-ship Company, besides establishing a new branch of service between San Francisco and the ports of Cape

St. Lucas, Guaymas, San Blas, Mazatlan, Acapulco, and other Mexican ports.

The service between San Francisco, Oregon, Washington Territory, and Vancouver is performed thrice monthly by the steamers Sierra Nevada, Cortez, and Columbia, and connects with the steamers of the Pacific Mail Steamship Company as heretofore.

Ports of entry.	Price of passage from San Francisco.		Freight, per ton.	
	Cabin.	Steerage.	Upward.	Down.
In Oregon, Humboldt Bay (town of Eureka)	$30	$15	$15	$15
" Crescent City	30	15	10	15
" Port Orford	40	15	10	15
" Umpqua and Gardiner City	50	25	15	15
In Vancouver, Victoria	50	25	12½	15
In Washington Territory, Port Townsend	50	25	15	15
" " " Steilacoom	50	25	15	15
" " " Olympia	50	25	15	15

The Mexican branch of this Company's service is not yet fully reported. The first steamer left San Francisco May 1st, 1861.

4th. THE PANAMA RAILROAD COMPANY'S CENTRAL AMERICAN LINE OF STEAMSHIPS, RUNNING SEMI-MONTHLY BETWEEN THE PORTS OF GUATEMALA, SALVADOR, COSTA RICA, NICARAGUA, AND PANAMA.

The steam propellers Guatemala, 1021 tons, J. M. Dow, commander, and Columbus, 460 tons, J. W. Ludwig, commander, arrive at and depart from Central American ports on or about the following days of each month, forming a semi-monthly line :*

Departure.			Arrival.		
From	Guatemala.	Columbus.	At	Guatemala.	Columbus.
Panama	15th	30th	Punta Arenas	17th	2d
Punta Arenas	18th	3d	Realejo	19th	4th
Realejo	20th	5th	La Union	20th	5th
La Union	21st	6th	La Libertad	22d	7th
La Libertad	22d	7th	Acajutla	22d	7th
Acajutla	22d	7th	San José	23d	8th
San José	25th	10th	Acajutla	25th	10th
Acajutla	26th	11th	La Libertad	27th	11th
La Libertad	27th	12th	La Union	28th	13th
La Union	30th	15th	Realejo	30th	15th
Realejo	1st	16th	Punta Arenas	2d	17th
Punta Arenas	3d	18th	Panama	5th	20th

Prices of Passage.

From Panama to Punta Arenas..............................$40 00
"   "   Realejo...................................... 65 00
"   "   La Union.................................... 70 00
"   "   La Libertad................................ 75 00
"   "   Acajutla.................................... 80 00
"   "   San José de Guatemala................ 85 00

Payable in American gold.

* The Company have contracted for the building of another vessel (first-class iron steamer), 214 feet in length, 32 feet beam, 21 feet hold, to be completed and ready for service at Panama early in the spring of 1862; burden about 1200 tons.

Prices of Freight (including Lighterage in Panama).

From Panama to	Punta Arenas,	per ton measurement	......	$14 00
" "	Realejo,	"	"	......	16 00
" "	La Union,	"	"	......	16 00
" "	La Libertad,	"	"	......	18 00
" "	Acajutla,	"	"	......	18 00
" "	San José,	"	"	......	18 00

And five per cent. primage.

Prices of Return Freight (including Lighterage at Panama).

From San José, Acajutla, and La Libertad, to Panama: For cochineal and indigo, 1¼ cents per lb. on the net weight; hides, 32 cents each; other merchandise in cases, bales, etc., 45 cents per cubic foot; and 5 per cent. primage.

From La Union and Realejo to Panama: Cochineal and indigo, 1¼ cents per lb. net weight; hides, 30 cents each; merchandise in cases, bales, etc., 40 cents per cubic foot; and 5 per cent. primage.

From Punta Arenas to Panama: Coffee, ⅞ cent, gross weight; hides, 24 cents each; merchandise in cases, bales, etc., 35 cents per cubic foot.

Produce and other merchandise for Panama will be landed at the railroad wharf, where it must be received by the consignees immediately; in default of which, it will be taken to the depôt at the expense and risk of the owner.

All freight and passage payable in American gold or its equivalent.

Prices of Freight from the Ports of Central America to Aspinwall (Colon), including the Expense of Landing and Transportation by the Railroad.

From San José, Acajutla, and La Libertad: Indigo and cochineal, 2⅞ cents per lb. net weight; hides, 47 cents each; merchandise in cases, etc., 45 cents per cubic foot, and the regular transportation charges established by the tariff of the railroad.

From La Union and Realejo: Indigo and cochineal, 2⅞ cents per lb. net weight; hides, 45 cents each; merchandise in cases, etc., 40 cents per cubic foot, and the transportation charges established by the tariff of the railroad.

From Punta Arenas: Coffee, 1½ cents per lb. gross weight; hides, 39 cents each; merchandise in cases, etc., 35 cents per cubic foot, and the transportation charges established by the tariff of the railroad.

Through Rates of Freight from Central America to the South American Ports.

To Guayaquil,	cochineal, per ceroon	......	$3 75
" Callao,	" "	......	4 75
" Valparaiso,	" "	......	5 75
To Guayaquil,	coffee, per pound	......	1½ cts.
" Callao,	" "	......	1¾ "
" Valparaiso,	" "	......	2¼ "
To Guayaquil,	crude sugar	......	1½ cts.
" Callao,	"	......	1¾ "
" Valparaiso,	"	......	2¼ "

Rates of Through Freight from New York, by the Company's sailing Vessels to Aspinwall, including Lighterage in Panama.

	To Punta Arenas.	Realejo, La Union.	La Libertad, Acajutla, San José (Guatemala).
Dry-goods, hats, boots, shoes, drugs, and other goods, included in railroad tariff as first class, per ton of 40 feet	$40 00	$42 00	$44 00
Unbleached domestics, per ton of 40 feet	32 00	34 00	36 00
Furniture, carriages, agricultural implements, wooden-ware, clocks, etc., per ton of 40 feet	30 00	32 00	34 00
Iron in bars, sheets, and bundles, iron castings, nails, spikes, copper, zinc, and lead, per ton of 2000 lbs.	30 00	32 00	34 00
Steel in bars and bundles, coarse machinery, common hardware, earthen-ware, sugar-mills, -moulds, and -pans, shot, etc., per ton of 2000 lbs	34 00	36 00	38 00
Butter, cheese, lard, fish, ham, soap, and candles, per ton of 2000 lbs.	35 00	37 00	39 00
Refined sugar, per ton of 40 feet	30 00	32 00	34 00
Flour and rice, per barrel	4 20	4 50	4 80
" " per half barrel	2 20	2 35	2 50
Wine in boxes and baskets, per ton of 40 feet	32 00	34 00	36 00
" in casks, and other liquors, per ton of 40 feet	35 00	37 00	39 00
Tobacco, manufactured, per ton of 40 feet	40 00	42 00	44 00
" unmanufactured, per ton of 40 feet	32 00	34 00	36 00
Ship-bread, crackers, etc., per ton of 40 feet	28 00	30 00	32 00

Goods can be shipped three times per month, by steamers of the Atlantic and Pacific Steam-ship Company, to Aspinwall, at an addition of 35 cents per foot, or $14 per ton, to the above rates.

Rates of Return Freights, by the Company's sailing Vessels from Aspinwall to New York, including Lighterage in Panama.

	To Panama.	Aspinwall.	New York.
Lumber, from La Union, per M.	$20 00		
" " Punta Arenas, per M.	18 00		
Cochineal and indigo, from either port, per lb. net.	1¼	$0 02¾	$0 03½
Hides, from San José, Acajutla, and La Libertad, each	32	47	62
Hides, from La Union and Realejo, each	30	45	60
" " Punta Arenas	24	39	54
Coffee, from Punta Arenas, per lb. gross	⅞	1½	1¾
Deer and goat skins, from Punta Arenas, per lb.	1	1¾	2¼
" " " other ports, "	1½	2¼	3
Cigars, balsam, and first class goods, per railroad tariff, per foot	50	1 00	1 16

No primage on through rates.

Through bills of lading are given from Central American ports to Liverpool (by propellers Saladin and Plantagenet from Aspinwall) at 4 cents per lb. on net weight of indigo and cochineal, and 2½ cents per lb. on gross weight of coffee; and to London (by the Royal Mail Steam Packet Company's steamers) at 2⅜ pence sterling **per lb.** on gross weight of indigo and cochineal.

Produce and other merchandise for Panama will be landed at the railroad wharf, where it must be received by the consignees immediately; in default of which, it will be taken to the depôt **at the expense** and risk of the owner.

All freight and passage payable in **American gold or its equivalent.**

For farther information, apply to

    Jos. F. Joy, *Secretary*, 88 Wall St., New York.
    Wm. Nelson, *Commercial Agent*, Panama.
    Crisanto Medina, Punta Arenas.
    Courtade y Clavera, La Union.
    H. J. Foote and J. Mathi, Sonsonate.
    J. Saragia, San José de Guatemala.
        Or to the commanders on board.

For a description of the countries touched at by the Central American Line, also an account of the ports, port regulations and charges, tariffs, commerce, etc., etc., see page 181, et seq.

5th. **THE PACIFIC STEAM NAVIGATION COMPANY, PLYING BETWEEN PANAMA, CALLAO, VALPARAISO, AND INTERMEDIATE PORTS.**

The steam-ships destined for the **service are the** following: Bogotá, 1600 tons; Lima, 1600 tons; Callao, **1200 tons;** Valparaiso, 1200 tons; Guayaquil, 1000 tons; San Carlos, 1000 tons; **Bolivia, 800 tons;** Anne, 500 tons; Cloda, 900 **tons;** New Granada, **750 tons;** Inca, 300 tons; Morro, 150 tons.

Voyage to the South.

	Days of each Month.
Departure from Panama...............	9th and 24th.
Arrival at....... Guayaquil...............	13th and 28th.
Departure from Guayaquil...............	14th, 29th, and 2d.
Arrival at....... Payta...............	15th, 30th, and 3d.
" .... Lambayeque...............	17th and 4th.
Departure from Lambayeque...............	18th and 5th.
Arrival at....... Pacasmayo...............	18th and 5th.
" .... Huanchaco...............	19th and 6th.
" .... Santa...............	20th.
" .... Samanco...............	7th.
" .... Casma...............	20th and 7th.
" .... Supe...............	21st and 8th.
" .... Huacho...............	21st and 8th.
" .... Callao...............	18th, 22d, 2d or 3d, and 9th.
Departure from Callao...............	20th, 26th, 5th, and 11th.
Arrival at.. ..... Cerro Azul...............	27th and 12th.
" .... Islas de Chincha...............	21st, 27th, 6th, and 12th.
" .... Pisco...............	21st, 27th, 6th, and 12th.
" .... Chala...............	29th and 14th.
" .... Islay...............	23d, 30th, 8th, and 15th.
" .... Arica...............	24th, 31st or 1st, 9th, and 16th.
" .... Pisagua...............	1st or 2d, and 17th.
" .... Mejillones...............	1st or 2d, and 17th.
" .... Iquique...............	1st or 2d, and 17th.
" .... Tocopillo...............	2d or 3d, and 18th.
" .... Cobija...............	25th, 2d or 3d, 10th and 18th.
" .... Caldera...............	27th, 4th or 5th, 12th, and 20th.
Departure from Caldera...............	27th, 4th or 5th, 12th, and 20th.
Arrival at....... Carrizal bajo...............	5th or 6th, and 21st.

PANAMA RAILROAD. 153

		Days of each Month.
Arrival at.......	Huasco................................	5th or 6th, and 21st.
"	.... Coquimbo	28th, 6th or 7th, 13th, and 22d.
"	.... Tongoy..............................	6th or 7th, and 22d.
"	.... Valparaiso	29th, 7th or 8th, 14th, and 23d.

Voyage to the North.

		Days of each Month.
Departure from Valparaiso		3d, 11th, 18th, and 27th.
Arrival at.......	Tongoy...............................	12th and 28th.
"	.... Coquimbo	4th, 12th, 19th, and 28th.
"	.... Huasco............................	13th and 29th.
"	.... Carrizal bajo.................	13th and 29th.
"	.... Caldera...........................	5th, 14th, 20th, and 30th.
"	.... Cobija.............................	7th, 16th, 22d, 1st or 2d.
"	.... Tocopillo	16th, and 1st or 2d.
"	.... Iquique	17th, and 2d or 3d.
"	.... Mejillones	17th, and 2d or 3d.
"	.... Pisagua	17th, and 2d or 3d.
"	.... Arica..............................	8th, 18th, 23d, and 3d or 4th.
"	.... Islay...............................	9th, 19th, 24th, and 4th or 5th.
"	.... Chala..............................	20th, and 5th or 6th.
"	.... Pisco...............................	11th, 21st, 26th, and 6th or 7th.
"	.... Islas de Chincha..............	11th, 21st, 26th, and 6th or 7th.
"	.... Cerro Azul.......................	21st, and 6th or 7th.
"	.... Callao.............................	12th, 22d, 27th, and 7th or 8th.
Departure from Callao		14th, 24th, 29th, and 13th.
Arrival at.......	Huacho.............................	25th and 14th.
"	.... Supe...............................	25th and 14th.
"	.... Casma............................	26th and 15th.
"	.... Samanco........................	26th.
"	.... Santa.............................	15th.
"	.... Huanchaco.....................	27th and 16th.
"	.... Pacasmayo.....................	27th and 16th.
"	.... Lambayeque..................	28th and 17th.
"	.... Payta.............................	17th, 19th, and 1st or 2d.
"	.... Guayaquil......................	30th.
"	.... Panama..........................	22d, and 6th or 7th.

Rates of Passage.

		First Saloon.	Second Saloon.			First Saloon.	Second Saloon.
Panama to Guayaquil...		$105	$100	Panama to Islay...........		$220	$210
"	Payta..........	115	110	"	Arica..........	230	220
"	Lambayeque	135	130	"	Iquique......	245	230
"	Huanchaco..	135	130	"	Cobija.........	255	240
"	Casma	140	135	"	Caldera.......	265	250
"	Huacho......	145	140	"	Huasco	270	255
"	Callao.........	160	150	"	Coquimbo...	275	260
"	Pisco	175	165	"	Valparaiso..	290	270

Passage for any of the above ports can be secured at the office of the Panama Railroad Company, 88 Wall Street, New York.

The Pacific Steam Navigation Company will issue *through bills of lading* for produce from the above-mentioned ports—To New York, to be conveyed from Aspinwall by sailing vessels of the Panama Railroad Company; to Liverpool, to be conveyed from Aspinwall by propellers Saladin and Plantagenet; to Southampton, to be conveyed from Aspinwall by steamers of Royal Mail Steam Packet Company.

An arrangement has also been made by which produce can be shipped under *through bills of lading* from ports in Central America touched at by steamers Guatemala and Columbus to the above ports on the west coast.

Rates of Freight in Dollars from Panama to Valparaiso and intermediate Ports.

		Buenaventura.	Guayaquil.	Payta.	Lambayeque.	Huanchaco.	Casma.	Huacho.	Callao.	Pisco.	Islay.	Arica.	Iquique.	Cobija.	Caldera.	Huasco.	Coquimbo.	Valparaiso.
Panama	per ton.	20	25	25	25	25	30	30	30	30	35	35	40	40	40	45	45	45
Buenaventura	"	...	20	20	25	25	25	25	25	30	30	35	35	35	40	40	40	40
Guayaquil	"	...	...	12	15	15	15	15	15	20	20	20	25	25	25	25	25	25
Payta	"	...	...	...	15	15	15	15	15	20	20	20	25	25	25	25	25	25
Lambayeque	"	...	...	...	...	15	15	15	15	20	20	20	20	20	20	20	20	20
Huanchaco	"	...	...	...	...	...	15	15	15	20	20	20	20	20	20	20	20	20
Casma	"	...	...	...	...	...	...	15	15	20	20	20	20	20	20	20	20	20
Huacho	"	...	...	...	...	...	...	...	12	15	20	20	20	20	20	20	20	20
Callao	"	...	...	...	...	...	...	...	...	15	20	20	20	20	20	20	20	20
Pisco	"	...	...	...	...	...	...	...	...	...	20	20	20	20	20	20	20	20
Islay	"	...	...	...	...	...	...	...	...	...	...	15	20	20	20	20	20	20
Arica	"	...	...	...	...	...	...	...	...	...	...	...	15	15	20	20	20	20
Iquique	"	...	...	...	...	...	...	...	...	...	...	...	...	20	20	20	20	20
Cobija	"	...	...	...	...	...	...	...	...	...	...	...	...	...	20	20	20	20
Caldera	"	...	...	...	...	...	...	...	...	...	...	...	...	...	...	12	12	12
Huasco	"	...	...	...	...	...	...	...	...	...	...	...	...	...	...	...	12	12
Coquimbo	"	...	...	...	...	...	...	...	...	...	...	...	...	...	...	...	...	12

Rates of Freight in Dollars from Valparaiso to Panama and intermediate Ports.

		Coquimbo.	Huasco.	Caldera.	Cobija.	Iquique.	Arica.	Islay.	Pisco.	Callao.	Huacho.	Casma.	Huanchaco.	Lambayeque.	Payta.	Guayaquil.	Buenaventura.	Panama.
Valparaiso	per ton.	12	12	12	20	20	20	20	20	20	25	25	25	25	25	25	30	30
Coquimbo	"	...	12	12	15	15	15	15	15	15	18	18	18	18	18	18	25	25
Huasco	"	...	...	12	15	15	15	15	15	15	18	18	18	18	18	18	25	25
Caldera	"	...	...	...	15	15	15	15	15	15	18	18	18	18	18	18	25	25
Cobija	"	...	...	...	...	15	15	15	15	15	18	18	18	18	18	18	25	25
Iquique	"	...	...	...	...	...	15	15	15	15	18	18	18	18	18	18	25	25
Arica	"	...	...	...	...	...	...	15	15	15	15	15	15	15	15	18	25	25
Islay	"	...	...	...	...	...	...	...	15	15	15	15	15	15	15	18	25	25
Pisco	"	...	...	...	...	...	...	...	...	12	15	15	15	15	15	18	25	25
Callao	"	...	...	...	...	...	...	...	...	...	12	12	12	12	12	15	20	20
Huacho	"	...	...	...	...	...	...	...	...	...	...	12	12	12	12	12	18	18
Casma	"	...	...	...	...	...	...	...	...	...	...	...	12	12	12	12	18	18
Huanchaco	"	...	...	...	...	...	...	...	...	...	...	...	...	12	12	12	18	18
Lambayeque	"	...	...	...	...	...	...	...	...	...	...	...	...	...	12	12	18	18
Payta	"	...	...	...	...	...	...	...	...	...	...	...	...	...	...	12	15	18
Guayaquil	"	...	...	...	...	...	...	...	...	...	...	...	...	...	...	...	15	15
Buenaventura	"	...	...	...	...	...	...	...	...	...	...	...	...	...	...	...	...	15

Through Rates of Freight from New York to Valparaiso and intermediate Ports.

The Panama Railroad Company are now prepared to issue *through bills of lading* to all the ports touched at by the steamers of the Pacific Steam Navigation Company, at the following rates:

	To Buenaventura, Guayaquil, Payta, and intermediates.	To Callao, Valparaiso, and intermediates, south of Payta.
General merchandise, and all goods embraced in first class of Panama Railroad tariff, per ton of 40 cubic feet, or 2240 lbs. gross weight, at the option of the Company.....	$40 00	$50 00
Beef and pork, per barrel...	5 00	7 00
" " per half barrel.......................................	2 75	3 75
Flour, per barrel...	4 00	5 00
" per half barrel...	2 25	2 75
Biscuit, per 100 lbs..	2 50	3 50
Butter, lard, hams, bacon, cheese, salt fish, tallow, and rice, per ton of 2000 lbs.	30 00	40 00
Refined sugar, per ton of 2000 lbs................................	40 00	45 00
Wines and other liquors, in boxes and barrels, per ton of 40 cubic feet..	30 00	40 00
Manufactured tobacco, per ton of 40 cubic feet...............	30 00	40 00
Cigars, per ton of 40 cubic feet.....................................	35 00	45 00
Unbleached domestics, per ton of 40 cubic feet...............	25 00	32 00
Soap, per ton of 2000 lbs.	30 00	40 00
Candles, per ton of 40 cubic feet...................................	30 00	40 00
Carriages and furniture, per ton of 40 cubic feet.............	30 00	40 00
Agricultural implements, per ton of 40 cubic feet............	25 00	35 00
Pitch, tar, and rosin, per barrel....................................	3 00	4 00
Earthen-ware and glass-ware (coarse), in crates and boxes, per ton of 40 cubic feet...	25 00	35 00
Turpentine and oil in cases, per ton of 40 cubic feet	30 00	40 00
Turpentine and oil in tins only, per ton of 40 cubic feet.....	35 00	45 00

All weights to be the gross weight.

Articles not enumerated to be charged **at rates** assimilating to the above.

From New York to Aspinwall shipments **are made** by the sailing vessels of the Panama Railroad Company, leaving **at intervals** of from eight to ten days.

All freight to be prepaid.

No bill of lading signed for less than five dollars.

Farther particulars may be learned on application to the secretary at the office of the Panama Railroad Company, No. 88 Wall Street, New York.

Weekly Line between Callao, Lambayeque, and Guayaquil.

Departure from Callao......	6th, 13th, 19th, and 24th	of each month.	
Arrival at Huacho............	7th, 14th, 20th, and 25th	" "	
" Supe...............	7th, 14th, 20th, and 25th	" "	
" Casma	8th, 15th, 21st, and 26th	" "	
" Samanco.........	.... 26th	" "	
" Santa...............	...... 15th	" "	

Arrival at Huanchaco......	9th, 16th, 22d, and 27th	of each month.
" Malabrigo........	9th and 22d	" "
" Pacasmayo......	...... 16th, ... and 27th	" "
" Lambayeque...	10th, 17th, 23d, and 28th	" "
" Payta	.... 29th	" "
" Guayaquil......	.... 30th	" "
Departure from Guayaquil	.... 2d or 3d	" "
Arrival at Payta............	.... 3d or 4th	" "
" Lambayeque....	.... 4th or 5th	" "
Departure fr. Lambayeque	10th, 17th, 23d, and 4th or 5th	" "
Arrival at Pacasmayo......	...... 18th ...... and 5th or 6th	" "
" Malabrigo.......	...... 18th ...... and 5th or 6th	" "
" Huanchaco......	11th, 19th, 24th, and 6th or 7th	" "
" Santa	...... 20th	" "
" Samanco	.... 7th or 8th	" "
" Casma	12th, 20th, 25th, and 7th or 8th	" "
Departure from Casma	12th, 20th, 25th, and 7th or 8th	" "
Arrival at Supe	13th, 21st, 26th, and 8th or 9th	" "
" Huacho	13th, 21st, 26th, and 8th or 9th	" "
" Callao............	14th, 22d, 27th, and 9th or 10th	" "

Rates of freight: From Callao to Guayaquil and the intermediate ports, $8 per ton; from Guayaquil to Callao and the intermediate ports, $10 per ton; from Guayaquil, and the intermediate ports as far south as Callao, to Valparaiso, $15 per ton.

Semi-monthly Line between Valparaiso, Talcahuano, and Puerto Montt.

Departure from Valparaiso..	10th and 30th	of each month.
Arrival at Constitucion	11th	" "
" Tomé.................	12th and 31st or 1st	" "
" Talcahuano.........	12th and 31st or 1st	" "
" Coronel	...... 1st or 2d	" "
" Lota	13th	" "
" Valdivia............	14th	" "
" Ancud...............	15th	" "
" Calbuco............	16th	" "
" Puerto Montt	16th	" "
Departure from Puerto Montt	18th	" "
Arrival at Calbuco............	18th	" "
" Ancud...............	18th	" "
" Valdivia............	20th	" "
" Lota	21st	" "
" Coronel	...... 1st or 2d	" "
" Talcahuano.........	22d and 2d or 3d	" "
Departure from Talcahuano.	22d and 3d or 4th	" "
Arrival at Tomé	22d and 3d or 4th	" "
" Constitucion........	23d	" "
" Valparaiso	24th and 4th or 5th	" "

Monthly Line between Panama and Guayaquil—Steam-ship Anne.

Departure from Panama.....................	12th of each month.	
Arrival at Buenaventura.....................	14th " "
Departure from Buenaventura	15th " "
Arrival at Tumaco	16th " "
" Esmeraldas........................	17th " "
" Manta..............................	18th " "
" Guayaquil	20th " "

Departure from Guayaquil .... 24th of each month.
Arrival at Manta .... 26th   "   "
  "   Esmeraldas .... 28th   "   "
  "   Tumaco .... 29th   "   "
  "   Buenaventura .... 30th   "   "
Departure from Buenaventura .... 31st   "   "
Arrival at Panama .... 2d or 3d   "

Prices of Passage by the Anne.

	Buenaventura.	Tumaco.	Esmeraldas.	Manta.	Guayaquil.
From Panama to	$50 00	$60 00	$70 00	$80 00	$85 00
" Buenaventura to		30 00	40 00	50 00	60 00
" Tumaco to			20 00	30 00	40 00
" Esmeraldas to				20 00	30 00
" Manta to					25 00

	Manta.	Esmeraldas.	Tumaco.	Buenaventura.	Panama.
From Guayaquil to	$25 00	$30 00	$40 00	$50 00	$85 00
" Manta to		20 00	30 00	45 00	80 00
" Esmeraldas to			20 00	35 00	70 00
" Tumaco to				30 00	60 00
" Buenaventura to					50 00

Rates of Freight.

From Guayaquil and intermediate ports to Panama..... $10 00 per ton.
  "   Panama   "   "   Guayaquil.. 12 00   "

The Pacific Steam Navigation Company was organized in April, 1839, but the charter of incorporation was not obtained until February, 1840. In November, 1839, the directors, under assurance that the charter would be granted, contracted for two steam vessels, which were completed and dispatched from England for service on the Pacific in July, 1840, and commenced their voyages on the coasts of the Pacific in November of the same year, since which time the line has been in regular and successful operation. Its business has increased to such an extent that a fleet of eleven large steam-ships, with a semi-monthly service, are now employed on the through route between Panama and Valparaiso, besides a monthly steam-ship (the Anne) plying between Panama and Guayaquil, a weekly line of four steamships plying between Callao and Guayaquil, and a semi-monthly line between Valparaiso and Puerto Montt, touching at the intermediate ports for the collection of freight, which, from the increase of the through business, caused too much delay for the ships of the through line.

The machine and repair shops, and other facilities for keeping the vessels of the Company in order, are very extensive and well appointed. They are situated on the island of Toboga, in the Bay of Panama.

The head-quarters of the Company are at
Liverpool .... WILLIAM JUST, *General Manager.*
Callao .... GEORGE PETRIE, *Resident Manager on the Pacific.*
Panama .... CHARLES H. BIDWELL, *Agent.*

6th. **THE ROYAL MAIL STEAM PACKET COMPANY, PLYING BETWEEN THE WEST INDIES, MEXICO, CENTRAL AMERICA, AND PANAMA.**

Offices—55 Moorgate Street, London, R. T. Reep, Secretary; Canute Road, Southampton, Captain W. Vincent, Superintendent.

Foreign Agencies on the Continent of Europe, and at the termini of Routes in the West Indies.

Paris...............	Messrs. Pritchard and Monneron, 4 Rue Rossini.
Havre	Messrs. Davidson and Co.
Hamburg........	Messrs. Hundeiker and Abegg.
St. Thomas......	J. B. Cameron, Esq., Superintendent.
Aspinwall........	W. Ritchie, Esq., Resident Traffic Manager.
Panama...........	C. A. Henderson, Esq., H.B.M.'s Consul.
Havana	J. T. Crawford, Esq., C.B., H.B.M.'s Consul General.
Vera Cruz.......	C. Markoe, Esq.
Tampico.........	Messrs. Jolly and Co.
Jamaica..........	Captain Cooper, R.N., Superintendent.
Trinidad.........	Messrs. H. Scott and Son.
Barbadoes......	Messrs. M. Cavan and Co.
Demerara........	Messrs. Rose, Duff, and Co.
Belize.............	Captain A. W. Cox.

List of Ships.

No.	Station.	Names.	Registered Tonnage.	Horse Power.	Names of Captains.
1.	On West India service.	Shannon ...	3472	800	G. Abbott.
2.	" "	Seine........	3440	800	R. Revett.
3.	" "	Atrato.......	3126	800	F. Woolley.
4.	" "	La Plata....	2404	1000	
5.	" "	Tasmanian.	2253	550	C. G. Weller.
6.	" "	Tamar	1707	400	P. M. Woolcott.
7.	" "	Thames.....	1889	430	A. Hole.
8.	" "	Trent........	1856	430	J. T. Moir.
9.	" "	Solent.......	1689	400	E. M. Leeds.
10.	" "	Teviot.......	1744	450	J. M. Gillies.
11.	" "	Clyde........	1371	430	H. P. Lewis.
12.	" "	Conway.....	895	260	W. Heenan.
13.	" "	Wye.........	752	180	J. Thwaites.
14.	" "	Derwent	794	260	E. West.
15.	" "	Prince.......	398	200	
16.	On Brazil service.......	Magdalena.	2567	800	R. Woolward.
17.	" "	Oneida......	2284	530	T. A. Bevis.
18.	" "	Tyne.........	1916	400	J. H. Jellicoe.
19.	On transport service...	Avon	1834	440	F. Reeks.
20.	On River Plate route..	Mersey......	1001	250	R. Curlewis.
21.		Parana......	2730	800	
22.		Dee..........	1699	440	
23.		Medway	1895	430	

The following are the estimated Dates of Arrival of the outward Mails at the principal Stations, commencing from Southampton March 2d, 1860.

(The mails are sent on from St. Thomas by the Company's intercolonial ships.)

From Southampton:
2d and 17th of each month, arriving at St. Thomas...............17th and 2d.
"   "   "   "   Aspinwall (Isthmus of
                                          Panama)..............22d and 7th.
"   "   "   "   Jamaica..................21st and 6th.
"   "   "   "   Barbadoes...............20th and 5th.
"   "   "   "   Trinidad.................22d and 7th.
"   "   "   "   Demerara.................22d and 7th.
2d of each month, arriving at Havana (one mail each month) 22d idem.
"   "   "   Vera Cruz   "   26th "
"   "   "   Tampico   "   28th "
"   "   "   Carthagena   "   24th "
"   "   "   Santa Martha   "   26th "
17th   "   "   Belize   "   10th following m'th.
"   "   "   Greytown   "   10th "

The following are the estimated Dates of Departure of the homeward Mails from the principal Stations, commencing with the Mails in reply to those from Southampton March 2d.

(The mails are conveyed to St. Thomas by the Company's intercolonial ships.)

From:
Tampico (one mail each month) 29th, reaching Southampton 29th following m'th.
Santa Martha   "   27th,   "   "   29th   "
Vera Cruz   "   2d,*   "   "   29th idem.
Havana   "   8th,*   "   "   29th   "
Carthagena   "   5th,*   "   "   29th   "
Belize   "   17th,*   "   "   14th following m'th.
Greytown   "   19th,   "   "   14th   "
Demerara........................ 9th* and 24th of each month. ⎫
Trinidad......................... 9th* and 24th   "   "   ⎪ Reaching
Barbadoes.......................11th* and 26th   "   "   ⎬ Southampton
Jamaica.........................10th* and 25th   "   "   ⎪ 29th and 14th
Aspinwall (Isthmus of Panama).. 9th* and 24th   "   "   ⎪ respectively.
St. Thomas......................15th* and 30th   "   "   ⎭

N.B.—The estimated dates of departure which are marked thus * above will be a day earlier when the preceding month comprised 31 days.

Notice.—The Company will not be responsible for the maintenance of passengers, or for their loss of time during any detention consequent upon the occurrence of any cause to prevent the vessels from meeting at the appointed places; nor for any delay arising out of accidents; nor for any loss or damage arising from perils of the seas, or from machinery, boilers, or steam, or from any act, neglect, or default whatsoever of the pilot, master, or mariners; nor from any consequences arising from sanitary regulations or precautions which the Company's officers or local government authorities may deem necessary, or should such sanitary regulations or precautions prevent embarkation or disembarkation; and if, in consequence of such sanitary regulations or precautions, passengers should have to be conveyed to their destination by a circuitous route, or to remain (with the consent of the Company's officers) on board the Company's vessels beyond the time at which, under ordinary circumstances, they would disembark, the Company will, in lieu of additional passage-money, etc., charge only at the rate of 10s. per diem for victualing during the extra time each adult cabin passenger may have been on board, and in proportion for other classes of passengers.

PASSENGER FARES, WHICH INCLUDE THE USE OF BEDDING AND LINEN, STEWARD'S FEES, AND ALL OTHER CHARGES EXCEPT FOR WINES, SPIRITS, MALT LIQUORS, AND MINERAL WATERS.

Atlantic Voyages (see *Regulations*, pages 163 and 164).

OUTWARD.		FARES OUT OR HOME.		HOMEWARD.	
Leaves Southampton each Month.	Destination.	Berths* in after Cabins (except outside Cabins on the main Deck) and in main Deck forward Cabins. Each Berth.†	Berths in lower Deck forward Cabins. Each Berth.	From what Places.	Due at Southampton each Month.
		£ s.	£ s.		
2d and 17th	Antigua	38 10	33 0	Antigua	14th and 29th
2d and 17th	Barbadoes	38 10	33 0	Barbadoes	14th and 29th
17th	Blewfields	44 0	38 10	Blewfields	14th
2d and 17th	Carriacou	38 10	33 0	Carriacou	14th and 29th
2d	Carthagena	44 0	38 10	Carthagena	29th
2d and 17th	Aspinwall	44 0	38 10	Aspinwall	14th and 29th
2d and 17th	Demerara	38 10	33 0	Demerara	14th and 29th
2d and 17th	Dominica	38 10	33 0	Dominica	14th and 29th
		18 14	18 14	Fayal (if touched at)	
2d and 17th	Granada	38 10	33 0	Granada	14th and 29th
17th	Greytown	44 0	38 10	Greytown	14th
2d and 17th	Guadaloupe	38 10	33 0	Guadaloupe	14th and 29th
2d	Havana	44 0	38 10	Havana	29th
17th	Honduras	44 0	38 10	Honduras	14th
2d and 17th	Jacmel	38 10	33 0	Jacmel	14th and 29th
2d and 17th	Jamaica	38 10	33 0	Jamaica	14th and 29th
2d and 17th	Martinique	38 10	33 0	Martinique	14th and 29th
2d and 17th	Porto Rico	38 10	33 0	Porto Rico	14th and 29th
2d and 17th	St. Kitts	38 10	33 0	St. Kitts	14th and 29th
2d and 17th	St. Lucia	38 10	33 0	St. Lucia	14th and 29th
2d and 17th	St. Thomas	38 10	33 0	St. Thomas	14th and 29th
2d and 17th	St. Vincent	38 10	33 0	St. Vincent	14th and 29th
2d	Sta. Martha	44 0	38 10	Sta. Martha	29th
2d	Tampico	49 10	44 0	Tampico	29th
2d and 17th	Tobago	38 10	33 0	Tobago	14th and 29th
2d and 17th	Trinidad	38 10	33 0	Trinidad	14th and 29th
2d	Vera Cruz	49 10	44 0	Vera Cruz	29th

* A whole after cabin secured for the exclusive use of one passenger (not being an outside cabin on the main deck) is to be charged as a berth and a half, calculated at the rate shown in the column marked † above.

† For an outside cabin, or for a berth therein on the main deck aft, an additional charge of £5 is to be made to each passenger beyond the fares indicated respectively in the preceding clause and in the column marked † above.

In future, no whole cabins on the main deck forward, or on the lower deck forward, of any of the Company's ships, are to be let as single cabins.

The above distinctions in accommodation apply more particularly to the Atlantic voyages between Southampton and St. Thomas, and *vice versa*, but they will also be adhered to as far as practicable on board the intercolonial vessels.

The difference in the rates of passage-money shown above refers merely to the sleeping-cabins; in all other respects the passengers will be precisely on the same footing.

Return Tickets.—Return tickets issued to cabin passengers for Atlantic voyages with an abatement of 25 per cent. on the passage-money. Such tickets to be paid for when issued, and not to be transferable. To be available if the parties holding the same embark on the return voyage within six calendar months (but in the case of Colon [Aspinwall] within twelve calendar months) from the date of their first embarkation; and no allowance will be made to such parties if they do not make the return voyage by the Company's vessels. Should there be no available accommodation in the ship by which the holder wishes to embark on the return voyage, he will be entitled to a passage by the first subsequent opportunity. In all such cases certificates must be obtained from the Company's agents or captains, specifying the dates of application, and that no accommodation could then be afforded.

Children.—Of the children of cabin passengers under three years of age, one to be carried free of charge; any other under that age to be charged as three years and under eight; those three years and under eight years, to pay one fourth the cabin-passage rate paid by their parents, and four such children to be entitled to one berth.

Passengers on Warrant-officers' Scale.—A limited number of artisans, emigrants, etc., to be victualed on the same footing as the ship's warrant-officers, and supplied with bunks and bedding, will be conveyed, when there is room for them, from Southampton to the West Indies, Colon (Aspinwall), or Mexico for £25 each.

Return tickets are not to be issued to passengers of this class.

Servants.—Passengers' servants can not be booked as deck passengers.

Passengers' male servants to pay one half, and female two thirds of the lowest rates established for adult saloon passengers, and no abatement to be made on account of age. Men servants will be berthed in the fore part of the ship; women servants will have beds made up in the ladies' saloon.

Deck Passengers can only be conveyed intercolonially.—Only troops, common sailors, or laborers to be conveyed as deck passengers; to find their own provisions and bedding, and not admitted abaft the chimney, and to pay one fourth the cabin fare. Children of deck passengers to pay half the deck fare, when three years or above, and not exceeding twelve years of age, and when under three years to be taken free. N.B.—No deck passenger is to be booked for St. Thomas.

Dogs, Carriages, Horses, Cattle, etc.—Dogs to be charged at one eighth the fare paid by their owners.

Carriages, horses, live-stock, etc. (for the shipment of which special permission must be obtained from Captain W. Vincent, the Company's superintendent at Southampton), will be conveyed only under special form of ticket, which provides for the owner's undertaking all risk of conveyance whatsoever, as the Company will not be responsible for any injury or damage (however caused) occurring while on board the Company's ships, or in embarkation, transfer, or disembarkation; and the shippers must in all cases provide food, boxes, pens, or coops.

Carriages measuring 3 tons or under, £12 each.

Carriages measuring above 3 tons, at the rate of £4 per ton measurement.

Horses, colts, and heifers, to St. Thomas, £20 each; to other West Indian ports, £25 each. Rams, sheep, and pigs, £5 each; poultry, 15s. each.

☞ In all cases where passengers are subject in the ordinary course of the mail service, as per tables, to a detention of more than four days, that is, while waiting the arrival of the vessel by which they are to prosecute their voyage, they will have to defray the expenses of their victualing during such period of detention.

Intercolonial Voyages.—Fares in Silver Dollars for Cabin Passengers. (Return Tickets are not granted to intercolonial Passengers.)

Places.	Antigua.	Barbadoes.	Blewfields.	Carriacou.	Carthagena.	Colon (Aspinwall).	Demerara.	Dominica.	Granada.	Guadaloupe.	Greytown.	Havana.	Honduras.	Jacmel.	Jamaica.	Martinique.	St. Juan's.	St. Kitts.	St. Lucia.	Sta. Martha.	St. Thomas.	St. Vincent.	Tampico.	Tobago.	Trinidad.	Vera Cruz.
Antigua	...	25	85	25	65	85	40	12	25	8	75	65	80	40	50	15	25	10	15	65	15	25	115	35	30	110
Barbadoes	20	...	100	20	80	95	20	15	15	20	90	80	95	55	65	15	40	25	10	80	30	12	130	25	20	125
Blewfields	110	120	...	120	50	25	135	115	120	110	10	135	150	110	120	115	95	105	115	60	85	120	185	130	130	180
Carriacou	25	20	100	...	80	...	35	20	5	20	90	80	95	55	65	20	40	20	20	80	30	5	130	25	12	125
Carthagena	85	95	40	95	...	25	110	90	95	85	30	110	125	85	95	90	70	80	90	10	60	95	160	105	105	155
Colon (Aspinwall)	85	95	25	95	25	...	110	90	95	85	15	100	125	85	95	90	70	80	90	35	60	95	160	105	105	155
Demerara	40	20	120	30	75	110	...	40	30	40	110	100	115	75	85	35	60	45	30	100	50	30	180	35	30	145
Dominica	12	25	95	25	80	90	40	...	25	8	85	75	90	50	60	8	35	15	8	75	30	25	125	35	30	120
Granada	25	20	100	5	75	90	35	20	...	25	90	75	95	55	65	20	40	25	20	80	30	10	130	20	10	125
Guadaloupe	8	25	90	25	80	85	40	8	25	...	80	70	85	45	55	8	30	12	12	70	20	25	120	35	30	115
Greytown	100	110	10	110	40	15	125	105	110	100	...	125	140	100	110	105	85	95	105	50	75	110	175	120	120	170
Havana	85	95	130	95	110	95	135	90	120	95	125	...	95	85	95	90	70	80	90	110	60	95	45	105	105	40
Honduras	110	120	155	120	135	120	135	115	120	115	140	40	...	85	110	115	95	105	115	135	85	120	130	130	105	75
Jacmel	55	65	100	65	80	85	80	60	65	60	100	20	50	...	20	60	40	50	60	80	30	65	125	75	75	120
Jamaica	70	80	115	80	95	95	95	75	80	75	105	...	30	25	...	75	35	65	75	95	45	80	140	90	90	135
Martinique	12	25	95	20	75	85	40	8	25	8	85	75	90	50	60	...	35	15	8	75	25	25	125	35	25	120
St. Juan's, Pto. Rico	35	50	80	50	60	60	60	40	50	40	70	60	90	25	50	40	...	30	40	60	12	50	105	60	55	100
St. Kitts	12	30	80	30	60	60	50	20	30	20	80	65	75	35	60	20	30	...	20	60	12	30	115	40	35	110
St. Lucia	15	10	100	20	80	80	30	10	20	20	80	80	95	55	65	20	40	20	...	80	30	20	130	30	20	125
Santa Martha	85	95	50	95	8	25	110	90	95	85	40	110	125	85	95	90	70	80	90	...	60	95	160	105	105	155
St. Thomas	25	35	70	35	50	50	50	30	35	30	60	50	65	25	35	30	10	20	30	50	...	35	95	45	45	90
St. Vincent	20	15	105	5	85	85	30	15	10	25	95	85	100	60	70	15	45	25	15	85	35	...	135	25	15	130
Tampico	145	155	190	155	170	155	180	150	155	145	180	65	100	145	155	150	115	140	150	170	120	155	...	165	165	12
Tobago	30	25	110	25	90	80	35	25	15	30	100	90	105	65	75	25	50	35	25	90	40	25	140	...	10	135
Trinidad	30	25	110	12	90	90	35	30	10	30	100	90	105	65	75	25	50	35	25	90	40	15	140	15	...	135
Vera Cruz	140	150	185	150	165	150	165	145	150	140	175	60	180	140	150	145	110	135	145	165	115	150	12	160	160	...

Dogs, when conveyed intercolonially, to be charged one eighth of the fare paid by their owners.

Horses, colts, and heifers, when conveyed intercolonially, to be charged five sixths of the saloon passenger rate.

Carriages, ditto, measuring three tons or under, £9 each. Ditto, ditto, above three tons, at the rate of £3 per ton measurement.

Rams, sheep, and pigs, £3 each. Poultry, 10s. each.

For Conditions of Conveyance, see page 161.

PASSENGER REGULATIONS, ETC.

Each ship carries an experienced surgeon.

No berth is considered engaged until the whole fare is paid.

Passengers not proceeding after taking their passage, to forfeit half the passage-money.

Passengers are earnestly recommended to conform to established regulations as respects passports, etc.

Passengers are not allowed to take on board wines, spirits, or other liquors for use during the voyage, an ample stock thereof being provided on board at moderate prices.

There are French and English cooks on board.

No person can be received on board the Company's ships when suffering from any infectious disorder; and if, in the course of the voyage, any passenger should be found to be suffering from a disorder of that character, he will be required, at his own expense, to find accommodation at any port in which the vessel may happen to be at the time of, or at the first port she may reach after discovery of the existence of the disorder, it being understood that, when sufficiently recovered, such passenger will be conveyed to his destination in one of the Company's vessels.

The captains will be most careful to avoid all personal preference or partiality in allotting accommodation on board the Company's ships. Within the prescribed limits, priority is always to be given according to the dates on which passengers were originally booked and the passage-money paid. If paid through the Company's agent, he will be careful, when he hands the money to the captain, to furnish also the date when it is paid for notation on the passage ticket.

The respective classes of cabin accommodation in the homeward steamer from St. Thomas will be apportioned as follows, viz.: the passengers from routes Nos. 2 and 4, and those booked at St. Thomas, are to be allowed priority of berths on the starboard side, according to the date of their tickets, that is to say, the oldest date from No. 2 route to have the first allotment, the oldest date from No. 4 route the second, and the oldest date from St. Thomas the third; this plan to be repeated until the whole of the cabin accommodation on that side has been disposed of. The passengers from all other sources are to be allowed berths on the port side in the same manner. Should there be an excessive demand on the one side and a deficiency on the other, the available berths are to be allotted to passengers from each route alternately according to priority in date of tickets.

No passenger booking for a berth in a cabin is to be accommodated in a cabin by himself, so long as he can be placed in a cabin of the same class or price with another passenger not booked for a whole cabin.

Transatlantic passengers are always to have priority of cabins over intercolonial passengers, whether previously booked or not. This is not, however, to extend to the displacing of any intercolonial passenger while any other cabin berth of similar description is vacant.

Transatlantic passengers desiring it may, on taking their tickets, secure to themselves the privilege of remaining at an intermediate port from the time of arrival at such port till the next steamer of the Company calls there, viz., for a fortnight or a month, as the case may be, but in such cases the place must be specified, and a corresponding notation made on the ticket, upon the understanding, moreover, that on re-embarking the passenger must be content with inferior accommodation if there should be none vacant similar to that originally engaged. In the event of there being no room on board the vessel by which the passenger may be entitled to proceed, they will be allowed accommodation by the first subsequent vessel able to afford it.

Homeward passengers taking a whole or single after cabin are not to have another passenger intruded upon them, unless the number of passengers should accumulate by successive transhipments so as to render it unavoidble to occupy the remaining berth or berths in the cabin, in which case the charge will be only as for one berth in a cabin throughout. Passengers, however, may secure to themselves the exclusive right to a whole cabin by the payment of £10 extra at or prior to their first embarking.

Should any homeward-bound passenger, upon subsequent transhipment, fail to obtain accommodation similar to that for which he originally paid, he is to be charged the inferior fare throughout.

Whenever there may be more passengers than can be accommodated with cabin berths, and who may, in consequence, be obliged to sleep in cots, or otherwise not in any cabin, an abatement of £5 from the lowest cabin rate will be made upon such occasions, but no passenger will be allowed this abatement so long as there is a cabin bed berth unoccupied.

When passengers fail to obtain on board the ship conveying them to England the same sort of accommodation as that for which they originally paid, the captains will furnish to each of such persons a certificate specifying the description of berth paid for and the accommodation subsequently afforded on the voyage to Southampton, which document will entitle the respective parties, on its production at the Company's office in London, to payment of the abatements. Certificates are likewise to be granted to contract passengers when *compelled* to share *fore* cabin accommodation with others.

Should any outward-bound passenger upon subsequent transhipment fail to obtain accommodation similar to that for which he originally paid (as this can only occur when the voyage is nearly finished), he is to be allowed a deduction of five shillings per day for every day he is compelled to occupy such inferior accommodation.

Should any outward or homeward bound passenger shift from the accommodation for which he was originally booked to a berth for which a higher charge is established, or from a berth in a cabin to a whole cabin, he is to be charged the superior fare throughout.

There is to be no difference in the fares between the fore, after, and main deck cabins, nor between a whole cabin and a berth in a cabin, so far as mere intercolonial passages are concerned; the difference of fares being only intended to apply to transatlantic passages out and home.

Although ladies may have sleeping berths allotted to them in the ladies' saloon, yet it is to be open for the use of all the ladies on board between 9 A.M. and 9 P.M. every day.

Intercolonial passengers must not be booked farther than they can be conveyed by the vessel in which they embark, or by other vessels, expected to be met with, to which they can be directly transferred.

Passengers intending to embark abroad will apply to the agents, but the passage-money is to be paid on board, either by the agents (if they have received it) or by the passengers themselves.

Embarkation at Southampton.—The Company's steam tender will convey passengers on board free of charge at Southampton, leaving the docks for that purpose not later than 30 minutes after 11 A.M. on the day of sailing.

Baggage, except carpet-bags and hat-boxes, must be shipped the previous day. No heavy baggage will be received on board on the day of sailing.

Baggage.—Any passenger is liable to a penalty of £100 who carries gunpowder or other goods of a dangerous nature (stat. 17 and 18 Vic., c. 104); for example, lucifer matches, chemicals, or any articles of an inflammable or damaging nature.

Baggage for shipment at Southampton must be addressed to the care of shipping agents there, and, as before stated, must be shipped the day previous to the ship's departure.

Arrangements have been made by which passengers can effect insurance on their baggage at the Company's office in London.

Each adult saloon passenger allowed to carry luggage free of charge to the extent of 20 cubic feet measurement, children and servants in proportion; and each adult passenger on the warrant-officers' or artisans' scale, 10 cubic feet. With a view to prevent mistakes on landing or transhipment, passengers are strongly recommended to label each parcel of their luggage with their name and destination.

Each deck passenger is allowed 56 lbs. of baggage.

All luggage will have to pass through the Custom-house at the port of destination.

All extra luggage to be charged as for measurement goods, but without primage.

Merchandise can not be carried under the name of luggage, but must be shipped according to the Company's regulations for cargo, etc. Whenever an attempt may be discovered to carry merchandise as luggage, freight will be charged at the rate of 4s. per cubic foot. All specie, bullion, or other treasure carried by passengers, above the value of £150, to be shipped as treasure, and charged for at the established rates of freight.

The Company will not be responsible for any loss, damage, or detention of luggage under any circumstances; nor for specie, bullion, jewelry, or other treasure belonging to passengers, unless the same be shipped as such at the established rates of freight.

Foreign Currency.—The Spanish dollar is to be taken every where at the rate of 4s. 2d. sterling; the doubloon at 64s.; the American eagle and its fractional parts at the rate established by H. M. proclamation, dated 19th of August, 1853, viz.: the eagle at 41s. sterling; the half eagle at 20s. 6d., the quarter eagle at 10s. 3d.; and the gold dollar at 4s. 1d.

In foreign ports the fares specified in the intercolonial table are to be paid in silver dollars, or their equivalent in other current coin; this rule applies also to the British colonies, except that notes of the West India Colonial Bank are to be taken as equivalent. Gold or silver five-franc pieces are to be received at the rate of four shillings each when tendered in payment of passage-money, but only by persons embarking at or for Martinique or Guadaloupe.

SPECIE, TREASURE, CARGO, AND PARCELS.

Outward.

For through rates to ports in the Pacific, see pages 170, 171.

Specie and treasure may be forwarded by the packets from Southampton to any port at which they touch at the following rates, viz.:

Quicksilver .... 2 per cent. on value from Southampton.
Plate.. 2   "   "   "   "
Specie, Jewelry, and Precious Stones............................ } 1   " from Southampton, or 1¼ when received by the Company in London.
Copper Coin .... £7 per ton from Southampton.

For particulars, apply at 55 Moorgate Street, or to Mr. W. Ritchie, the Company's Cargo Superintendent, Southampton.

When packages of specie or treasure are sent to Southampton, they must be forwarded to the care of shipping agents there.

No bills of lading will be given for less freight than £1 1s.

Packages for Aspinwall will not be received when consigned "to order," but a consignee must be named.

Outward Cargo.

A limited quantity of goods can be forwarded by the packets of the 2d and 17th of each month from Southampton to Barbadoes, Granada, Jamaica, Demerara, Trinidad, St. Thomas, Aspinwall; by the packet of the 2d of each month to Carthagena and Santa Martha; and by that of the 17th to Honduras and Greytown.

For through rates to ports in the Pacific, see pages 170, 171.

No package above five hundred weight to be received, and none to exceed a cube of 27 feet, nor in length 4 feet 4 inches.

Packages cubing more than 4 feet can not be taken to Greytown.

No bills of lading will be given for less freight than £1 1s.

Packages for Aspinwall will not be received when consigned "to order," but a consignee must be named.

Wine and beer can be shipped at Southampton only by special permission from Captain Vincent, the Company's superintendent there.

The following are the *Rates of Freight*, which must be prepaid: By measurement, £6 per ton, or 3s. per cubic foot, with 5 per cent. primage; by weight, £5 per ton and 5 per cent. primage—the Company reserving the right to charge by measurement or by weight. Cinnamon, 1d. per pound.

Goods for shipment must be addressed to the care of agents at Southampton, and must be there, at latest, at noon on the last day of each month if for shipment by the steamer of the 2d, and at noon on the 15th if for shipment by the steamer of the 17th of the month; but when the day of departure falls on a Monday, the latest period will be one day previous to the above dates.

For particulars, apply to Mr. W. Ritchie, the Company's Cargo Superintendent, Southampton.

Outward Parcels and Periodicals are received at the Company's offices in London and Southampton for transmission by the steamers of the 2d and 17th of each month, to St. Kitts, Antigua, Guadaloupe, Dominique, Martinique, St. Lucia, Tobago, St. Vincent, Barbadoes, Demerara, Granada, Trinidad, Jacmel, Jamaica, St. Thomas, and Aspinwall; by the steamer of the 17th for Honduras and Greytown; and by the steamer of the 2d for Havana, Vera Cruz, Tampico, Santa Martha, and Carthagena. The weight of a package or parcel for St. Kitts, Antigua, Guadaloupe, Dominique, Martinique, St. Lucia, Tobago, and St. Vincent, must not exceed half a hundred weight. The cube of a package or parcel for Greytown must not exceed 4 feet.

To Havana, Vera Cruz, and Tampico, parcels containing only samples and periodicals can be conveyed.

Packages and parcels (not exceeding 5 cubic feet) must be delivered at the London office before noon upon the 14th if intended for transmission by the steamer leaving Southampton upon the 17th of the month, and before noon upon the 28th if intended for shipment by the vessel leaving upon the 2d of the following month.

Periodical publications, with the covers open at both ends, can be booked at the London office until 2 o'clock on the day previous to the sailing of the packet, excepting when the day of sailing falls on Monday, in which case not later than 2 o'clock on the previous Saturday.

Parcels and periodicals, if sent to the care of an agent at Southampton, can be received at the Company's cargo office at that place until 10 A.M. on the day of the departure of the steamers for the West Indies.

Rates (which must be prepaid).

For through rates to Panama and ports in the South Pacific, see pages 172, 173.

The following rates include all charges except insurance (which, however, can be effected at the Company's office in London), whether the packages are received at London or Southampton: By measurement, 1 cubic foot and under, 7s. 6d. per package; above 1 foot and not exceeding 2, 11s. 6d.; above 2 feet and not exceeding 3, 15s.; above 3 feet, 5s. per foot, up to 14 feet, beyond which measurement no packages can be received at the parcel rate.

Packages can not be received at the London office if they exceed 5 cubic feet, but in that case they must be sent to Southampton.

By weight, at the rate of 10s. per cwt.

No package weighing more than 5 cwt. can be received at the parcel rate.

The Company reserves to itself the right to charge by measurement or by weight.

Quarterly publications and pamphlets, 2s. each; monthly publications, 1s. each.

Each package must be fully and distinctly addressed, and contents and value declared.

No parcels are to contain letters or bills.

The Company will not be responsible for the act of God, the queen's enemies, fire on shore or afloat, or any other dangers and accidents of the seas, rivers, and steam navigation. All parcels must be applied for to the agents of the Company at the port of delivery, except those for St. Thomas and Carthagena, which must be taken from alongside at consignee's risk and expense. At Martinique, the landing charges are to be paid by the consignee, and at Greytown the packages will be landed by the Company, but at the consignee's risk. All parcels subject to duty must be cleared from the Custom-house in the usual manner by the parties to whom they are addressed, they paying all duties and other expenses attendant upon the same. The Company will not be answerable for any package, in case of loss, damage, or detention, beyond the value of £5, unless by special agreement.

REGULATIONS IN REGARD TO CARGO AND PARCELS.

Packages, of whatever description, sent to Southampton, must be forwarded to the care of shipping agents there for delivery by them to the Company.

Shippers are earnestly recommended to have their goods packed securely in tin or wooden cases, to prevent the possibility of damage in shipment, transfer, or disembarkation.

Brown paper parcels will not be received, and the use of canvas wrappers is strongly recommended to shippers as a means of security.

All deeds must be packed in tin cases.

The Company decline to take on board their vessels medicinal fluids, oil, balsam, sugar, molasses, cotton, spirits, gunpowder, vitriol, tar, pitch, turpentine, acids, ether, chloroform, Lucifer matches, percussion caps, or any other articles of a dangerous, damaging, or inflammable nature. Any person or persons forwarding such commodities for shipment, without giving notice to the Company, will be liable, by the Merchant Shipping Act of 1854, to a penalty of £100.

Wine and beer can not be shipped at Southampton except by special permission of the Company's superintendent there.

Packages containing plants can not be shipped, unless by special agreement exempting the Company from all liability in the event of damage.

Double freight will be imposed in all cases of detection, where attempts may be made, by smuggling specie, etc., to evade the Company's established charges.

No article of any kind to be received on board without going through the established Customs' regulations and formalities.

Packages on arrival at destination will be lodged in the Custom-house, whence they will have to be retired by the consignees, or by agents commissioned by them to do so, at their expense.

All packages must have the port of destination distinctly marked thereon, or they can not be received for shipment.

No package above five hundred weight to be received, and none to exceed a cube of 27 feet, nor in length 4 feet 4 inches.

Homeward and Intercolonial Freight.

☞ It is to be understood that all regulations or notices relating to outward traffic will hold good, where applicable, to homeward and intercolonial traffic, although they may not be repeated under the latter heads.

Homeward Specie and *Treasure* can be shipped at any of the ports touched at by the Company's steamers at the following rates, viz.:

Specie, bullion, platina, diamonds, pearls, emeralds, and all other precious stones, unset, being exempt from duty, deliverable at the Bank of England or Southampton, and jewelry subject to duty deliverable at Southampton only.....on value $1\frac{1}{8}$ per cent.

Ditto ditto, deliverable at the Branch Bank of France, Havre... $1\frac{5}{16}$ "

Specie or bullion, from Martinique or Guadaloupe, deliverable ditto..on value

    Consignments under £50 in value............................. £1 1s.
    " " £100 " .... £1 10s.
    " " £150 " .... £2 2s.
    " of and above £150 in value................ $1\frac{1}{16}$ per cent.

Plate, subject to duty, deliverable at Southampton.....on value 2 "
Ditto, deliverable at the Branch Bank of France, Havre......... $2\frac{3}{16}$ "
Copper coin, deliverable at Southampton.......................£7 per ton weight.
Copper ore, mineral sand, etc............................see Homeward Cargo.

No primage is charged on the foregoing.
For rates on treasure from the Pacific, see pages 172–174.

No package of specie, jewelry, etc., to be conveyed, and no bills of lading to be granted, for less freight than £1 1s., or five silver dollars.

Homeward Cargo can be shipped for Southampton at the following ports, viz.: Barbadoes, Jamaica, St. Thomas, Porto Rico, Tampico, Vera Cruz, Havana, Honduras, Trinidad, Carthagena, Santa Martha, Aspinwall, Greytown, Demerara, Granada.

No bills of lading granted for less freight than £1 1s.

The following are the rates payable on delivery of the goods at Southampton, viz.:

Copper ore, copper and silver alloy, cupel stuff, and mineral sand... £5 per ton weight.
Alpaca wool... { $1\frac{1}{2}d.$ per lb. or 1s. 9d. per foot measurement.
Ginger.. £7 per ton weight.
Coffee, cocoa, and arrow-root.............................. £5 " "

India-rubber in solid pieces	£5 per ton weight.
Sarsaparilla, jalap, and other dry drugs	1½d. per lb.
Divi divi	1d. "
Peruvian bark	1d. "
Pimento, cochineal, indigo, gums, and beeswax	1d. "
Plantain fibre	1½d. "
Pines, oranges, or other green fruits or plants, packed in hampers, barrels, or boxes	£5 per ton measurement of 40 cubic feet.
Cigars and leaf tobacco	£5 per ditto ditto.
Measurement goods	3s. 6d. per cubic foot.
Cases containing preserved turtle	2s. 6d. " "
Turtle, on the quantity landed alive at Southampton; but the Company not liable for losses by death or disaster	£1 5s. per cwt.
Vanilla .... on value	1⅛ per cent.
" deliverable at Havre .... "	1·3/16 "
Cochineal, " "	1½d. per lb.

Five per cent. primage is charged on all homeward freight except vanilla.
Balsam will not be received on board the Company's steamers.

Homeward Parcels and Periodicals, including small parcels of succades, arrow-root, etc., will be charged at the same rates as outward parcels, but deliverable at Southampton.

Freight must be prepaid. For rates, etc., see pages 166, 167.

Intercolonial Specie, Cargo, and Parcels.

Specie can be shipped for any port touched at by the packets.

No package of specie is to be conveyed, and no bills of lading are to be granted, for less freight than five silver dollars.

Freight on specie, jewelry, pearls, diamonds, and other precious stones, to be prepaid at the port of shipment: Exceeding 2500 miles, 1 per cent.; exceeding 1000 miles, and not above 2500 miles, ¾ per cent.; not exceeding 1000 miles, ½ per cent.

The distance between St. Thomas or intermediate places and Demerara is to be considered as not exceeding 1000 miles.

No sums under 5000 dollars are to be conveyed, however short the distance, at a lower rate than ½ per cent.; but when larger amounts are to be remitted from one British colony to another, or between any places visited by the Company's vessels eastward of Jamaica, provided, in either case, the distance is within 800 miles, the rate will be ¼ per cent. The tables of routes to determine the distances.

Copper coin, £7 per ton weight.

Intercolonial Rates on Goods to be prepaid at Port of Shipment.

Goods can be forwarded between Barbadoes, St. Thomas, Aspinwall, Demerara, Jamaica, Greytown, Trinidad, Granada, Carthagena, Honduras, Santa Martha, and to these places from Havana and other foreign ports; but cargo can not be carried to foreign ports, with the before-mentioned exceptions, except by special permission.

£3 10s. per ton measurement of 40 cubic feet.
Cocoa and coffee, £3 10s. per ton, on the gross weight.
Indigo and other dry drugs, cochineal, 1d. per lb.
Divi divi, ½d. per lb.
Beeswax, ¾d. per lb.

Dry and wet provisions,	From St. Thomas to Barbadoes, Trinidad, Demerara, or Jamaica	1 silver dollar per barrel.
	From St. Thomas to Greytown	1½ do. do.

No primage is charged.

No bills of lading for merchandise will be granted for less freight than 2½ silver dollars.

Balsam will not be received on board the Company's steamers.

Intercolonial Parcels carried to all the places named under the head of "Outward Parcels," to be prepaid at the port of shipment, to be charged one fifth less than the transatlantic scale, and to be restricted in size and weight, as indicated under that head for different ports. See p. 166, 167.

Preference is always to be given to transatlantic over intercolonial cargo.

ISTHMUS OF PANAMA AND THE PACIFIC.

Trains now run daily across the Isthmus of Panama, thus affording an easy means of transit for passengers, specie, goods, etc.

Under arrangement with the Pacific Steam Navigation Company, whose vessels run from Panama southward, through tickets (comprising the privilege of stopping at an intermediate port, as stated in "General Passenger Regulations," page 163) can be obtained to or from Southampton and ports on the west coast of South America, but not including the providing or expense of the transit of passengers or their luggage across the Isthmus of Panama. Also, return tickets to or from those ports (including Panama), with an abatement of 25 per cent. on the Royal Mail Steam Packet Company's proportion of passage-money, available for twelve months, under the conditions mentioned in page 161.

Goods, etc., for San Francisco and Victoria (**British Columbia**).

The Royal Mail Steam Packet Company have completed arrangements for granting *through bills of lading* for measurement goods, jewelry, and plate, shipped by their steamers leaving Southampton on the 2d and 17th of each month, to be delivered at San Francisco and Victoria (British Columbia) at the following rates of freight:

To be paid on shipment of goods, etc.:

Goods: From Southampton to Aspinwall, £6 per ton measurement, with 5 per cent. primage.

Jewelry, on value: From London to Aspinwall, 1¼ per cent.; from Southampton to Aspinwall, 1 per cent.

Plate, on value: From Southampton to Aspinwall, 2 per cent.

And in addition,

To be paid on delivery of goods, etc., at destination.

Goods: From Aspinwall to San Francisco, $80 per ton measurement, with 5 per cent. primage; from Aspinwall to Victoria, $100 per ton measurement, with 5 per cent. primage.

Jewelry, on value: From Aspinwall to San Francisco, 2 per cent.; from Aspinwall to Victoria, 2½ do.

Plate, on value: From Aspinwall to San Francisco, 4 per cent.; from Aspinwall to Victoria, 5 per cent.

No bill of lading will be issued for less freight than one guinea to Aspinwall.

Specie, Goods, etc., from England or the West Indies, for Ports in the Pacific south of Panama, viz., Buenaventura, Tumaco, Guayaquil, Payta, Lambayeque, Huanchaco, Callao, Islay, Arica, Iquique, Cobija, Caldera, Coquimbo, Valparaiso.

Cargo for Lambayeque and Huanchaco is carried on to Callao, where it is transhipped to the steamer proceeding northward.

The Royal Mail Steam Packet Company have effected an arrangement with the Panama Railroad Company and the Pacific Steam Navigation

Company for the delivery of treasure, measurement goods, and quicksilver, from Southampton and the West Indian ports hereafter specified,* under *through bills of lading*, at ports in the South Pacific, and at the respective rates of freight under-mentioned, which must be paid on shipment of the goods, whether at Southampton or in the West Indies.

Measurement Goods from Southampton, shipped by Steamer of 2d and 17th of each Month.

Per ton measurement (with 5 per cent. primage):
To Buenaventura..	£12 15s.
To ports south of Buenaventura, including Guayaquil.....	13 5
To Payta..	13 15
To ports south of Payta, including Callao.......................	14 5
To ports south of Callao, including Valparaiso...............	15 5

No bill of lading for goods to any of the above ports will be granted for less freight than £2 2s.

From the West Indies, viz., *St. Thomas, Havana, Jamaica, Barbadoes, Trinidad, Demerara, Greytown, Carthagena, and Santa Martha.*

To any of the above-mentioned Pacific ports south of Panama, the rate of freight for measurement goods will be £2 10s. per ton less than from Southampton to those places, and no primage will be charged.

No bill of lading for goods from the West Indies to any of the above ports will be granted for less freight than £1 11s. 6d.

Treasure from England, or the before-mentioned West Indian ports, at a uniform rate, viz.: For specie (gold) and jewelry, when received in London, 2¾ per cent. on value.

No bill of lading for gold or jewelry will be granted in London for less freight than £2 7s. 6d.

Of jewelry only small packages will be received in London.

For specie (gold) and jewelry, when received in Southampton or the West Indies, 2¼ per cent. on value.

No bill of lading for gold or jewelry will be granted in Southampton or the West Indies for less freight than £2 5s.

For specie (silver), one eighth per cent. is to be added to the above respective rates for gold.

Quicksilver, which must be delivered to the Company at Southampton for shipment: To ports as far as Callao inclusive, 5¼ per cent. on value; to ports beyond Callao, 5¾ per cent. on value.

No bill of lading for quicksilver will be granted in Southampton for less freight than £5 5s. in the one case, and £5 15s. in the other.

Parcels not exceeding three cubic feet in measurement will be received at the Company's offices in London and Southampton for the ports above-mentioned at the under-mentioned rates, which must be paid on shipment, and which include all charges except insurance (which, however, can be effected at the Company's office in London), whether the packages are received at London or Southampton: One cubic foot and under, £1; above 1 cubic foot and not exceeding 2, £1 10s.; above 2 feet and not exceeding 3, £2.

Under arrangement between the Royal Mail Steam Packet Company and the Panama Railroad Company, *through bills of lading,* are granted at Southampton as follows: To Central American (Pacific) ports, touched at by the steamers of the Panama Railroad Company, viz., Punta Arenas, Realejo, La Union, La Libertad, Acajulta, San José de Guatemala.

For goods, at £13 per ton measurement (with 5 per cent. primage), which must be paid on shipment.

No bill of lading will be granted for less freight than £2 2s.

There is no through parcel or specie rate to these ports.

Through bills of lading are also granted at Southampton, and in the West Indies at St. Thomas, Havana, Jamaica, Barbadoes, Trinidad, Demerara, Greytown, Carthagena, and Santa Martha, as far as Panama, for specie, jewelry, measurement goods, and quicksilver, destined for Panama and the North Pacific, at the following rates of freight, which must be paid on shipment:

For goods, etc., from Southampton, £10 per ton measurement (with 5 per cent. primage).

No bill of lading will be granted for less freight than £1 11s. 6d.

For goods, etc., from the above West Indian ports, £7 10s. per ton measurement (without primage).

No bill of lading will be granted for less freight than £1 1s.

For specie (gold) and jewelry, when received in London, 1⅜ per cent.

No bill of lading will be granted for less freight than £1 7s. 6d.

For specie (gold) and jewelry, when received in Southampton or at the above West Indian ports, 1¼ per cent.

No bill of lading will be granted for less freight than £1 5s.

For specie (silver), one eighth per cent. is to be added to the above respective rates for gold.

For quicksilver, which must be delivered to the Company at Southampton for shipment, 3¼ per cent. on value.

No bill of lading will be granted for less freight than £3 5s.

Parcels for Panama not exceeding 3 cubic feet in measurement will be received at the Company's offices in London and Southampton at the following rates, which must be paid on shipment, and which include all charges except insurance (which, however, can be effected at the Company's office in London), whether the packages are received at London or Southampton: One cubic foot and under, 12s.; above 1 foot and not exceeding 2, 18s.; above 2 feet and not exceeding 3, £1 4s.

NOTE.—For farther information as to when goods, etc., must be ready for shipment, and general regulations in regard to cargo and parcels, etc., see pages 166, 167, and 168, or apply to 55 Moorgate Street, or to Mr. J. K. Linstead, the Company's Cargo Superintendent, Southampton.

No package above 5 cwt. to be received, and none to exceed a cube of 27 feet, nor in length 4 feet 4 inches.

Specie, etc., from Panama and the South Pacific.

The following rates have been established by the Royal Mail Steam Packet Company, in addition to the freight charged by the Pacific Steam Navigation Company, or other parties delivering treasure to the agent of the Royal Mail Steam Packet Company at Panama, for conveyance to the under-mentioned places, such charges to include transport across the Isthmus, and all other expenses thence to the place of destination:

		To Branch Bank of France, Havre.
Specie and bullion from Panama to Southampton or Bank of England	1¾ per cent.	1⅞ per cent.
Pearls, emeralds, and all other precious stones, unset being exempt from duty, from Panama to Southampton or the Bank of England, on value	1½ "	2¹⁄₁₀ "
Jewelry, subject to duty, from Panama to Southampton, on value	1¾ "	1⅞ "

Specie, bullion, precious stones, etc., from Panama to British
 Guiana, Vera Cruz, and Tampico..................................... 1¼ per cent.
Ditto ditto to St. Domingo, Porto Rico, St. Thomas, Wind-
 ward Islands, Havana, Honduras, and Jamaica.................. 1⅜ "
Ditto ditto to Carthagena and Greytown......................... ⅞ "

N.B.—The Pacific Steam Navigation Company's charge on specie, etc., from any port in Chili or Peru, etc., to Panama, for transfer to the Royal Mail Steam Packets, is ⅞ per cent., which, being added to the rates from Panama above stated, will make the charges by *through bill of lading*,

To Southampton or the Bank of England.......... 2⅛ per cent.
To the Branch Bank of France, Havre.............. 2 1/16 "

The through charge on jewelry, pearls, and all other precious stones from the South Pacific ports is the same as that on specie and bullion.

Double freight will be imposed in all cases of detection where attempts may be made, by smuggling, etc., to evade the Company's established charges.

Gold, etc., from San Francisco (California).

Gold, etc., can be shipped at San Francisco, under the *through bills of lading* of the United States Pacific Mail Steam-ship Company and the Royal Mail Steam Packet Company, for conveyance to England, Havre, or the West Indies.

For particulars as to through rates of freight, etc., apply in San Francisco to W. L. Booker, Esq., H.B.M. Consul, or at the office of the Pacific Mail Steam-ship Company.

Goods from South Pacific Ports to Southampton.

Through bills of lading are granted at South Pacific ports by the Pacific Steam Navigation Company, in conjunction with the Panama Railroad Company and the Royal Mail Steam Packet Company, at the following through rates of freight, payable on delivery of the goods at Southampton:

Description of goods, etc.	Shipped at ports between Payta and Panama, including Payta.	Shipped at ports between Callao and Payta, including Callao.	Shipped at ports between Valparaiso and Callao, incl. Valparaiso.
	Per ton weight. £ s. d.	Per ton weight. £ s. d.	Per ton weight. £ s. d.
Copper and tin, bars................	7 2 8	7 9 4	7 19 4
Copper and tin ore, in bags.....	8 2 8	8 9 4	8 19 4
Silver ore................................	8 16 0	9 4 0	9 16 0
Coffee, cocoa, and India-rubber	9 16 0	10 4 0	10 16 0
Orchilla...................................	9 0 0	9 6 5	9 16 0
Bark*.....................................	15 8 8	15 18 8	16 8 8
Tobacco in leaf.......................	15 16 0	16 8 0	17 6 0
	Per ton measurement.	Per ton measurement.	Per ton measurement.
Whalebone.............................	11 2 8	11 13 4	12 9 4
Panama hats..........................	18 9 4	19 10 8	21 2 8
Sarsaparilla............................	11 16 0	12 8 0	13 6 0
General merchandise..............	13 8 0	14 0 0	15 0 0

Primage at the rate of 5 per cent. will be charged in addition to the above rates of freight.

* Bills of lading will be granted for bark to Havre at an advance of a farthing per lb. on the above rates.

Parcels from South Pacific ports to Southampton at the same rates as "Outward Parcels" to those places (see pages 171, 172).

From Central American (Pacific) Ports to Southampton.

Through bills of lading are granted by the Panama Railroad Company, in conjunction with the Royal Mail Steam Packet Company, at the following ports, touched at by the Panama Railroad Company's steamers, namely, Punta Arenas, Realejo, La Union, La Libertad, Acajutla, San José de Guatemala.

The through rates of freight from the above places to Southampton are as under-mentioned, and the freight is payable on delivery of the goods at that port:

On silver ore, £9 per ton weight, with 5 per cent. primage.
On coffee, £10 per ton weight, with 5 per cent. primage.
On cochineal and indigo, $2\frac{1}{16}d.$ per lb., with 5 per cent. primage.
Measurement goods, 7s. 6d. per foot, with 5 per cent. primage.

Also on treasure (gold and silver) from the above places to Southampton or the Bank of England, London, $2\frac{1}{4}$ per cent. on value, payable on delivery of the treasure.

Cochineal and indigo, deliverable at Havre, $2\frac{1}{16}d.$ per lb., with 5 per cent. primage.

Balsam will not be received on board the Company's steamers.

7th. **LIVERPOOL AND WEST INDIA LINE OF SCREW STEAM-SHIPS (HOLT'S), PLYING MONTHLY BETWEEN LIVERPOOL AND ASPINWALL** *via* **THE WEST INDIES.**

The Saladin, the Plantagenet, the Talisman, and the Crusader.
One of the steamers of this line will generally be at Aspinwall from the 9th to the 17th of each month.

TARIFF OF FREIGHT,

under *through bill of lading*, from San José de Guatemala, Acajutla, La Libertad, La Union, Realejo, and Punta Arenas, to Liverpool and London, by the Panama Railroad Company's steamers to Panama, thence by railroad to Aspinwall, and to their destination by vessels of the Liverpool and West India Line and the London and Northwestern Railway.

From San José, Acajutla, and La Libertad to Liverpool.

Indigo and cochineal, 4 cents per lb. net; hides, 77 cents each; merchandise in cases, etc., 85 cents per cubic foot, and the regular transportation charges established by the tariff of the railroad.

From La Union and Realejo to Liverpool.

Indigo and cochineal, 4 cents per lb. net; hides, 75 cents each; merchandise in cases, etc., 80 cents per cubic foot, and the transportation charges established by the tariff of the railroad.

From Punta Arenas to Liverpool.

Coffee, $1\frac{11}{16}$ cents per lb. net; hides, 69 cents each; merchandise in cases, etc., 75 cents per cubic foot, and the transportation charges established by the tariff of the railroad.

Indigo and cochineal, from any ports, $4\frac{3}{4}$ cents per lb. gross weight.
Coffee in bags, from Punta Arenas to London, $2\frac{1}{4}$ cents per lb. gross weight.

The above rates include every charge on the Isthmus of Panama, also in Liverpool.

Freight to be collected on the weights delivered or measurements taken in Liverpool, at the rate of $4 80 to the pound sterling.

Primage will not be charged on produce or merchandise shipped from the ports above mentioned under *through bills of lading.*

For farther information, apply to

    WILLIAM NELSON, *Commercial Agent*, Panama.
    CRISANTO MEDINA, Punta Arenas.
    COURTADE Y CLAVERA, La Union.
    H. J. FOOTE and J. MATHI, Sonsonate.
    J. SARAGIA, San José de Guatemala; and the captains of the Panama Railroad Company's steamers on board, or to
    ALFRED HOLT, No. 1 India Buildings, Liverpool.

N.B.—The rate of freight from Liverpool to the above ports, under *through bills of lading,* is £7 10s. per ton of 40 cubic feet, including all charges on the Isthmus, without primage.

THE PANAMA RAILROAD COMPANY'S LINE OF SAILING VESSELS BETWEEN NEW YORK AND ASPINWALL.

To accommodate shippers and facilitate trade, especially with the Pacific coast, the Panama Railroad Company have established a line of sailing vessels between New York and Aspinwall, composed of the following:

Bark Xantha .... Captain Chapman .... 321 tons.
  " Magdalena .....   "   Day 285   "
  " Golden Rule ....   "   Whiteberry 254   "
Brig Arabella ....   "   Lindsley 291   "
  " Costa Rica ......   "   Peel 260   "
  " E. Drummond ..   "   Cormay 244   "
  " Caroline ....   "   Porter 220   "

These vessels are all of the first class, sailing at intervals of from a week to ten days. The average passage from New York to Aspinwall is twenty days, and from Aspinwall to New York twenty-five days.

The freight from New York to Aspinwall is 15 cents per cubic foot, and 5 per cent. primage. The freight from Aspinwall to New York is from $6 to $8 per ton.

Whale-oil will be received and forwarded from Panama to New York by the road and the Company's Line of Sailing Vessels, at the rate of 8 cents per gallon, if received in the harbor alongside from ship's tackles, and at 7 cents per gallon if received at the pier, in full of all expenses, charging for the capacity of the cask, without allowing for wantage.

Whalebone will be taken from ship at Panama through to New York at 1½ cents per lb.

By these vessels the Panama Railroad Company issue *through bills of lading* to the ports of South America touched at by the steam-ships of the Pacific Steam Navigation Company, at the following rates:

	To Buenaventura, Guayaquil, Payta, and intermediates.	To Callao, Valparaiso, and Intermediates, south of Payta.
General merchandise, and all goods embraced in first class of Panama Railroad tariff, per ton of 40 cubic feet, or 2240 lbs. gross weight, at the option of the Company.....	$40 00	$50 00
Beef and pork, per barrel...	5 00	7 00
" " per half barrel.....................................	2 75	3 75
Flour, per barrel..	4 00	5 00
" per half barrel..	2 25	2 75
Biscuit, per 100 lbs..	2 50	3 50
Butter, lard, hams, bacon, cheese, salt fish, tallow, and rice, per ton of 2000 lbs.	30 00	40 00
Refined sugar, per ton of 2000 lbs...............................	40 00	45 00
Wines and other liquors, in boxes and barrels, per ton of 40 cubic feet...	30 00	40 00
Manufactured tobacco, per ton of 40 cubic feet................	30 00	40 00
Cigars, per ton of 40 cubic feet..................................	35 00	45 00
Unbleached domestics, per ton of 40 cubic feet................	25 00	32 00
Soap, per ton of 2000 lbs.	30 00	40 00
Candles, per ton of 40 cubic feet................................	30 00	40 00
Carriages and furniture, per ton of 40 cubic feet..............	30 00	40 00
Agricultural implements, per ton of 40 cubic feet.............	25 00	35 00
Pitch, tar, and rosin, per barrel..................................	3 00	4 00
Earthen-ware and glass-ware (coarse), in crates and boxes, per ton of 40 cubic feet...	25 00	35 00
Turpentine and oil in cases, per ton of 40 cubic feet	30 00	40 00
Turpentine and oil in tins only, per ton of 40 cubic feet.....	35 00	45 00

All weights to be the gross weight.
Articles not enumerated to be charged at rates assimilating to the above.

The Pacific Steam Navigation Company will issue *through bills of lading* for produce *from* the above ports.

Goods arriving at Aspinwall by the Company's vessels, and consigned to parties at Panama, under *through bills of lading*, will be forwarded to them free of charges and commissions by the Company other than such as are expressed in the bills of lading.

Residents and agents at Panama can forward goods through the commercial agent of the Company at Panama to foreign ports beyond Aspinwall, on *through bills of lading*, by the Company's line of sailing vessels to New York, or by any other lines or vessels with which the Company has made the necessary arrangements.

Rates of Through Freight from New York, by the Company's sailing Vessels to Aspinwall, including Lighterage in Panama.

	To Punta Arenas.	Realejo, La Union.	La Libertad, Acajutla, San José (Guatemala).
Dry-goods, hats, boots, shoes, drugs, and other goods, included in railroad tariff as first class, per ton of 40 feet	$40 00	$42 00	$44 00
Unbleached domestics, per ton of 40 feet	32 00	34 00	36 00
Furniture, carriages, agricultural implements, wooden-ware, clocks, etc., per ton of 40 feet	30 00	32 00	34 00
Iron in bars, sheets, and bundles, iron castings, nails, spikes, copper, zinc, and lead, per ton of 2000 lbs.	30 00	32 00	34 00
Steel in bars and bundles, coarse machinery, common hardware, earthen-ware, sugar-mills, -moulds, and -pans, shot, etc., per ton of 2000 lbs	34 00	36 00	38 00
Butter, cheese, lard, fish, ham, soap, and candles, per ton of 2000 lbs.	35 00	37 00	39 00
Refined sugar, per ton of 40 feet	30 00	32 00	34 00
Flour and rice, per barrel	4 20	4 50	4 80
" " per half barrel	2 20	2 35	2 50
Wine in boxes and baskets, per ton of 40 feet	32 00	34 00	36 00
" in casks, and other liquors, per ton of 40 feet	35 00	37 00	39 00
Tobacco, manufactured, per ton of 40 feet	40 00	42 00	44 00
" unmanufactured, per ton of 40 feet	32 00	34 00	36 00
Ship-bread, crackers, etc., per ton of 40 feet	28 00	30 00	32 00

Goods can be shipped three times per month, by steamers of the Atlantic and Pacific Steam-ship Company, to Aspinwall, at an addition of 35 cents per foot, or $14 per ton, to the above rates.

Rates of Return Freights, by the Company's sailing Vessels from Aspinwall to New York, including Lighterage in Panama.

	To Panama.	Aspinwall.	New York.
Lumber, from La Union, per M.	$20 00		
" " Punta Arenas, per M.	18 00		
Cochineal and indigo, from either port, per lb. net.	1¼	$0 02¾	$0 03½
Hides, from San José, Acajutla, and La Libertad, each	32	47	62
Hides, from La Union and Realejo, each	30	45	60
" " Punta Arenas	24	39	54
Coffee, from Punta Arenas, per lb. gross	⅝	1¼	1½
Deer and goat skins, from Punta Arenas, per lb.	1	1¾	2½
" " " other ports, " ...	1½	2¼	3
Cigars, balsam, and first class goods, per railroad tariff, per foot	50	1 00	1 16

No primage on through rates.

Officers and Directors of the Panama Railroad.

DAVID HOADLEY, President.
JOSEPH F. JOY, Secretary.
GEORGE M. TOTTEN, Chief Engineer.
HENRY SMITH, Treasurer.
WM. PARKER, General Superintendent.

DIRECTORS.

WILLIAM H. ASPINWALL,	HENRY CHAUNCEY,
EDWIN BARTLETT,	WM. FELLOWES,
GOUVERNEUR KEMBLE,	SAMUEL W. COMSTOCK.
WILLIAM WHITEWRIGHT JR.,	JAMES T. SOUTTER,
EDWARD CUNARD,	JOSEPH W. ALSOP,
THEODORE W. RILEY,	JOHN STEWARD,

DAVID HOADLEY.

TOWER OF SAN JEROME.

BRIEF ACCOUNT

OF THE

REPUBLICS OF CENTRAL AMERICA,

CONNECTED WITH THE PANAMA RAILROAD BY THE STEAMERS OF THE CENTRAL AMERICAN LINE.

THE course of the Panama Railroad Company's Central American steamers, for their upward voyages from Panama, is due south across the Bay of Panama to Point Mala, its western boundary; from thence, following the coast-line, within distinct view of the rugged mountain range which bounds it, a northwesterly course is pursued to San José de Guatemala, the terminus of the route.

The 1st port of entry is Punta Arenas, in the Republic of COSTA RICA, distant from Panama 450 miles.

The 2d port of entry is Realejo, in the Republic of NICARAGUA, distant from Panama 692 miles.

The 3d port of entry is La Union, in the Republic of SALVADOR, distant from Panama 762 miles.

The 4th port of entry is Libertad, in the Republic of SALVADOR, distant from Panama 862 miles.

The 5th port of entry is Acajutla, in the Republic of SALVADOR, distant from Panama 902 miles.

The 6th port of entry is San José de Guatemala, in the Republic of GUATEMALA, distant from Panama 966 miles.

COSTA RICA.

THE Republic of Costa Rica, lying between 8° 30' and 10° 40' N. latitude, and 82° and 85° W. longitude, has an area of about 23,000 sq. miles. Population about 150,000, composed of whites of Spanish descent, Indians, Negroes, and Mestizoes, the latter estimated at about one fifth of the whole. Costa Rica is politically divided into five departments, viz., San José, Cartago, Heredia, Alajuela, and Punta Arenas.

The prevailing religion is Roman Catholic. There are about 50 churches in the republic. Protestants are protected from molestation or annoyance on account of their religion by treaties with Great Britain and the United States. Its educational facilities consist of a University, with a government endowment of $46,310, besides one fourth of the receipts of the tobacco monopoly; there are also reported about 80 primary schools in the republic.

The city of San José, the capital of the republic, is situated in the department of the same name, about midway between the Atlantic and Pacific Oceans, on a table-land 45,000 feet above their level. It is regularly laid out. The buildings are generally of one story, on account of the frequency of earthquakes. The University is located at San José; there are also a government palace, a hospital, a mint, a national bank, and several churches. The city is connected with Punta Arenas, the sea-port, by a cart-road 70 miles in length. On this road, five leagues from the capital, is the government custom-house, at a place called Garita del Rio Grande.

Punta Arenas, the only available sea-port of the Republic of Costa Rica, is situated on a small peninsula in the Gulf of Nicoya. This peninsula is a low sandy point a little more than four miles in length by from one fourth to a mile in breadth, its highest point about 16 feet above the level of the sea. Upon this the town is situated, and contains about 3000 inhabitants, one tenth of whom are Spanish, the remainder a mixed race of Spanish, Indian, and Negro.

The soil of Costa Rica is exceedingly productive. On

the "tierras calientes," or torrid lands, which run back from the Pacific up to an elevation of 3000 feet, almost all the tropical productions abound. Above these are the "tierras templadas," which are terraces making out from the main Cordilleras (following very nearly the longitudinal axis of the state in a northwest and southeast direction), and are from 3000 to 5000 feet above the level of the sea, producing sugar-cane, potatoes, corn, coffee, oranges, etc., etc., in great perfection.

Still above the tierras templadas are the tierras frias, or frigid lands, which are from 5000 to 6000 feet above the ocean level, among which several volcanoes shoot up, varying from 8000 to 11,000 feet in height. The forests, which extend over a large portion of the republic, abound in timber suitable for ship-building; also mahogany, Brazil, and various other valuable dye-woods.

The cultivated portion of Costa Rica lies principally within the valley of the Rio Grande, which flows down the western slope of the main mountain range into the Gulf of Nicoya. "Fully seven eighths of all the inhabitants are here concentrated, in a district not exceeding fifty miles in length by an average of twenty in breadth."

CLIMATE.

"The topographical features of the country indicate the variety of climate to be found in this state. In the district around the capital the thermometer generally ranges during the forenoon from 65° to 75° of Fahrenheit; from noon until 3 P.M., during the hottest season, sometimes as high as 82° Fahrenheit; during the night, at the coldest periods, never below 57°. Upon both the Atlantic and Pacific coasts the average mean temperature is, of course, much higher, but on the Pacific the thermometer seldom rises above 85° Fahrenheit. The seasons are well defined. On the Pacific the dry season lasts from November to April, and the rainy from April to November. On the Atlantic slope these periods are nearly reversed. Here, too, a much larger amount of rain falls, and the climate is hot and insalubrious."* The Pacific coast has, however, the reputation of being much more healthy, and the table-lands and upland valleys are, for a tropical country, said to be especially salubrious.

The mineral wealth of Costa Rica is almost wholly undeveloped. Mines of gold, copper, iron, lead, and coal have been discovered, but no intelligent efforts have as yet been made to ascertain their value.

The commercial products of Costa Rica are coffee, hides, dye-woods, sarsaparilla, tortoise-shell, pearl-shells, and mahogany. The principal of these, however, is coffee, which is of very fine quality, and scarcely second to the celebrated Mocha. The cultivation of this great staple was introduced in 1829. By 1845 about five millions of pounds were exported; in 1848, ten millions; and in 1850, fourteen millions. Up to the year 1856 the coffee was transported by a tedious and expensive voyage around Cape Horn to European markets. Since the establishment of the Central American Steam-ship Line, in connection with the Panama Railroad, much of the coffee-crop has been exported through this direct channel, and not a small portion has thereby found its way to the United States. Large quantities have been sent to Panama for reshipment on the Pacific mail steamers for the California market. The impetus given by greatly increased facilities and increased demands have, notwithstanding the disturbed political condition of the country, resulted in a growing increase in the number and extent of the coffee estates; and almost solely by means of its coffee trade, from one of the poorest, Costa Rica has become, relatively, one of the richest of the Central American states. The present export of coffee from Costa Rica yearly is estimated

* Squier's **Central America**.

at over a million of dollars, and, with all its other exports combined, about $1,350,000. Its imports, which are chiefly from Great Britain and the United States, present a total of about $1,200,000 per annum. A bank of discount, deposit, and loans on real estate was established at the capital in 1858, and its notes are the legal currency of the republic. The specie currency is mostly made up of American half eagles, British sovereigns, and French Napoleons: the two former have a fixed value of $5 25, the latter a conventional one of $4 25. The silver currency of the country is the peso = $1, the real = $12\frac{1}{2}$ cents, $\frac{1}{2}$ and $\frac{1}{4}$ reals.

HARBOR AND COMMERCIAL REGULATIONS.

The harbor at Punta Arenas is separated into two anchorage grounds by the point of land on which the town is located. That between the town and the main land affords accommodation only to vessels under seven feet draught. Those drawing more anchor in the outer harbor, which is protected by two small islands lying to the westward. Goods from thence are brought by lighters to the landing-place in the inner harbor, a distance of about two miles, at a cost of about $1 per ton.

Port Charges for both National and Foreign Vessels.

No anchorage or tonnage dues are imposed.
1. Quarantine fees, 75 cents for each foot of depth.
2. Clearance duty, $3.
3. Hospital dues, 50 cents per head.

No fees are exacted for the landing of passengers or their baggage, and a free permit is granted except when the latter exceeds 2 cwt., when all above that weight is subject to inspection.

All foreign merchandise in packages, when landed, is required to be deposited in the public warehouses for the purpose of registry; and, after being duly entered, may again be withdrawn, the party interested presenting the required certificates. The charge made for the above is 1 real ($12\frac{1}{2}$ cents) on each gross cwt.

Merchandise may be deposited on storage for any length of time on payment of ½ real (6¼ cents) per month per cwt.; subject, however, to existing laws.

Open articles of merchandise, such as iron in bars and unpacked goods, are exempt from registry.

Light-house dues are 6¼ cents per ton.

Any vessel, whether foreign or national, may compromise the hospital and light-house dues for $25 annually, paid in advance.

Municipal and bridge tolls (intended for turnpikes), 37½ cents for each quintal (of 101 pounds).

A fine of $25 is imposed for violation of any one of the above regulations.

There is, besides, a heavy penalty for sealing in packages of powder or tobacco in quantities over 2 cwt.

CUSTOM-HOUSE REGULATIONS OF COSTA RICA (1857).

FREE LIST.

1st. All printed books for instruction or entertainment, if not in opposition to religion and morals; all periodicals and papers.

2d. Foreign music and musical instruments.

3d. Foreign seeds and plants.

4th. Gold and silver in coins and dust.

5th. All kinds of complete machines, and iron wheels with teeth.

6th. Quicksilver, stone coal, pack-thread, empty sacks or sacking materials.

7th. Instruments of art and science.

8th. All kinds of carriages, coaches, cars, etc.

PROHIBITED LIST.

Imports.

1st. Tobacco in leaf or manufactured.

2d. All spirits of molasses or rum, such as is manufactured in Costa Rica; all books and other things offending public morals; eatables of spoiled or bad quality; fire-arms and munitions of war, if not ordered by government.

By a decree bearing date September 21st, 1857, all foreign spirits are placed upon the same footing as gunpowder, rum, and tobacco, which are contraband except when imported on account of the government.

The authorities are required to prosecute and punish those who sell liquor clandestinely, and without previous permission.

The government will cause to be procured, on account of the state, all the various kinds of foreign spirits in common use, in order that the same may be expended in such public places as shall be instituted for this purpose, and the proprietors of hotels and restaurants will purchase at wholesale in those places for the supply of their establishments.

Exports.

Tobacco in leaves or stems, unless by especial permit.

Gold in coin pays at exportation 2 per cent. ad valorem; in ingots, dust, or jewelry, 4 per cent. ad valorem; silver in coin, 8 per cent. ad valorem.*

Coffee pays export duty 12½ cents on 101 pounds, duty paid in 3, 6, or 9 months, according to amount.

All vessels arriving at Punta Arenas having any prohibited articles on board are required to deposit them in a government store-house at a cost of $2 per month for each cwt. (although they may be destined for other ports), or to leave the port within twelve hours.

Coins and Weights.

Coins.—1 peso fuerto, $1; 1 real, 12½ cents.

Weights.—1 quintal = 4 arrobas = $101\frac{44}{100}$ lbs.; 1 arroba = 25 lbs. 7 oz.; 1 libra = $1\frac{014}{1000}$ lb.; 1 onza = 1 oz.

Measure.—1 vara, 33½ inches.

Tariff on Articles received in Costa Rica from the United States.

Denomination of Merchandise.	Number, Weight, or Measure.	Rate of Duty.
Bread, ship	1.014 lb.	$0 03
Brandy in bottles	of sugar-cane,	prohibited.
" " barrels	1.014 gall.	11
Candles, tallow	1.014 lb.	02
" stearine	"	03
Cider	in bbls. of 101 lbs.	1 00
Copper, manufactures of	101 lbs.	(stills)10 00
Cotton goods, white	1.014 lb.	07
" " colored	"	08
Cheese	"	04
Cloths and cassimeres, fine	"	25
Fish in oil	101 lbs.	2 00
Flour		free.
Gold and silver coin		"
Glass, window	101 lbs.	1 50
Hides and skins		not defined.
Indigo	1.014 lb.	03½
Pork, salt	101 lbs.	62½
Printing-presses		free.
Paper, writing	101 lbs.	3 00
Rice		not defined.
Soap, common	1.014 lb.	02
Silk, raw	"	20
Shoes, calf-skin, for men	"	25
" patent-leather	"	25
Sheathing, metal	"	06
Spirits in casks	see Brandy.	
Teas	101 lbs.	2 00

* A recent act is reported abolishing the export duties upon gold and silver in coin or bullion, and jewels.

Denomination of Merchandise.	Number, Weight, or Measure.	Rate of Duty.
Tobacco, unmanufactured............	} prohibited.	
" manufactured................		
Tin, crude....................................	101 lbs.	$2 00
Wines in casks.............................	"	2 00
Wood, manufactured as furniture....	"	5 00

Price Current of Commodities exported to the United States.

Coffee, per cwt., $8 to $10.
Lumber, cedar and mahogany, per M. ft., $45 to $50.
Sarsaparilla, per cwt., $14.

Hides, dry, per cwt., $6 50 to $7.
Turtle-shell, per lb., $4 50
Old copper, per cwt. $15.

Freight to Atlantic States, $25 per ton; California, $20; Lumber to California, $10 to $12 per ton. Terms: Cash on delivery.

Rates of Wages.

Clerks, $500 per annum; engineers, $1000 to $1500; wheelwrights, $5 per day; carpenters, $3 50; blacksmiths, $2 to $3 per day; seamen, $25 per month.

NICARAGUA.

THE Republic of Nicaragua has the states of Honduras and Salvador on the north, and Costa Rica on the south, the Pacific Ocean on the west, and the Caribbean Sea on the east, and lies between 83° 20' and 87° 30' west longitude, and 9° 45' and 15° north latitude, embracing an area of about 48,000 square miles, and is estimated to contain a population of 300,000 souls:*

Whites..	30,000
Negroes..	18,000
Civilized Indians..	96,000
Mestizoes..	156,000

This republic, like Costa Rica, is divided administratively into five departments:

* The last census, however, taken in 1846, shows only 257,000; but it fell short of the true number, as the people feared it a preliminary step to taxation or conscription.

	Population.
The Oriental (census of 1846)	95,000
" Occidental	90,000
" Meridional	20,000
" Septentrional of Matagalpa	40,000
" " Segovia	12,000

The prevailing religion is Roman Catholic, although all other religious denominations receive the protection of the government.

The educational interests are at a very low ebb. There are reported two universities, one of which has a library of 15,000 volumes. Their course of instruction is said to be extremely defective. The expenses are paid partly by old endowments, and partly by a fee of $12 from each pupil. Besides the universities there are sixty primary schools, with a total of 2800 pupils, and five schools for females in the entire republic.

Its chief city and capital (though not invariably the seat of government) is Leon, in the Occidental department, about a day's journey from Realejo, the Pacific sea-port of the republic. It was, under the ancient Spanish rule, one of the finest cities of Central America, but has greatly declined, though many marks of its former estate remain. It is regularly laid out, the houses usually of one story. The public edifices are numerous and imposing: the great Cathedral of St. Peter covers an entire square, and is said to have cost $5,000,000; besides this there are sixteen churches, two hospitals, and a University. Population about 35,000. The capitals of the different departments are,

	Population.
Rivas, in the Meridional department (census of 1846)	20,000
Granada, in the Oriental "	10,000
Matagalpa, in the Septentrional of Matagalpa	2,000
Segovia, in the Septentrional of Segovia	8,000
Other considerable towns { Massagua	15,000
Managua	12,000
Granada	10,000
Chinandega	11,000
Realejo	1,200

Realejo, the principal sea-port town, is situated at the head of an estuary about three miles from the harbor of the same name; the low and swampy coast-lands prevented its establishment at a nearer point. It contains about 1200 inhabitants. The transportation between the harbor and the town is by bongoes and canoes.

TOPOGRAPHY, CLIMATE, AGRICULTURE, AND NATURAL PRODUCTIONS.

The northeastern portion of the republic is mountainous in its character, with a climate of the temperate zone. It abounds in mines of gold, silver, copper, iron, and lead. Precious stones, such as the opal and jasper, have been discovered; also extensive beds of anthracite coal. None of these deposits have yet been effectively worked, on account of the ignorance and indolence of the inhabitants. The great Sierra Madre range (bristling with high volcanic peaks, several of which are active) passes through the western portion of the republic; it is broken, however, by a broad valley, 300 miles in length by 150 in width, which contains the Lakes of Managua and Nicaragua, the latter well known as traversed by the old San Juan transit-route in former times. This valley is made up of fertile slopes, beautiful and productive plains, well adapted to agricultural and grazing purposes, and contains within its limits the chief cities and the greater portion of the inhabitants of the republic. It has a tropical climate. The seasons are divided into the wet and dry, the wet embracing the months from May to November, and the dry the remaining part of the year. The temperature is equable, seldom rising above 90°, or falling below 74°.

The soil is admirably adapted to the growth of all the great staples of the tropics. Indigo, sugar, cacao, tobacco, rice, coffee, cotton, etc., may all be successfully grown, but ignorance, indolence, and political disturbance have so

NATIVE BONGO, PANAMA.

dwarfed the agricultural interests of the republic that at present few articles are raised in amount beyond the immediate necessities of the people. The chief exports are indigo, sugar, cotton, hides, dye-woods, and bullion; small quantities of sarsaparilla, cacao, ginger, gum acacia, gum copal, and caoutchouc are also exported. Crude sulphur is obtained in considerable quantities from the vicinity of the volcanoes, also nitre and sulphate of iron; but the entire exports of the republic do not exceed one million of dollars annually.

The imports in manufactured goods and liquors amount to about half that sum.

From Great Britain are imported calicoes and other manufactured cottons, hardware, lead, gunpowder, etc., etc.; and from the United States, soap, candles, hardware, brandy, gunpowder, etc.

SAN SALVADOR.

THE Republic of San Salvador has Guatemala on the north and west, and Honduras on the east. It is separated from Nicaragua on the southeast by the Bay of Conchagua. It lies between 13° and 14° 10′ north latitude, and 87° and 90° west longitude, embracing an area of about 9600 square miles, and is estimated to contain 294,000 inhabitants — Spanish whites, Indians, and mixed races. It is divided into eight departments:

Departments.	Capitals.	Population.
San Miguel	San Miguel	80,000
San Vicente	San Vicente	56,000
La Paz	Sacatecoluca	28,000
Chalaltenango	Chalaltenango	75,000
Suchitoto	Suchitoto	
San Salvador	San Salvador	80,000
Sonsonate	Sonsonate	75,000
Santa Ana	Santa Ana	

The capital of the republic is San Salvador, situated about twenty-two miles from the port of La Libertad, on the Pacific coast. Formerly it contained about 25,000 inhabitants, having eight or ten fine church edifices, a flourishing University, a female seminary, several hospitals, and the buildings of the general government, and was a place of considerable trade; but in 1854 it was almost totally destroyed by an earthquake, when it was deserted by many of its inhabitants, and the seat of government transferred to Cojutepeque, twelve leagues distant. San Salvador is now in process of rebuilding, its inhabitants having mostly returned, and it promises speedily to regain its former condition.

TOPOGRAPHY.

San Salvador has a coast-line on the Pacific 160 miles in length, along which, for the most part, lies a belt of low alluvial land, varying in breadth from ten to twenty miles; back of this is a broad plateau, about 2000 feet above the ocean level, and along which numerous high volcanic peaks arise. Farther beyond is a broad and beautiful valley, from twenty to thirty miles in width, and over one hundred in length, drained by the Lempa (a large river, navigable for vessels of light draught for upward of 100 miles, and emptying into the Pacific). The northern border of the state rises up into a range of mountains, which separates it from Honduras. In the eastern and western portions are also well-watered valleys of great beauty and considerable extent.

The soil of the mountain slopes, the valleys, and the coast alluvions is fertile and productive in the highest degree, and well adapted to the growth of the tropical staples. Cotton is cultivated to some extent along the coast, and with good results. The chief productions, however, are indigo, sugar, tobacco, balsam, cacao, maize, and frijoles. The usual fruits of the tropical and several of the temperate zones are abundant. Indigo is the chief article of export. Under the Spanish rule this product was exported to the amount of over $3,000,000 per annum, but since the independence of the state, owing to intestine wars and political disturbances, but little more than $1,000,000 per annum has been produced. A district along the coast, between the ports of La Libertad and Acajutla, called "Costa del Balsimo," produces an article known commercially as the "balsam of Peru." It is collected solely by the aboriginal Indians who inhabit that district. About 20,000 pounds (valued at 50 cts. per pound) are obtained for annual export.

The mineral productions of San Salvador are not extensive. It has, however, in the northeastern part of the state, valuable mines of silver and gold. Iron of a very superior quality is abundant. Vast deposits of coal are also said to exist there.

In general, the inhabitants of Salvador have more intelligence and industry than those of the previously-described states of Central America. Their government is more liberal, and the rights of person and property are more respected, and the privileges extended to foreigners are greater than those above mentioned. Under a treaty negotiated by Mr. Squier, United States minister to Salvador in 1850, all the rights, privileges, and immunities of the citizens of Salvador in commerce, navigation, mining, holding and transferring property, are extended to the citizens of the United States in that republic.

"The commerce of San Salvador is chiefly carried on through means of fairs established by the government in the districts best suited for the exhibition of the products of the state. The principal fairs are held at Chalaltenango, San Vicente, and San Miguel. The two former take place on the first of November of each year; the latter, called

'Fair of La Paz,' on the 21st of the same month. It lasts about two weeks, and is far the most important of any held in the country. It attracts buyers and sellers not only from all parts of Central America, but from nearly every part of the Pacific coast, as well as from England, Germany, France, and the United States. England sends calicoes, shirtings, drills, linens, hosiery, cutlery, iron, and steel; France, silks, cambrics, wine, and spirits; the United States, coarse cottons, sperm-oil, and hardware; Spain, paper, wine, oil, and spirits; Germany, glass, hardware, and toys; Italy, oil, preserves, and liquors; Chili and Peru, hats, hammocks, pellons, etc. About the only product given in exchange for them is the staple of the state, indigo. A second fair, called 'Ceniza,' takes place in San Miguel about the beginning of February. To both of these fairs large numbers of cattle are brought from Honduras and Nicaragua. In 1857 the number amounted to 17,844, averaging in value from $5 to $8 each."* The amount and value of the imports and exports of the state may be estimated from the following table:

Years.	Imports.	Exports.
1854	$1,015,925	$ 786,711
1855	698,219	765,324
1856	1,046,720	1,285,485
1857	860,104	1,304,102

TARIFF REGULATIONS.

Import Duties of San Salvador on Articles received from the United States. Rate of Duty 24 per cent. ad valorem.

Denomination of Merchandise.	Number, Weight, or Measure.	Rate of Duty.
Bread, ship	101 lbs.	$3 00
Brandy in bottles	dozen,	2 50
" in barrels	gallon,	1 00
Candles, tallow		prohibited.
" stearine	1,014 lb.	30
Cider in bottles	dozen,	2 00
Copper, manufactures of	101 lbs.	25 to 37 cts.
Cotton goods, white	yard,	12
" colored	"	12

* Squier's Central America.

SAN SALVADOR. 197

Denomination of Merchandise.	Number, Weight, or Measure.	Rate of Duty.
Cheese...	25 lbs. 7 oz.	$4 00
Cloths and cassimeres, fine...............	yard,	1 00
Fish in oil.......................................	101 lbs.	4 00
Flour..	barrel,	4 00
Gold and silver coin.........................		free.
Glass, window...................................	dozen panes,	38 cts. to $1.
Hides and skins.................................	dozen,	$12 to $24.
Indigo...		not defined.
Pork, salt..	101 lbs.	5 00
Printing-presses................................		free.
Paper, writing...................................	ream,	2 00
Rice...	25 lbs. 7 oz.	3 00
Soap, common	101 lbs.	8 00
Silk, raw..		not defined.
Shoes, calf-skin, for men..................	dozen,	$6 to $18.
" patent-leather	"	"

HARBORS.

San Salvador has three ports of entry:

1st. That of *La Union*, at the southeastern extremity of the state, in the Bay of Fonseca. This possesses an excellent and extensive anchorage-ground, from three to twelve fathoms deep, free from shoals, and nearly ten miles in diameter. It is surrounded on three sides by high lands, and its entrance is protected by a number of islands. It is decidedly the best harbor in Central America. Its waters abound in fine fish and excellent oysters.

2d. *La Libertad*, 100 miles from La Union, is an open roadstead. It is connected with the city of San Salvador by a cart-road 26 miles in length.

3d. *Acajutla*, 40 miles from La Libertad, is also a roadstead. It is protected from all winds except from the southwest; but there is frequently a heavy swell prevailing, which often renders the landing difficult. It is connected by a good road with Sonsonate (chief city of one of the richest districts in the state), 12 miles distant.

COMMERCIAL REGULATIONS.

All vessels of the United States, no matter whence they may have come or how laden, are to be treated in all the ports of San Salvador, as to all duties of tonnage, lighthouse, or any other charges of whatsoever denomination or character, as national vessels. From this equality the coasting-trade is excepted, which is reserved to the national flag; but should any favors of navigation be hereafter granted to any other foreign nation, it will immediately apply to the United States.

Imports into San Salvador in vessels of the United States, no matter whence imported or of what origin, to be subject to the same duties, charges, and fees of every description as similar imports in vessels of San Salvador; and if these imports consist of articles the growth, produce, or manufacture of the United States, to be subject to no higher or other duties than other similar imports the growth, produce, or manufacture of any other foreign nation.

PORT CHARGES.

All sea-going vessels, without distinction of burden or flag, pay $17, in full of tonnage and other port dues. There are no pilots.

GUATEMALA.

THE State of Guatemala, lying between latitude 14° and 18° north, and longitude 89° and 93° west, is bounded north by the Mexican provinces of Tobasco, Chiapas, and Yucatan, east by the British establishment of Honduras, south by the states of Honduras and Salvador, and west by the Pacific Ocean, and embraces an area of 43,380 square miles. It is estimated to contain about 907,500 inhabitants, made up of between 7000 and 8000 whites (principally of Spanish descent), 150,000 Ladinos, or mixed bloods, and 750,000 Indians.

The Pacific coast-line of Guatemala is about 250 miles in

length, trending northwest, and is bordered by a strip of alluvial land from twenty to thirty miles in width, broken, however, by occasional spurs from the coast-range of mountains by which it is bounded, and which, spreading out into broad table-lands, form the greater portion of the surface of the state. These great plateaux in the southern part have an elevation of from 2000 to 5000 feet, gradually attaining a still greater height toward the northeastern part, where they are more than 8000 feet above the ocean level. They are frequently separated by deeply-cut and extensive valleys of great fertility. Toward the eastern boundary they subside into the low lands bordering the coast of the Bay of Honduras. Along the Pacific several volcanic peaks arise, the highest of which is more than 14,000 feet above the level of the sea.

There are several lakes in the interior, the largest of which, that of Atitlan, in the department of Solola, is said to be thirty miles in length by ten or fifteen in breadth, and no less than 1800 feet in depth.

There are also numerous rivers in the state. These, for the most part, flow into the Bay of Honduras or the Gulf of Mexico. The rivers emptying into the Pacific are small and few. None have much importance in a commercial point of view.

CLIMATE.

The climate of Guatemala varies greatly with its varying elevations, from the tropical heat of the coast-lands and lower valleys, through the intermediate spring-like temperature of the interior plateaux and higher valleys, to the cold and sometimes almost wintry climate of the most elevated table-lands and mountains. The plateau on which the capital is situated is in the interior, about 90 miles from the Pacific coast. There the average maximum temperature throughout the year is 88.7° Fahrenheit, and the average minimum is 38.9°. The average mean is 65°. The average temperature of the coast-lands is probably between 80° and 85° Fahr., but data do not exist for exact calculation of this. On the highest table-lands and mountains in the northeastern part, ice and snow are not uncommon in certain seasons of the year. Here the productions of the temperate zones abound. Wheat of a superior quality is produced, and sheep are raised extensively. The wool-crop for 1857 was 1,500,000 pounds, but, from the lack of roads, the expense of getting these products to market bars their being raised for exportation. Cattle-raising is also carried on to a considerable extent. On the lower plateaus and valleys coffee, cochineal, tobacco, sugar-cane, and indigo are luxuriantly grown, also the vegetables and fruits of both tropical and temperate zones. On the low coast-lands cotton and rice flourish. The chief staple production of the state is the cochineal insect. The yearly produce of this is variable, on account of various contingencies to which it is subject. The crop in 1849 was 1,469,100 lbs.; in 1851, 1,231,610 lbs.; in 1852, 567,000 lbs.; in 1853, 312,700 lbs.; in 1854, 1,757,300 lbs.; in 1855, 1,204,510 lbs. It is nevertheless abundantly profitable, as its cultivators aver that if one crop is successfully gathered out of three raised, the receipts from its sale repay for the entire labor and capital expended on the whole. Cacao, silk, dye-woods, balsam, various gums, and many other minor articles, are produced to some extent.

The mineral productions of Guatemala are not extensive. Deposits of gold, silver, copper, lead, and iron exist. Some have been worked with considerable profit, but the mining interest is greatly neglected.

The seasons are divided into the wet and dry, the former commencing at about the middle of May, and continuing until the middle or end of October; the dry season then sets in, and lasts for the remainder of the year.

POLITICAL DIVISIONS.

Guatemala is divided into seven departments, those of Guatemala, Solola, and Quezaltenango extending along the Pacific coast; Sacatepequez and Totonicapam in the interior; Vera Paz, the largest of all, in the northern part; and Chiquimula in the eastern. The chief towns are:

In the Department of Guatemala—Guatemala City; Escuintla, population 6000; Amatitlan, population 15,000; and Jalpatagua.

In the Department of Solola—Solola; Atitlan; Masatenango.

In the Department of Quezaltenango—Quezaltenango, population 25,000; San Marcos; Tejutla; Tapachula.

In the Department of Sacatepequez—Old Guatemala (or Antigua), population 20,000; Chimaltenango; Patsun.

In the Department of Totonicapam—Totonicapam, population 15,000; Momostenango; Gueguetenango; Jacaltenango.

In the Department of Vera Paz—Salama; Rabinal; Copan, population 14,000; Cajabon, population 4000.

In the Department of Chiquimula—Chiquimula, population 6000; Zacapa, population 5000; Gualan, population 4000; Casaguastlan; Esquipulas, population 1800; besides many other large towns.

Guatemala City, the capital of the state, is 90 miles distant from San José, the sea-port of the Pacific coast, and 220 from Izabal, on the Atlantic, and has a population of about 40,000. It is beautifully situated on a broad table-land 4372 feet above the ocean level. The volcanoes of Agua and Fuego, 12,000 and 14,000 feet in height, tower up on the northern side 40 miles distant; the other sides present low mountains and hills in beautiful variety. The climate is one of perpetual spring, the thermometer averaging 65° Fahrenheit, and perfectly salubrious. It is regularly laid out in a quadrilateral form, with its sides facing the cardinal points; the streets are forty feet broad, crossing each other at right angles. The main plaza is 150 yards square, the east side occupied by the Cathedral, the palace of the archbishop, and other buildings of the Church authorities; on the west is the government house, offices, etc., of the government officials; on the north, the cabildo, or town-hall, prison, etc.; and on the south a range of stores of various kinds. In the middle of the square is a fountain, elaborately and artistically sculptured of gray stone, furnishing an abundant supply of water; besides this, in each of the seven or eight lesser squares are fountains well supplied with water, which is brought to the city by two aqueducts a distance of five and six miles. The dwellings are all of one story. There are twenty-six churches, some of large size, with elegantly ornamented interiors; to several are attached monasteries and convents; a University, two colleges, one public and several private elemental schools, three hospitals, one alms-house, two theatres (one of which, just finished, is a large and elaborate Corinthian building, said to have cost $200,000), and a large amphitheatre for bull-fights.

CHARACTER OF THE INHABITANTS.

The Indians are the cultivators of the lands, and are, in general, industrious and peaceable; some are owners of estates, but the landholders are principally whites. The mixed bloods are mostly mechanics and petty traders. As a people the Guatemaltecos are courteous, affable, and hospitable to strangers.

The prevailing religion is the Roman Catholic, and there are few countries in the world where the exercises and ceremonials of that Church are more universally and elaborately practiced.

THE PORTS OF GUATEMALA.

The commerce of Guatemala previous to the establishment of the Panama Railroad Company's line of steamers on the Pacific coast of Central America was almost entirely carried on through the port of Izabal, on the Atlantic. This port is inaccessible except to vessels of very light draught. It is over 200 miles from the capital (surrounding and to the westward of which the great proportion of the staples of the country are principally produced), and is reached by mule-paths, through a mountainous and uninhabited region, with great labor and expense. It is now, however, rapidly losing its importance, on account of the more accessible port of San José, on the Pacific, through which much of the commerce of the state is already carried on. San José lies in latitude 13° 56′ north, and longitude 90° 42′ west. It is an open roadstead. The coast is very clear, running east and west. The anchorage is about three quarters of a mile from shore, in eleven to fifteen fathoms of water. The swell breaks very heavily upon the shore, and out as far as forty or fifty fathoms, making it necessary to use a girt-line for landing and leaving. The currents are very strong, and vary with each change of the moon, the variations sometimes taking place within the short period of six hours. From November to February the landing is easy. In March the ebb and flow of the tide extends from 90 to 100 yards, and at the flood tide the surf is so heavy as to dash up the beach a distance of 100 to 120 yards; after March the sea is again calm until July, and from July to December it is again rough, and the landing difficult. An iron screw-piled pier is now, however, in process of construction at this place by the government of Guatemala (if it is not already finished), which will extend from the shore to a point beyond the breakers, thus enabling the transportation between ship and shore to be performed at every season of the year with facility and safety.

The town of San José has a population of between two and three hundred. Supplies for vessels are, however, procured with much difficulty here, unless provision be previously made to obtain them from Escuintla, a town forty miles distant, on the road to the capital. There are no means at this port for refitting or repairing vessels at present. The modes of conveyance from the port of San José to the interior are by mules and stages, and the arrangements are convenient and ample. Diligences for the transportation of passengers are in waiting on the arrival of the Panama Railroad Company's steamers for conveyance to the capital, 90 miles distant, and the intermediate points, and the roads throughout the dry season are excellent. In the wet season the journey from San José to Escuintla is performed on mules, owing to the deep mud on the low land to that place; from thence to Guatemala City the diligence is in operation throughout the year.

A small trade is carried on through the minor ports of Santa Tomas on the Atlantic and San Luis on the Pacific.

HARBOR REGULATIONS.

"Every vessel which shall anchor in the ports of this republic, no matter whence it may come, shall pay a tonnage duty of two reals (25 cents) for each ton of measurement. This measurement shall be ascertained from the register, the certificate of nationality, the patent or clearance under which it sails."

"*Shall be free of tonnage duty:* 1st. Small vessels engaged in transporting merchandise from one port to another of the republic; 2d. Vessels which shall anchor in ballast to take in water, provisions, or fruits of the country, provided they discharge no cargoes; 3d. Vessels of war, and regular mail or steam packets, provided they do not discharge merchandise over twenty tons; 4th. Merchant vessels which, exceeding 150 tons measurement, discharge not exceeding twenty tons of merchandise; 5th. Vessels which receive on board for exportation produce of the country, excepting *cochineal*." Cochineal pays an export duty of five reals on each ceroon to the Church.

TARIFF REGULATIONS OF GUATEMALA.

PROHIBITED LIST.

Guns, muskets, and all other arms for military purposes; munitions of war, as lead, balls, gunpowder, and rifles; prints, cuts, pictures, etc., bearing against public morals and religion; books, manuscripts, etc., especially interdicted.

FREE LIST.

Anchors, cable, rigging, and all other articles belonging to ships' material not comprehended in the tariff; quicksilver, barometers, fire-engines, staves and heading of all kinds; scientific instruments and agricultural implements; books, music, maps, and geographical charts; machines and steam-engines; gold and silver coins; barrels, hogsheads, etc., etc., for exporting the products of the country.

Duties on Articles received from the United States.

Denomination of Merchandise.	Number, Weight, or Measure.	Rate of Duty.
Bread, ship	arroba of 25 lbs. 7 oz.	$0 50
Brandy in bottles	dozen,	72
" in barrels	15 to 18 gallons,	3 44
Candles, tallow	1.014 lb.	03
" stearine	"	05
Cider	dozen bottles,	05
Copper, manufactures of	1.014 lb.	12½
Cotton goods, white	yard,	02½
" colored	"	03
Cheese	101 lbs.	2 88
Cloths, cassimeres, fine	yard,	78
Fish in oil	1.014 lb.	04½
Flour	25 lbs. 7 oz.	25
Gold and silver coin		free.
Glass, window	box of from 137 to 150 lbs.	3 60
Hides and skins	1.014 lb.	12
Indigo	"	2 00
Pork, salt	25 lbs. 7 oz.	48
Printing-presses		free.
Paper, writing	ream,	25
Rice	25 lbs. 7 oz.	24
Soap, common	"	72
Silk, raw	1.014 lb.	72
Shoes, calf-skin, for men	pair,	04
" patent-leather	"	57
Sheathing, metal	1.014 lb.	08
Spirit in casks	12 to 15 gallons,	3 44
Teas	1.014 lb.	18
Tobacco, unmanufactured	24 per cent. on the invoice value, with an addition of 20 per cent. on the aggregate amount.	
Tin, crude	101 lbs.	5 00
Wines in casks	12 to 15 gallons,	2 16
Wood, manufactured as furniture	40 per cent. ad val.	

IMPORTS AND EXPORTS.

The official statement of the imports into Guatemala for the year 1860 shows the amount to have been $1,495,191; exports, $1,870,631. Imports from Great Britain, $802,305; France, $295,651; Germany, $108,649; the United States, $50,235; Spain, $47,702; and small amounts from various other countries. Of the exports about two thirds were of cochineal, the remainder consisting of ores, sugar, coffee, sarsaparilla, dye-woods, and hides. The following comparative statement will show the increase of trade since the establishment of the Central American Steam-ship Line in 1856:

	Value.	Value.
Ores exported in 1855............	$6,600;	in 1860... $92,575
Sarsaparilla exported in 1855...	1,890;	" ... 13,800
Dye-woods " " ...	5,000;	" ... 27,672
Hides " " ...	26,000;	" ... 76,582
Sugar " " ...	none;	" ... 52,377
Coffee " " ...	none;	" ... 15,352

The coffee of Guatemala is of very fine quality, and promises soon to become a prominent article of export.

By a contract between the government of Guatemala and the Panama Railroad Company, a drawback of ten per cent. on tariff rates is allowed on all merchandise passing over the Panama Railroad en route for that state.

Rates of wages are much the same as in Costa Rica (p. 188). Laborers on estates receive from $1\frac{1}{2}$ to 2 reals per day.

REPUBLICS OF SOUTH AMERICA

CONNECTED WITH THE PANAMA RAILROAD.

NEW GRANADA.

NEW GRANADA, the most northerly, as well as the most important of the South American republics, is situated mostly between the equator and 12° north latitude, and between 70° and 83° west longitude, containing an estimated area of 480,000 square miles. Its greatest length is about 800 miles, and its greatest breadth about 600. It is bounded on the north by the Caribbean Sea, on the east by the Republic of Venezuela, on the southeast by Brazilian Guiana, on the south by the Republic of Ecuador, and on the west by the Pacific Ocean. Along the western portion, the Andes, divided into three great chains, pass in a northeast and southwest direction through the republic. To the east of the most eastern chain the country is spread out into vast llanos or plains, about 300 feet above the ocean level, gradually descending to the River Orinoco, one of its eastern boundaries. These immense plains are said to be unfit for cultivation, but large herds of cattle and horses are raised upon them. The wet season on the llanos lasts from November till April, and the dry the remainder of the year. The average annual temperature is 80° Fahrenheit; the wet season averages about 8° hotter than the dry. This section is principally watered by the tributaries of the River Orinoco.

Upon the sides and summits of the Cordilleras are vast table-lands, varying in climate and productions with their elevation, and embracing every grade of temperature, from that of the torrid zone to the regions of perpetual snow and ice, and, with the exception of the snowy regions, these plains are said to be remarkably fertile, producing in great abundance and perfection the fruits and agricultural staples of every zone. Between the mountain ranges are broad and beautiful valleys: that of Magdalena between the eastern and central ranges, and Cauca and Atrato between the central and western. These valleys are drained each by large navigable rivers of the same names. In the territories comprehended between the eastern and western Andes there are two wet and two dry seasons, the wet coming on at the approach of the equinoxes, and the dry at that of the solstices; each continues about ninety days.

The northeastern portion of the republic, bordering the Atlantic, is low and unhealthy, but of great fertility. At the northwestern portion the Cordilleras become depressed, and frequently disconnected, forming the low hill and valley country of the Isthmus, where, like the northeast portion, the climate is hot, and, in the lower lands, insalubrious, but richly productive. The seasons in these portions of the republic are divided into the dry and rainy, each occupying about six months of the year.

The population of New Granada, which has increased greatly during the past few years, is now estimated at 2,747,500, of whom 1,648,519 are said to be whites, mostly of Spanish descent; 183,166 pure Indian; 97,583 Negro; 366,332 Mulattoes and Samboes; 451,900 of different races mixed with Indian.

The Republic of New Granada is politically divided into eight states, viz.:

	Population.	Capitals.
Panama	168,500	Panama.
Cauca	404,000	Popayan.
Cundinamarca	635,000	Bogotá.
Boyaca	465,000	Tunja.
Santander	463,000	Bucaramanga.
Magdalena	89,900	Santa Martha.
Bolivar	222,100	Carthagena.
Antioquia	300,000	Medellin.

Agriculture holds the first place in the industrial interests of New Granada. Rice, cotton, coffee, tobacco, cocoa, sugar, and the tropical fruits are the principal cultivated productions of the low valleys and coast-lands, which also produce spontaneously caoutchouc, vanilla, anise, balsams, dye and cabinet woods, ivory-nuts, Peruvian bark, etc. The elevated valleys and plains yield wheat, maize, and almost all the other products of the temperate zone. The cultivation of the soil is, however, very rudely and indifferently managed, and the reclaimed lands bear a very small proportion to the whole.

The manufacturing interests of the republic are also in a very low condition, and consist of little more than coarse woolen and cotton cloths, earthen-ware, and cigars for the use of the lower classes, and the straw hats known in commerce as Panama hats.

The mineral productions of the republic are gold, silver, and platinum; it also possesses valuable mines of emeralds and of salt; but the mining interest is sadly neglected, being mostly left to the lower classes. Turtle-shell and pearls of fine quality are procured in considerable abundance. The entire annual exports are estimated as follows:

Gold	$5,000,000	Cacao	$200,000
Platinum, silver ore, and emeralds	1,000,000	Caoutchouc, maize, cotton, ivory-nuts, anise, rice, balsam, etc.	200,000
Pearls and turtle-shell	800,000		
Tobacco	3,500,000	Sugar, flour, preserves, rough woolen and cotton cloths, brandies, etc.	50,000
Straw hats	1,400,000		
Peruvian bark	600,000		
Coffee	600,000		
Hides	500,000		$14,350,000
Dye and building woods	500,000		

Education in New Granada is at a low ebb, though, nominally, liberal provisions for public instruction are made by the government. By law a free public school is established in every parish throughout the republic; in all there are said to be 800 public schools, and 60 high-schools and colleges, and 47 printing-offices.*

The capital of the republic is Bogotá, in the State of Cundinamarca, in lat. 4° 36' 6'' north, and long. 74° 10' west, which is situated on a broad plateau 8655 feet above the level of the sea. It is regularly laid out, the houses mostly built of sun-dried bricks, and of two stories, and is amply supplied with water. It contains twenty-four churches, one fine cathedral, a national college, with a library of 33,000 volumes in fourteen different languages, mostly ancient, an observatory, eleven high-schools, besides a seminary, and two public schools in each ward (eight), fourteen hospitals, three lazarettos (both the schools and hospitals are very indifferent), seven printing-offices, three lithographic offices, a fine theatre, one manufactory of woolen cloths, and one of earthen-ware. It has a good market, supplied with fruits and vegetables of both the temperate and tropical zones. Population 60,000. The city of Bogotá is distant from the nearest sea-port on the Atlantic (Carthagena) about 700 miles, and from Buenaventura, on the Pacific, 800. From Carthagena the route is up the Magdalena River by steam-boats to Honda, 700 miles distant, and from thence 100 miles to Bogotá by mules: this is the usual route for merchandise and passengers from foreign ports to the capital. That from Buenaventura is long, difficult, and expensive, much of the distance over the Cordilleras having to be accomplished on mules or the backs of the natives. The roads throughout the republic are very bad.

* The foregoing statistics of population, exports, etc., were made out from official data kindly furnished by Señor Raphael Pombo, Secretary of New Granadian Legation.

The rivers of New Granada are numerous and important. The rivers Rio Negro, Caqueta, and Putumayo connect the eastern and southeastern portions of the republic with the Amazon. The Guaviare, the Meta, and their affluents, connect the east and southeast with the Orinoco. The Orinoco and the Amazon are connected at the boundary of New Granada with Venezuela by the Rio Cassequiare. Commercially, the most important rivers are the Magdalena and its tributary, the Cauca, each over 1000 miles in length, and crossing almost the whole of the most fertile and productive portion of the republic from south to north. The Magdalena empties by three mouths into the Atlantic, and is navigated by steam-boats for 700 miles of its length. It is through this river and the Cauca that the principal part of the interior commerce of the country is carried on. At its western mouth is the port of Sabanilla. It also communicates with the port of Carthagena by a dike or connected chain of lagoons 92 miles in length, and navigated by boats and small steamers.

The Rio Atrato, in the State of Antioquia, is about 300 miles in length, and is navigable for small vessels for about 150 miles. It empties into the Gulf of Darien. Besides these, emptying into the Atlantic, are the Chagres, in the State of Panama, and several other small rivers at present of little commercial importance. Emptying into the Pacific are the rivers Patia and San Juan, draining rich and extensive regions in the State of Cauca.

The principal sea-ports of the republic of New Granada are Rio Hacha and Santa Martha in the State of Magdalena, Sabanilla and Carthagena in Bolivar, and Aspinwall in the State of Panama, on the Atlantic coast; and Panama in Panama, and Buenaventura and Tumaco in the State of Cauca, on the Pacific.

Rio Hacha is an open roadstead. Vessels have to anchor one and a quarter miles from shore, at which distance large vessels can ride. Cargoes are landed by means of bongoes or canoes. This can only be done between 8 A.M. and 2 P.M., on account of northeast winds, which prevail almost all the year. The landing of cargoes is best effected during the summer season.

The aspect of the town is very pleasing, as most of it is of recent construction. Its business is principally with the interior, through the Indians of La Goajira. Its principal exports are divi divi, dye-woods, hides, skins, and mules. Population between 3000 and 4000.

Santa Martha, 90 miles southwest from Rio Hacha, has a good harbor, with the exception of being exposed to the northeast winds. Vessels are laden and unladen at the wharves. Merchandise is shipped from this port in large decked boats up the Magdalena River, from the mouth of which it is distant about 40 miles. Besides the staples of the country, from this place are exported considerable numbers of horses, mules, and cattle to Jamaica and other West India islands. It ranks as one of the first ports of New Granada.

The city of Santa Martha is the capital of the State of Magdalena. There is a good hospital, a college, and a printing-office here. Population 4340.

Sabanilla, at the western mouth of the Magdalena River, is a roadstead. On account of a bad bar at the mouth of the Magdalena, goods have to be transhipped for their transportation up the river. The town is low and unhealthy. The residences of the principal merchants are at Baranquilla, twelve miles interior.

Carthagena is the finest port and harbor and the chief naval arsenal of New Granada, and is connected with the Magdalena by the canal before mentioned, navigated by steamers of light draught. It is the principal depôt for the products of the provinces watered by the Magdalena and Cauca Rivers, and exports sugar, cotton, coffee, tobacco, hides, specie, bullion, Peruvian bark, anise, balsams, dye-woods, etc., etc. The port is defended by two forts, and is the only port of New Granada on the Atlantic which has facilities for the repair of vessels. Vessels are laden and unladen by means of flat-boats and bongoes. The town is well fortified and well laid out, the houses mostly of stone. It has a massive citadel, several churches, a college, various seminaries, and two hospitals. Population 10,000. There is a charity hospital at Carthagena, where sick American seamen are admitted at a charge of 40 cents per diem; accommodations very indifferent. The usual charge for storage of dry goods is about one per cent. on gross sales; drayage from wharf to store, 28 to 30 cents per ton; boat for landing, cartage to wharf, and storing at custom-house, about 11 cents per barrel. From the United States to this port are imported flour, codfish, hams, butter, cheese, glass-ware, earthen-ware, iron-mongery, pitch, tar, rosin, cordage, copper, and a great variety of articles from France, Spain, Italy, and Germany.

The ships of the Royal Mail Steam Packet Company, plying between Southampton, the West Indies, and the east coast of South and Central America, stop here monthly with mails, passengers, and freight. See Itinerary of said Company, p. 158, et seq.

Aspinwall, the Atlantic terminus of the Panama Railroad, in the harbor of Navy Bay, is a free port. The shelter here for shipping is extensive, and the anchorage good. Nothing obstructs the entrance to the harbor for vessels of the largest draught. No pilots are required. The wharf and storage accommodations are ample. Reference to connections of Panama Railroad, page 145, will give the principal maritime movements of this port. Harbor regulations, freight, wharfage, storage, light dues, etc., etc., will be found on page 88, et seq.

Panama is a free port. This port derives its importance

from being the Pacific terminus of the Panama Railroad. It is situated in the Bay of Panama, latitude 8° 56' north, longitude 79° 37' west. Its harbor is protected by a group of islands of considerable extent, distant about two and a half miles from the place of embarkation. The nearest secure anchorage for vessels of heavy draught is distant from shore one and three quarters of a mile, on account of coral reefs which extend for that distance out into the bay. The average tides at this point have a rise and fall of twelve feet,* and transportation between ship and shore is carried on at from one half to high tide by means of small steamers and large iron-decked launches, which discharge at the wharves of the Panama Railroad Company. Storms are unknown in the harbor of Panama, and the transportation between ship and shore is performed at every season with perfect ease and safety. The group of islands before mentioned furnishes the rendezvous for the vessels of the Panama Mail Steam-ship Company. About nine miles to the southeast of the harbor is the beautiful and productive island of Toboga, at which place is the rendezvous of the British Pacific Steam Navigation Company. At this place facilities are afforded for the repair of vessels of the heavi-

*	Table of the Tides on the		
	Pacific at Panama.		Atlantic at Aspinwall.
	May and June.	Nov. and Dec.	Aug. and Sept.
	Feet.	Feet.	Feet.
Greatest rise of tide...................	17.72	21.30	1.60
Least " "	7.94	9.70	0.63
Average " "	12.08	14.10	1.16
Mean tide of Pacific above mean tide of Atlantic.....................	0.759	0.140	
High spring tide of Pacific above high spring tide of Atlantic	9.40	10.12	
Low spring tide of Pacific below low spring tide of Atlantic........	6.55	9.40	
Mean high tide of Pacific above mean high tide of Atlantic	6.25	6.73	
Mean low tide of Pacific below mean low tide of Atlantic........	4.73	5.26	
Average rise of spring tides..........	14.08	17.30	
" " neap tides	9.60	12.40	

est draught by means of a "gridiron," which is rented at reasonable rates to vessels of all nations. There is also at Toboga a large machine-shop, where repairs for the largest varieties of machinery are effected at moderate charges. No pilots are required in the harbor of Panama. Fresh provisions and water are furnished to shipping in abundance, and at moderate rates.

Labor is cheap and easily procured; wages from eight to ten reals per day.

The city of Panama is a place of considerable commercial importance. Several mercantile houses of large capital are established here, which collect from the interior and the North and South Pacific coasts the various staple productions of South and Central America for exportation over the Panama Railroad to the United States and Europe, and receive from thence large quantities of merchandise for the use of the interior towns and different ports in the Pacific. For the maritime commercial movements of this port, see connections of Panama Railroad, page 145. Population of the city of Panama, 10,000.

About sixty miles southeast from the port of Panama is the group of islands called "Islas de las Perlas," or Islands of Pearls, where a pearl-fishery is carried on, producing about $100,000 worth of a fine quality of pearls per annum.

Besides Panama, on the Pacific coast of New Granada, are the ports of Buenaventura and Tumaco, in the State of Cauca, from which are exported Peruvian bark, cocoa, tobacco, hides, etc., to Panama, principally by the vessels of the Pacific Steam Navigation Company, which touch at each bi-monthly. The trade of these ports is chiefly with Panama, receiving from thence merchandise from the United States and Europe suitable to the demands of the country.

PORT REGULATIONS.

The port regulations of the Republic of New Granada are such as are deemed necessary, as well in view of the general convenience and safety of vessels as to answer proper police and harbor discipline.

There are no quarantine regulations at any of the ports of New Granada, and, consequently, no bills of health are required. Tonnage dues, port dues, pilotage, and visit fees are the same in all the ports of the republic, with the exception of the free ports of Aspinwall and Panama. Every vessel pays $6 40 for the visit of the captain of the port, and $11 pilotage in and out, besides $1 60 for an interpreter.

Every vessel pays 40 cents per New Granadian ton for her capacity for the first 100 tons, and 20 cents for every ton over the same. There are no light dues, except at the port of Aspinwall, where light fees are charged by the Panama Railroad Company (see p. 143). The river navigation of New Granada is free to flags of all nations, with the exception of vessels propelled by steam, the monopoly of which last is granted to certain individuals under contract with the government.

Tariff of New Granada on Articles received from the United States—1855.

Under this tariff weights and measures are, 1 pound = 1.014 pound; 100 pounds = 4 arrobas; 100 pounds = 101½ pounds avoirdupois; 1 vara = 33½ English inches; 1 quintal = 101.44 pounds; 1 kilogramme = 2⅕ pounds; 1 miriagramme = 26 lbs. 9 oz. 10 pwt.

Money.—1 peso = 8 reals = 100 cents = $1.*

Denomination of Merchandise.	Number, Weight, or Measure.	Rate of Duty.
Beef....................................		free.
Beer, ale, porter, in bottles.........	1.014 lb.	$0 00¾
" " " in casks...........	"	0 00⅜
Brandy in bottles.....................	1 kilogramme, or 2⅕ lbs.	0 16
" in casks.......................	"	0 16
Candles, wax...........................	2⅕ lbs.	0 40

* The French decimal system of weights, measures, and currency has been recently adopted by the New Granadian government.

NEW GRANADA.

Denomination of Merchandise.	Number, Weight, or Measure.	Rate of Duty.
Candles, spermaceti	2½ lbs.	$0 20
Cheese of all kinds	"	0 02
Cider in bottles	same as beer.	
" in casks	"	
Codfish		free.
Copper, manufactures of	2½ lbs.	0 15
" in bars		free.
Cotton, raw	no importation.	
" manufactures of	2⅛ lbs.	0 40
Flour, wheat		free.
Glass, window	box of from 100 to 125 lbs.	2 40
Hams and bacon		free.
Hats, straw	dozen,	0 60
Household furniture	chairs, dozen,	6 00
" "	1 lounge,	12 50
" "	1 table,	5 00
Indian corn		free.
Lard		"
Lead in bars and sheets	1 miriagram. 26 lbs. 9 oz.	0 32
" manufactures of	2½ lbs.	0 05
Nails, iron	26 lbs. 9 oz.	0 48
Oils, whale and other fish	1.014 lb.	0 06½
Pitch	"	0 00½
Paper, writing	ream,	0 40
" printing		free.
Paints	2½ lbs.	0 12
Pork		free.
Rice		"
Rosin	"	0 00½
Soap, common	26 lbs. 9 oz.	0 72
" perfumed	2½ lbs.	0 50
Shoes and boots, leather	10 per cent. additional to the duty on leather.	
Sugar, refined	1.014 lb.	0 02¾
Tallow	101 lbs.	2 00
Tar	26 lbs. 9 oz.	0 08
Teas	2½ lbs.	0 20
Tobacco, unmanufactured	"	0 20
" cigars, Havana	"	0 80
" " others	"	0 80
Umbrellas, silk	each,	0 60
" cotton	dozen,	2 00
Wax, raw, white	2½ lbs.	0 20
" " yellow	"	0 20
Wood, boards, pine		free.
" shingles		"
Wines, red	2½ lbs.	0 06
" white	"	0 10

Goods imported into the Isthmus of **Panama**, although a part of the New Granadian Republic, are exempt from duty; but if imported from the Isthmus into New Granada, they are charged the regular duties as if coming from foreign countries.

FREE LIST.

Animals for breed; beaver and other skins; bee-hives and bees; books, printed; carts; casks; coal; gold, silver, and platina, in dust; implements for agriculture and mining; scientific and surgical instruments; medals; mills; paintings and engravings; paper for printing; plants; seeds; statues and busts; steam-engines; wool; effects of embassadors, and equipage of travelers.

PROHIBITED LIST.

Arms; obscene books and prints; coin, defaced or clipped; rum; tobacco, raw.

Coasting trade free to foreign vessels.

By virtue of the tariff act which came into force in New Granada, June 25, 1856, an increase of duty from 25 to 100 per cent. was imposed on nearly every article of import, presenting an exception to the tariff modifications of almost every other commercial country for years past. The percentage increase of rates on the principal articles of merchandise, by virtue of this act, on the rates previously levied, has been noted as follows, fractions being disregarded:

On the following articles the increase is 25 per cent.: steel, not manufactured; needles and fish-hooks of certain descriptions; indigo; sugar-candy; phials; cocoa, manufactured; cocoanuts; padlocks of iron or brass; candlesticks of glass or crystal; brushes for the teeth, nails, etc.; locks; beer; copper in sheets; glasses, small, for liquors, cut or not; knives for shoemakers, etc.; spurs, cast iron; chisels; bottles; large forge bellows; carbine hooks; buckles of metal; watchmakers' tools; common lead-pencils; china-ware, small articles; mirrors of certain sizes; hammers of all kinds; mills, small, and coffee-mills, etc.; razors; brown paper; Jamaica pepper; pipes of clay, for smoking; dishes of glass or crystal; lead in pigs, plates, balls, and shot; metallic pens; reins for bridles; castors for tables, etc.; tallow or stearine; ink in powder, paste, or liquid; glasses, watch, magnifying, etc.

On the following articles the increase is 26 per cent.: spirits from cane and its compounds, in those provinces in which this article is not a monopoly; spirits of turpentine; scented waters of all kinds; iron wire; white lead in powder or oil; raw cotton in bulk and in seed; trunks with merchandise; bottles and demijohns; brooches for clasps, etc.; shoe-brushes, etc.; copper in bars or cakes; compasses; fine penknives; spoons of tin, iron, copper, etc.; large knives, and knives of ivory, etc., and balance-handle knives with forks; thimbles; snuffers; screw-drivers; fowling-pieces; mirrors with gilt frames; tin, pewter, etc., in bars or cakes; felts for hats; nails, brads, etc.; liquor cases; saddle-trees; toilet soap; sealing-wax; files;

linen manufactures, common; mustard; mainsprings for clocks and watches; paper, writing, hanging, etc.; umbrellas of silk of all sizes; pincers of all sorts; pistols, common; earthen pitchers, jars, etc.; salt-cellars of glass or crystal; saws, pit and frame; scissors, small, etc.; turpentine; zinc, manufactures of.

On the following articles the increase is 27 per cent.: cruet-stands; needles of wire, bone, etc.; silver, brass, and piano wire; door-bolts, small; carpeting in pieces; cotton manufactures; curry-combs of iron; plate-holders; pin-cases; chandeliers of glass or metal; harness for two beasts; **trunks without merchandise**; scales; bridle-bits; copper pumps for engines; **silk brocade**; **wax candles**; bedsteads; sofas; sieves of wire, silk, etc.; clothes-brushes, etc.; cranks of iron; clothes-presses; watch-guards; swords; small looking-glasses; iron pickaxes; stirrups; pianos; flasks; decanters; **small buckles for braces**, etc.; whips; lawn; lace; fringes, etc., of linen; porcelain; manufactures of German silver; saddles; dial-plates; razors in cases; organs; gilt paper-hangings; cotton umbrellas; pistols; powder-flasks; bottle-stands; watches; manufactures of silk of all kinds; **fine scissors**; **gold braid**; window-glass.

On a certain description of needles, packing, sailmakers', etc., the increase is 100 per cent.; on irons for **carpenters' planes**, etc., and small hand-bellows, 150; on fine gold wire, 154; and on sperm-oil, manufactured, 160 per cent.

There is a decrease of duty on buttons of from 40 to 80 per cent.; on chairs, of 68; augers, 36; common glass bottles, 40; gloves of buckskin, etc., 54 and 52; stirrup-leathers, 37; and on a few other unimportant articles.

ECUADOR.

THE Republic of Ecuador, joining that of New Granada on the south, is situated between latitude 1° 35′ north and 5° 50′ south, and has its name from its position under the equator. Its eastern boundary is formed by a portion of New Granada, Brazil, and Peru; its southern by Peru, and its western by the Pacific Ocean. Estimated area 250,000 square miles.

The three ranges of the Andes pass through the extent of the western part of the republic from north to south. As in New Granada, they abound in high fertile valleys and elevated plains of great productiveness and salubrity; they also shoot up into frequent lofty volcanic peaks, many of which are in active eruption: 17 of these have an average height of over 16,000 feet each, while several others range from 17,000 to 21,000 feet, their summits covered with perpetual snow. The lower valleys and plains yield all the staples and fruits of the tropics, while the higher produce the grains and fruits of the temperate zone, and afford the finest pasturage for numerous herds of cattle, horses, sheep, lamas, guanacos, and vicunas. Here the Peruvian bark, sarsaparilla, balsam of tolu, vanilla, canella, copaiva, gentian, and many other medicinal productions, are indigenous. There are also vast tracts of wooded lands, producing the finest timber for ship-building and cabinet-work, besides many excellent varieties of dye-woods, and numerous fibrous plants suitable for the manufacture of hats, cordage, cloth, paper, etc.

The mineral productions of Ecuador are gold, silver, mercury, iron, tin, lead, copper, antimony, manganese, sulphur, and salt.

Gold is abundant in the sands of almost all the rivers. From not being properly or efficiently worked, the produce from the mining interest of Ecuador is inconsiderable.

The navigable rivers of Ecuador are numerous. Flowing into the Pacific are the Esmeralda, the Rio Guayaquil and its tributary the Daule (emptying into a gulf of the same name), and the Tumbez, forming a part of the southern boundary, all of considerable importance, draining rich and productive districts, and affording for a considerable portion of their extent an easy passage for the productions of the Pacific slope to the coast. Flowing westward into the valley of the Amazon and uniting with that river are the Putumayo, navigable for the greater part of its extent; the Napo, navigable for steam-boats for 550 miles; the Tigre for 230 miles; and the Santiago, 400 for steam-boats, and

120 more for smaller vessels. The Amazon, which forms a large portion of the southern boundary of the republic, is navigable for large vessels as far as the River Tigre (about midway of the southern boundary), making the navigable portion of that river in Ecuador about 350 miles for steamboats, and nearly 300 farther for rafts or balsas.

The climate of Ecuador varies with the situation of different portions; that along the Pacific coast is decidedly tropical and insalubrious; but as the slopes of the Andes are ascended, the temperature is decreased, until, reaching the valleys and plains at a height of nine or ten thousand feet, a perpetual spring prevails. The valley of Quito, in which the capital is located, is said to possess the most equable and delightful climate in the world, having a temperature varying from 56° to 62° Fahrenheit.

The year is divided into two seasons. In the elevated lands the winter commences in December and lasts until May, and is a season of clear skies, with a delightful temperature; the summer begins in June and ends in November: during this season high winds prevail. In the low land the temperature is hot and moist, and in the winter incessant rains prevail.

The population of Ecuador is estimated at about 800,000, composed of

Whites of European descent	351,672
Indians, descendants of the "Quiches"	274,440
Indians of the Orient	135,000
Negroes	7,831
Mixed races	31,057
	800,000

The whites are the principal landholders, traders, etc. The Quiches are mostly mechanics and agriculturists.

The Indians of the Orient are wild, and warlike, and uncivilized.

The prevailing religion is Roman Catholic, and the open profession of no other is tolerated, but foreigners are not molested on account of their religious faith. Education is at a low ebb.

The chief city and capital is Quito, and is situated 9453 feet above the level of the sea, in a valley of the same name, 150 miles from Guayaquil, the chief sea-port. It is well built, and has several handsome squares, in one of which are the cathedral, the town hall, and palaces of the archbishop, etc. There are also in this city many churches and convents, a work-house, an orphan asylum, a university, and a large hospital. It has manufactories of coarse cotton and woolen goods, lace, hosiery, jewelry, etc., and a large trade in corn and other agricultural produce, which, with some of its manufactured goods, are sent by way of Guayaquil to Central America in return for indigo, iron, steel, and to Peru in return for brandy, wine, oil, and precious metals, etc. There is said to be much wealth among its inhabitants. The markets are well supplied. Population 50,000.

The chief sea-ports and harbors of Ecuador are Guayaquil, Manta, and Esmeralda.

Guayaquil, the principal port, is situated at the head of a bay of the same name, and at the mouth of the River Guayaquil, 50 miles from the sea. The harbor is excellent, and affords great facilities for ship-building, excellent timber being found within a few rods of the river, where building-yards of capacity for the largest ships have been constructed. The city consists of the old and the new town, and is intersected by five small creeks which are crossed by wooden bridges. The houses are mostly of wood. The principal edifices are a cathedral, several churches, two hospitals, and two colleges. The city is defended by three forts. It is unhealthy, with a mild, humid climate: mean annual temperature 88° Fahr. Population 22,000. Guayaquil is an important entrepôt for the trade between Lima and Quito.

The ports of Manta and Esmeralda are chiefly ports of export for silver ore and the produce of the country surrounding. The towns are of small size and of but little importance. The regular ships of the Pacific Steam Navigation Company touch at Guayaquil on the 13th and 28th of each month, and a special steamer plies monthly between Guayaquil and Panama, touching at the ports of Manta and Guayaquil (see Itinerary, page 152). In 1856 the foreign exports by the ports of Manta and Guayaquil were $2,333,141 50, of which $67,562 12 was silver and silver ore. The exports across the country to New Granada were about $300,000, and to Peru $100,000. The imports for the same year were, through the port of Guayaquil, $2,374,439 38; through Manta, $112,267 39; from New Granada, $40,000; and from Peru, 100,000.

The chief exports consist of silver and silver ore, cacao, sombreros (or Panama hats), tobacco, cascarilla, sarsaparilla, agave fibre, tamarinds, caoutchouc, canes, coffee, hammocks, etc.; the imports, textiles of cotton, wool, flax, and silk, wine, spirits, flour, hardware, paper, furniture, musical instruments, etc., etc.

Port Regulations at Guayaquil.—There are no quarantine regulations. Tonnage dues, 25 cts.; light money, 6¼ cts.; hospital, 50 cts. per day. Vessels lie in the stream, and are loaded or discharged by means of rafts, $4 to $5 per load.

The commercial charge for storage is 1 per cent. Merchandise is carried on by porters, who charge from 10 to 50 cents, according to bulk.

Passengers, on landing, are obliged to present themselves at the police-office, where their passports are examined. Their baggage is examined at the custom-house, and no fees are exacted with the exception of those for a new passport on leaving the country.

The currency is the same as in Mexico.

Coin.—1 peso = 100 cents = $1 00.
Weights.—1 quintal = 4 arrobas of 25 lb. 7 oz.
Measures.—1 vara = 33½ inches English.

Tariff on Articles received in Ecuador from the United States—1856.

FREE LIST.

Printed books and music, maps, ships' materials, fresh fruits, vegetables, fire-engines, surgical and mathematical instruments, agricultural implements, tools of emigrants, useful machines, inventions, etc.

Denomination of Merchandise.	Number, Weight, or Measure.	Rate of Duty.
Alcohol	gallon,	$1 50
Beef	quintal (101 lbs.),	2 00
Beer, ale, porter, in bottles	dozen,	75
" " " in casks	gallon,	25
Brandy in bottles	dozen,	2 00
" in casks	gallon,	50
Cables and cordage	101 lbs.	37½
Candles, wax	1.014 lb.	18¾
" tallow	"	03
" spermaceti	"	06¼
Cheese of all kinds	101 lbs.	2 00
Cider in bottles	dozen,	1 00
" in casks	gallon,	25
Codfish	101 lbs.	3 00
Copper, manufactures of	1.014 lb.	06¼
" in bars	101 lbs.	2 50
Cotton, raw	"	50
" manufactures of	yard,	(drills) 02½
Flour, wheat	barrel, about 200 lbs.	6 00
Glass, window	box of 100 feet square,	1 00
Hams and bacon	101 lbs.	50
Hats, straw	each, for ladies,	2 00
Household furniture	1 table,	4 50
Indian corn	101 lbs.	1 00
Lard	"	4 50
Lead in bars and sheets	"	1 00
" manufactures of	"	1 50
Nails, iron	"	1 00
Oil, whale and other fish	gallon,	05
Paper, writing	ream,	25
" printing	"	75
Paints	101 lbs.	2 00
Pitch	"	30
Pork	"	2 00
Rice	"	3 00
Rosin	"	20
Shoes, boots, leather	1 pair,	1 50
Soap, common	101 lbs.	1 50
" perfumed	dozen cakes,	12½ cts. to 25
Sugar, refined	101 lbs.	4 00
Tallow	"	2 00
Tar	"	25
Teas*	1.014 lb.	18¾
Tobacco, unmanufactured	101 lbs.	10 00
" cigars, Havana	1000,	5 00

* Teas, when imported direct from the place of production in American or equalized vessels, are *free*.

Denomination of Merchandise.	Number, Weight, or Measure.	Rate of Duty.
Umbrellas, silk	one,	$1 00
" cotton	dozen,	2 00
Wax, raw, white	101 lbs.	9 00
" yellow	"	9 00
Wines, red	gallon,	15
" white	"	15
Wood, boards, pine	1 foot,	02
" shingles	1000,	3 36

The duties are to be paid within 10 days when they amount to $100; within 30 when from $100 to $500; within 45 from $500 to $2000; within 75 from $2000 to $6000; 100 from $6000 to $12,000; over $12,000, 150 days. Besides the duties small sums are levied as toll tax.

Export duties: gold, ½ per cent. ad valorem; silver, 1 per cent.; manglewurzel, 50 cents per 100 lbs.; straw for hats, 10 per cent. ad valorem.

PERU.

The Republic of Peru, between latitude 3° 25′ and 21° 48′ south, and longitude 68° and 81° 20′ west, embraces an area of 520,000 square miles, and had, by the census of 1852, a population of 2,106,492. Peru is bounded on the north by Ecuador, on the east by Brazil and Bolivia, on the south by Bolivia and the Pacific, and on the west by the Pacific Ocean, and has a coast-line on the Pacific of 1240 miles.

The double cordillera of the Andes traverses Peru from northeast to southwest, separating it into three regions. The central has an elevation of about 12,000 feet; the eastern forms a part of the great plain of South America; and the western, between the Andes and the Pacific, has a breadth of from 60 to 70 miles. The Andes and their branches are estimated to occupy about 200,000 square miles of the surface of Peru. The whole of the coast region is arid and barren; the upland or central region abounds in fertile valleys and plains. To the east of the mountains the country is covered with vast forests, which have as yet been but imperfectly explored. Between the coast regions and the mountains are numerous valleys and plains of great fertility, where tobacco, sugar, maize, cotton, indigo, cocoa, cochineal, and various tropical fruits are produced, besides the copaiva, vanilla, balsams, etc., and valuable cabinet woods, which are indigenous. Here rain rarely falls, but fogs and dews are frequent. In the central region the grains of Europe are successfully cultivated, and the finest pasturage for sheep and cattle is abundant. The lama, alpaca, guanaco, and vicuna are natives of this region, where they abound in great numbers; their wool, especially that of the alpaca, is said to be the finest in the world except the Cashmere, and forms an important article of export. Here also are found the cinchona-trees, from which the Peruvian barks of commerce are obtained.

The mineral wealth of Peru is very great: gold, silver, copper, tin, iron, and saltpetre are found in abundance; the region between the mountain ranges is especially rich in mineral products.

A very great source of wealth to Peru is its deposits of guano, which occur on the islands of Chincha and Lobos along its coast. These were estimated in 1842 to contain no less than 46,632,000 tons, valued at $20 per ton; the annual consumption was then assumed to be about 300,000 tons.

Peru is politically divided into eleven departments and two littoral provinces, as follows, from north to south:

Departments.	Population.	Capitals.
Amazonas	43,074	Chachapoyas.
Libertad	266,553	Truxillo.
Ancach	219,145	Huaras.
Junin	222,949	Cerro de Pasco.
Lima	259,801	Lima.
Huancavelica	70,117	Huancavelica.

Departments.	Population.	Capitals.
Ayacucho	132,921	Huamanga.
Cuzco	349,718	Cuzco.
Puno	285,661	Puno.
Arequipa	119,336	Arequipa.
Moquega	61,432	Tacna.
Province littoral de Callao	8,453	
" " " Piura	76,332	
Total	2,106,492	

The population consists of Spaniards, native Indians, Negroes, and the mixed races resulting therefrom: whites about 400,000; Indians, 1,000,000; the remainder Negroes and mixed bloods.

Education in Peru is in a very low condition, though there are many Lancastrian schools in the republic, where the elemental branches are taught. At Lima, the capital, there is a University and several colleges, but they are poor and thinly attended. "Superior education is confined to a very few among the whites, and the ornamental almost universally takes the precedence of useful instruction. There are at the capital some good libraries and a medical college."

"The established religion is Roman Catholic, though other denominations are now tolerated. The clergy are said to be careless of their duty and lax in their morals."

Agriculture is in a very primitive state. Manufactures are also in a backward condition, principally confined to ponchos, or loose cloaks (some of which are of great fineness and beauty), coarse blankets, mats, hats, cordage, and the beautiful filigree silver-work for which the interior of Peru is celebrated.

Lima, the capital of Peru, is situated on a beautiful and extensive plain 560 feet above the ocean, and from Callao, its sea-port, distant about eight and a half miles. It is about two miles in length, about the same in breadth, and is surrounded by massive brick walls. The River Rimac flows through the city, and is crossed by a fine stone bridge 530 feet in length. The streets are regularly laid out, the houses low, and built of sun-dried bricks. The grand plaza is about 500 feet square, in the centre of which is a handsome stone fountain, surmounted by a bronze statue; besides this there are about thirty other open squares in the city. There are two foundling asylums and eleven public hospitals, one of which has 600 beds. The city contains fifty-seven churches, sixteen nunneries, and twenty-five chapels, many of which are rich in decorations of gold and jewels. The church of the Dominican convent is 300 feet in length by 80 in breadth, and has a steeple 180 feet in height. The convent of St. Francis covers two whole squares, and has magnificent cloisters. Lima has a University, numerous primary and two high schools, also three Latin schools, and four colleges. There are two theatres, an amphitheatre for cock-fighting, and another for bullfights capable of accommodating 12,000 spectators. The manufactures, which are very limited, consist of gold lace and fringes, glass, cotton cloth, cigars, chocolate, and paper. Its population is about 100,000, one fourth of whom are white, one fourth Negroes, and the remainder Indians and mixed races. The climate of Lima is delightfully mild and equable, ranging from 60° to 80° Fahrenheit. Rain is extremely rare. The communication between Lima and Callao, its sea-port, is by a railway eight and a half miles in length, built in 1850–51 by English engineers, with materials brought from England. There is another railway running from Lima to Chorillas, a favorite bathing-place on the coast, nine miles distant. The country in the vicinity of Lima is exceedingly pleasing and fertile, producing all the fruits and vegetables of the temperate zone in abundance. Earthquakes occasionally occur, but are usually so slight that they rarely create alarm.

The chief sea-ports of Peru are Payta, San José, Huanchaco, Callao, Islay, Arica, and Iquique. These are the ports of entry for foreign commerce, and are called "*los pu-*

erto mayores," or major ports. There are, besides these, open to the coasting trade and for the exportation of the products of the country, the minor ports of Ylo, Chala, Pisco, Huacho, Casma, Pacasmayo, and Tumbez, and the small harbors of Sechura, Samano, Santo, Supe, Huarmes, Echinique, Chancay, Ancon, Cerro Azul, Chincha, Cancato, Nasca, Quilca, Cototea, Morro de Sama, and Pisaque.

The steam-ships of the Pacific Steam Navigation Company touch at all the principal and at most of the minor ports of Peru (see Itinerary, p. 152, et seq.).

The chief staple of export from Peru is guano; crude wools, bar silver, copper, and tin, Peruvian bark, nitrate of soda, are exported in considerable quantities. The average annual value of exports, in round numbers, is $12,000,000. The chief imports are textiles of silk, linen, cotton, wool, gold and silver ornaments, fruits, provisions, timber, furniture, wines, and liquors. The average annual value of imports, in round numbers, is $9,500,000. Of this the United States imports to Peru about $500,000 per annum, and exports about $2,000,000.

The chief trade of Peru is with Great Britain.

PORTS.

The principal sea-port of Peru is Callao. The town is badly built, and contains about 7000 inhabitants. It is connected with Lima, the capital, by a good carriage-road and a single-track railway, which last is used almost exclusively for passengers. Callao possesses good shelter for shipping. Vessels lie at anchor in the harbor and discharge their cargoes by lighters and launches. There is a circular mole into which the launches go to be unloaded by cranes and winches upon a railroad track, which takes all goods to the custom-house, where they are deposited in the public stores for an indefinite time, under fixed rates of storage, from three to twelve cents a package per month.

The general features of commercial transactions at Callao, and at the ports of Peru generally, are set forth in a communication of a late date from the consul of the United States at that port as follows: "The most valuable articles imported into this consulate are assorted merchandise from England, France, Italy, and the United States, Chili, Spain, and Ecuador, viz., cottons, linens, silks, wines, hardware, etc.; from the United States, domestic cottons, furniture, lumber, provisions, etc. The export trade of Peru consists chiefly of guano, which is sent to England, the United States, France, and Spain, and in smaller quantities to Italy, India, and the West Indies. Crude wools are largely exported, but the high duty on them in the United States throws nearly all that trade into Europe, mostly to England, where wool is duty free. The same remark also applies to the barks of Peru and to copper. The bar silver all goes to England, because there is no *direct* steam navigation with the United States. Nitrate of soda is largely exported—at least 600,000 quintals annually, valued at $2 per 100 pounds; much of this goes to the United States. Dry and salted hides and straw hats are exported in small quantities."

Pisco, a port for exportation, about 100 miles south of Callao. A railway has been projected to connect this port with "Yca," a city in the interior, distant about 40 miles; this, when completed, will bring to the sea the products of a very rich agricultural district.

Arica, a major port, through which a large business for Bolivia is transacted, and the outlet of a large mining district. A railway was constructed in 1854–5 for an English company from Arica to Tacna, a distance of 40 miles, by Walton W. Evans, Esq., an American engineer. Six and a half per cent. on $2,000,000 was guaranteed by the government of Peru. This road overcomes an elevation of 1800 feet in its course. Over it large quantities of goods are carried to Bolivia. From the interior of Bolivia, coffee, tin, copper, and barilla are brought over it to Arica for exportation; besides this, all of the calisaya bark and alpaca wool known to trade finds its way to the sea through the same channel.

Iquique.—From this port immense quantities of nitrate of soda (saltpetre) are shipped to the United States and England, said in amount to exceed 30,000 tons annually. Out of a population of 15,000, more than four fifths are engaged in this trade. A railroad is projected from this port to "Terrapaca," the centre of the saltpetre region, distant from the sea-coast about fifty miles: this road, when completed, will greatly increase the trade.

There are no navigable rivers in Peru; the interior transportation is effected principally by means of mules.

There are no pilots (the nature of the ports rendering them unnecessary), no quarantine system, no light-houses, no hospital fees in Peru. There are no facilities for the repair of ships in Peru.

Tonnage dues in the ports of Peru are 25 cents per ton. Port charges, exclusive of tonnage, amount to about $25 at Callao, and $40 at Payta.

Passengers are allowed to land at all the ports of Peru as soon as the captain of the port has made his visit on board. No passports are required on arriving, but they are usually required on leaving Peru, and cost $3 at the offices of the local authorities. Passengers take their baggage on shore with them, or on board of vessels in the port; the inspector examines the luggage on the wharf. No fees are exacted.

CURRENCY.

The circulating currency, representing silver, and now the only money in common use in Peru, is below the nominal standard about 52 per cent. The rate of exchange fluctuates from five to fifteen per cent. on the dollar. The dollar of Peru in invoices of export to the United States is usually valued at from 80 to 85 cents of United States currency. The Peruvian dollar of pure silver (not in circulation) is worth about 87½ cents United States currency. Gold coins of Peru are not now in common use. Patriot doubloons pass current at $17, and of late are worth three per cent. premium, and but few to be obtained.

TARIFF REGULATIONS.

The tariff is that of November 25th, 1854, modified by a decree of May 1st, 1855.

Money.—1 peso = 100 cents = $1.

Weights and Measures.—1 quintal = 4 arrobas of 25 lbs. 7 oz. each = 100 libras = 101.45 lbs.; 1 pound = 1.014 lb. English.

FREE LIST.

Principal articles: tar; live animals; quicksilver; iron chains and cables; salted pork and beef in barrels; stone coal; geographical charts; lumber for house-building; cooking apparatus for vessels; scientific collections and objects of curiosity; staves and heading of all kinds; oakum; fresh fruits; printing-presses; scientific instruments of all kinds; cordage and tow; bricks; iron bars; timber for ship-building; hops; machines for agricultural and mining purposes; printed music; sheathing copper in sheets; seeds of all sorts.

If imported through the ports of Iquique, Arica, or Islay: fresh or salted meat; barley; beans; lard; lentils; and Indian corn.

In the port of Iquique, foreign goods in national vessels, if consisting of iron nails, steel, wood, tallow, and articles of food (flour excepted), pay only one half the ordinary duty. Empty sacks, gunny cloth, yarn for making bags, wood and stone coals, are free under all flags.

PROHIBITED LIST.

Gunpowder; all kinds of fire-arms and munitions of war; books offending public morals, and eatables of bad quality.

All merchandise imported direct from Europe, Asia, or North America, through the larger ports of the republic, are permitted to pay 10 per cent. of the total amount of duties levied in government bonds. Gold and silver in bullion or coin are exempt from export duty.

Tariff on Articles imported into Peru from the United States.

Denomination of Merchandise.	Number, Weight, or Measure.	Fixed Value on.	Percentage on fixed Value.
Beef......................................	101 lbs.	$6 50	$0 03
Beer, ale, and porter, in bottles	dozen,	specific duty,	1 50
" " in casks..	gallon,	"	0 25
Brandy in bottles..................	dozen, over 30°,	"	1 50
" in casks	gallon, "	"	1 50
" "	gallon, under 30°,	"	1 00
Cables and cordage		free.	
Candles, tallow	1.014 lb.	specific duty,	0 12¼
" spermaceti	"	"	0 12½
Cheese of all kinds................	101 lbs.	"	4 00
Cider in bottles	dozen,	"	1 50
" in casks....................	gallon,	"	0 25
Codfish...................................	101 lbs.	$5 00	0 10
Copper, manufactures of	1.014 lb.	0 37	0 15
" in sheets................		free.	
Cotton, raw	101 lbs.	$4 00	0 01
" manufactures of	fustian, dozen,	6 00	0 15
Flour, wheat..........................	101 lbs.	specific duty,	2 00
Glass, window		valuation,	0 25
Hams and bacon	1.014 lb.	20 cts.	0 03
Hats, straw		free.	
" other kinds		valuation,	0 30
Household furniture		"	0 30
Indian corn.............................	101 lbs.	$1 50	0 20
Lard..	"	specific duty,	1 00
Lead in bars and sheets	"	free.	
" manufactures of............	"	$7 00	0 20
Nails, iron..............................	"	5 50	0 06
Oil, whale and other fish	gallon,	0 35	0 20
Paints, common	101 lbs.	7 00	0 20
" fine, in pots...............	dozen,	0 75	0 20
Paper, writing.........................		valuation,	0 20
" printing........................	for music,	"	0 10
Pitch		free.	
Pork, salted		"	
Rice...		specific duty,	2 00
Rosin.......................................	barrel,	$4 00	free.
Shoes and boots, leather	dozen,	8 00	0 30
Soap, perfumed.....................	101 lbs.	25 00	0 20
Sugar, refined	arroba 25 lbs. 7 oz.	specific duty,	0 30
Tallow	101 lbs.	"	1 50
Tar..	barrel,	$4 00	free.
Teas*.....................................	1.014 lb.	specific duty,	0 18¾
Tobacco, unmanufactured......	101 lbs.	"	20 00
" cigars, Havana	1.014 lb.	"	0 62½
" " others...........	"	"	0 62½
Umbrellas, silk.......................	dozen,	$40 00	0 20
" cotton	"	10 00	0 20
Wax, raw, white....................	101 lbs.	50 00	0 20
" " yellow................	"	30 00	0 20

* Teas of all kinds, when imported direct from the place of production in American or equalized vessels, are free of duty.

Denomination of Merchandise.	Number, Weight, or Measure.	Fixed Value on.	Percentage on fixed Value.
Wines, red........................	dozen bottles,	specific duty,	$1 50
" white........................	"	"	1 50
Wood, boards, pine.............		free.	
" shingles....................		"	

BOLIVIA.

THIS republic extends from 10° 30′ to 25° south latitude, and from 57° 50′ to 71° 30′ west longitude, with an area of 473,298 square miles. Its greatest length is estimated at about 1000 miles, and its greatest breadth at 800. It has about 250 miles of sea-coast. Population, according to latest authorities, 1,425,758. Bolivia, in the general characteristics of its topography, soil, climate, productions, and inhabitants, does not differ materially from Peru, already described. Its facilities for internal navigation on the east of the Cordilleras are very great through the River Marmore and its affluents, whose waters flow into the Amazon, and the Pilcomayo, whose waters empty into the Paraguay, thereby affording communication with the Atlantic Ocean. The very liberal inducement offered to foreigners by the government of Bolivia for navigating these rivers and settling her rich and extensive eastern plains promise, at no distant day, to aid in developing her vast resources. By a decree promulgated by President Belzu in January, 1853, navigation through the above-named rivers was declared free and their ports free to all nations; a bounty of $10,000 to be awarded to the first steamer reaching any of her river ports from the Atlantic, and from one to twelve leagues square of Bolivian territory to the individuals or companies who, sailing from the Atlantic, shall arrive at any of the river ports and desire to found near them agricultural or industrial establishments. The commerce of Bolivia is carried on through its only available sea-port, Cobija, and through the port of Arica in Peru. All of the alpaca wool and calisaya bark known to commerce is produced in Bolivia, and finds its way to the market across the narrow strip of Peruvian territory which separates Bolivia from the Pacific at Arica. Deposits of guano exist along the coast, and form a considerable article of export. The mineral productions of Bolivia are similar to those of Peru. Its silver mines are world-famed, though from inefficient working their produce has of late years greatly declined; at present the export of silver and gold amounts only to about $1,400,000 per annum. The entire exports are estimated at $4,000,000 per annum. The imports by Cobija amount to about $500,000 per annum, and the internal traffic with Peru and Chili to about $1,500,000. Manufactures are carried on on a small scale: woolen and cotton cloths, hats made from the vicuna wool, tin-ware, and fire-arms, are the chief.

Agriculture is in low condition. Cocoa, cotton, rice, indigo, coffee, sugar, ginger, and tobacco, all of excellent quality, are cultivated.

Cobija, or "*Puerto del Mar*," the only legal sea-port of Bolivia, is a small town with a population of 2000. The harbor is bad, and the transportation of merchandise from this place to the interior, performed by means of mules, is difficult and expensive, from which cause most of the trade of Bolivia is carried on through the Peruvian port Arica. The steam-ships of the British Pacific Steam Navigation Company touch at Cobija four times a month on their upward and downward voyages (see Itinerary, page 152).

PORT CHARGES.

There are no pilots or wharves, but it is necessary to pay mole and tonnage dues—rates not ascertained. Passengers, before entering Bolivia, are required to have passports.

Money, weights, and measures, the same as in Peru.

TARIFF ON IMPORTS INTRODUCED INTO BOLIVIA

By way of Arica. Ad val.
Clothing, and men's boots and shoes........................30 pr. ct.
Perfumery, clocks, playing-cards, cigars, women's shoes, caps, and bonnets, iron and brass bedsteads, sofas, mirrors, lamps, candlesticks, and all other articles not enumerated in this class....20 pr. ct.
Woolens, silks, and linens.....15 "
All cotton goods except tucuyas or cotton shirtings......12 "
Tucuyas................................40 "
Earthen-ware, glass-ware, and writing-paper.................. 8 "
Silver and gold plate, jewelry, and watches....................16 "
Books..................................12 "
Quicksilver, musical instruments (except guitars), agricultural implements, and for the arts and trades, free.
Liquors and wines pay duty to Peru, as if intended for consumption there.

By way of Cobija. Ad val.
Clothing, and men's boots and shoes, saddles, hats, tucuyas.20 pr. ct.
All kinds of wines, liquors, etc. 18 "
Perfumery, clocks, playing-cards, cigars, women's shoes, caps, and bonnets, iron and brass bedsteads, sofas, mirrors, lamps, candlesticks, chandeliers, gold and silver lace, all kinds of haberdashery, and all other articles not enumerated in this class.10 pr. ct.
Cotton goods, except tucuyas. 5 "
Earthen-ware, glass-ware, writing-paper, silver or gold plate, jewelry, and watches.. 3 "
Quicksilver, iron not manufactured or wrought for manufactures, musical instruments (except guitars), implements of agriculture, the arts, and trades, carriages and printing-presses, types, etc., printed books (except the 2 per cent. on the library), free.

Specific Duties on Imports both by Arica and Cobija.

Description of Goods.	Quantities.	Rates.	Description of Goods.	Quantities.	Rates.
Alforgas (saddle-bags)...............	pair,	$2 50	Galloons...............	ounce,	$0 50
Sugar...................	arroba,	50	Caps of fur...........	each,	1 00
Boots...................	dozen,	6 00	Caps of silk or straw...............	"	1 50
Bootees for men......	"	4 00	Caps for children..	"	50
" " women.	"	1 50	Horseshoes...........	dozen,	4 00
Trunks.................	pair,	5 00	Toys of all kinds...	box,	15 00
Nails....................	pound,	12½	Picklocks..............	dozen,	1 50
Locks and keys......	dozen,	1 50	Trunks of hide......	pair,	2 00
Cigars..................	1000,	2 00	Gunpowder...........	pound,	50
Wax.....................	arroba,	1 00	Saddles................	each,	6 00
Sperm candles.......	dozen,	2 00	Hats.....................	"	2 50
Bridles or bits.......	"	1 50	Hat-bodies............	"	2 00
Matches................	gross,	2 00	Shoes for women...	dozen,	1 50
Saddle-frames.......	each,	2 00	" men......	"	3 00

There is no transit duty through Peru. The custom-house charges amount to about two per cent. The higher duties by Arica are for the purpose of encouraging commerce through the port of Cobija. All the foregoing duties took effect in **November, 1849.** On the 26th of June,

1854, five per cent. ad valorem was added to the rates by Cobija. All the ad valorem duties are on the value of goods at Pacific ports. Duties on all goods by Cobija are adjusted and paid there, for which bonds are received, payable one half in 30 and the other in 120 days. Payment may be made two thirds in the small coin and the other third in government scrip, issued for a contingent reserve from salaries, worth from 25 to 50 per cent. The duties on all goods by Arica for La Paz are adjusted and paid at La Paz, and those for all other points at Oruro.

CHILI.

This republic extends along the Pacific coast from latitude 24° to 56° south, varying in breadth from 80 to 130 miles. The Pacific Ocean forms its western and southern boundaries, Bolivia its northern, and the Andes its eastern, embracing (according to Lieut. Gilliss, U. S. N.) an area of 146,300 square miles. Population, by the census of 1857, 1,468,448, besides the tribes of independent Indians, estimated at 25,000 or 30,000.

Chili is divided into thirteen provinces and three colonies, named in the order of their situation from north to south, as follows:

Atacama	Pop. 55,567	Nuble	Pop.	110,219
Coquimbo	" 119,991	Concepcion	"	122,281
Aconcagua	" 121,654	Araucania	"	48,995
Santiago	" 203,113	Valdivia	"	31,983
Valparaiso	" 124,600	Chiloe	"	65,743
Colchagua	" 206,919	Juan Fernandez Colony.	"	136
Talca	" 84,461	Llanquihue "	"	3,826
Maule	" 168,807	Magellanic "	"	153
				1,468,448

The great Andean chain (which attains its maximum elevation in Chili) occupies quite two thirds of the surface of the republic. The two most northern provinces, Atacama and Coquimbo, are occupied by mountain ranges rich in mineral deposits, but mostly barren in their agricultural productions, and do not supply the necessities of one half of their limited population. But the remaining eleven provinces of the republic possess much fertile and cultivated land; besides raising enough for their own wants and supplying the northern deficiency, they export agricultural produce to the amount of over $2,250,000 annually. Santiago, Valparaiso, Colchagua, Nuble, Concepcion, and Chiloe comprise the chief agricultural districts. The principal grains raised are wheat, barley, oats, and maize; excellent potatoes are also produced. In the provinces of Aconcagua, Santiago, and Valparaiso fruits of both the temperate and tropical climates are abundant. Nuble, Concepcion, Valdivia, and Chiloe produce large quantities of valuable timber. In Aconcagua, Santiago, Colchagua, Maule, Nuble, Concepcion, and Araucania cattle-raising is extensively carried on.

Almost the whole extent of the Republic of Chili is rich in mineral productions, but the chief mining districts are in the provinces of Atacama and Coquimbo. The exports of gold, silver, and copper are estimated at over $15,000,000 per annum.

Coal of fair quality is abundant and extensively mined in the province of Concepcion. These mines were opened in 1840, at a heavy expense, by the Pacific Steam Navigation Company, and now produce over 300,000 tons annually.

The entire exports of the republic for the year 1857, which may be considered as the annual average, were as follows:

Bars of gold and gold coin...	$497,736	Butter and cheese............	$36,055
Silver and silver ore.........	4,725,655	Tallow and lard..............	2,729
Copper and copper ore.....	10,760,589	Hides, horns, and hoofs....	501,104
Wheat..........................	1,050,718	Goat, sheep, and chinchilla skins......................	40,861
Flour............................	798,112		
Biscuit, bread, and frangolio..............................	108,223	Wool...........................	397,643
		Assorted provisions	27,189
Barley...........................	257,970	Dried fodder...................	41,790
Beans	24,904	Cords, rope, and rigging ..	18,464
Potatoes........................	35,506	Planks and lumber...........	265,287
Wine and chicha..............	1,612	Coal	176,765
Nuts, dried and fresh fruits	89,052	Guano..........................	5,600
Salt beef........................	10,880	Miscellaneous..................	143,009
Jerked beef	104,173	Making a total of....	$20,121,626

The climate is equable and healthy. The interior is hotter than the coast. In the former, at the northern portion of the republic, the thermometer often rises to 90° and 95° in the shade during the summer months of January and February; on the latter, at the same season, it is seldom higher than 85°. North of the parallel of 27° it seldom or never rains, but heavy dews are frequent. In the central portion of the republic, during June, July, and August (the winter months of the southern hemisphere), occasional rains occur, and the thermometer falls as low as 49° Fahrenheit; and in December, January, and February it rises to about 90°. During these months no rain falls, but the night breezes from the sea render the temperature refreshing. The mean annual temperature at Santiago is 70°. From thence southward the mean temperature declines, and the humidity of the atmosphere increases, until, at the extreme southern portions, rains are frequent and severe at almost every season. Earthquakes are common.

The inhabitants of Chili are mostly descendants of the Spaniards, the aboriginal tribes, and admixtures of these. It is estimated that not more than one fourth are of pure Spanish blood. There is a small proportion of Negroes and Mulattoes. The foreign population was estimated in 1854 at 19,699, viz.: 11,324 natives of the Argentine Republic, 1934 English, 1929 Germans, 1650 French, 680 Americans, 915 Spaniards, 399 Italians, 168 Portuguese, 599 Peruvians, and 71 Chinese.

Agriculture and mining are the chief employments of the Chilenos. Manufactures of cotton, wool, glass, silk laces, fringes, gold and silver embroidery (wrought by hand), utensils and ornaments of gold and silver, copper utensils, leather, etc., are carried on to some extent, but do not form an important item in the resources of the country.

The Chilenos are more enterprising than the inhabitants of most of the South American states, and the haciendados, or planters, and merchants often accumulate large amounts of property. With the exception of those destined for the learned professions, they have generally but little education. Their educational system is, however, more efficient than any of the other South American states. There are in the republic 562 schools for males and 295 for females. The books are furnished by the government. There are two normal schools in a flourishing condition; a government university and theological seminary, a school of agriculture, a naval school under the direction of the minister of marine, and a military school under the care of the minister of war: these last are all at Santiago, the capital, where is also a government library of 22,000 volumes, founded by the Jesuits.

The established religion is Roman Catholic. While the public services of other denominations are not permitted, their private exercise is not interfered with.

The city of Santiago, situated 100 miles in the interior, southeast from Valparaiso, is the capital of the republic and seat of government. It occupies nearly seven square miles. It is regularly laid out into squares of 420 feet each way. Most of the houses are of one story, and built of sun-dried brick, plastered and whitewashed. Santiago possesses quite a number of fine public edifices, among which the Mint is the most extensive and imposing. Its architecture is of the Doric style, and covers about 400 square feet. It was built by the Spanish government at the close of the last century, and cost nearly a million of dollars. It has numerous churches, several extensive hospitals and alms-houses, and several institutes of learning, which have been already referred to. Connected by railway with the chief sea-port, Valparaiso, it is the chief mart for the interior commerce of the republic. Population about 90,000. An astronomical observatory was established at the city of Santiago by Lieut. Gilliss, U. S. N., under orders from the United States government, in 1851.

The ports of chief importance in Chili from north to south are as follows, viz.:

Caldera.—Here is a fine bay of nearly square form, about a mile across, with neither internal nor external dangers, and deep water. At the southeast quarter is a long pier, which serves for loading and discharging vessels. The exports are silver and copper. The Copiapo Railway, which was commenced in 1850 and completed in 1852, under the direction of Mr. William Wheelwright, connects Caldera with the city of Copiapo, fifty miles in the interior, since which time it has been run with great success, developing the wonderful mineral wealth of that region, and paying 16 per cent. dividends on its capital, which is equal to 20 per cent. on its cost. It overcomes 1300 feet elevation. Its chief business is bringing copper and silver ore to the coast, and carrying to the interior coal for smelting purposes, also provisions and building materials. In 1854 this railroad was extended to a point 24 miles in the interior, and 2195 feet above the sea. This extension, as well as the original line, was built and is still owned by a Chileno Company. In 1858 Walton W. Evans, Esq., of New York, constructed for an English company a branch line to this railway, 26 miles in length, terminating at Chanarcilla, one of the richest silver mining districts known. The summit is more than 1300 feet higher than any other summit in the world over which a locomotive has climbed, its elevation above the sea being 4467 English feet. Another branch to the Copiapo Railway is contemplated and has been surveyed; it is to connect Copiapo with the rich silver mining district of Tres-Puntas, in the desert of Atacama, and, if built, will give great activity to rich copper and gold mines in that region. It will be 54 miles in length, and terminate at a point 6400 feet above the level of the ocean.

Huasco is a port of entry, though scarcely more than an open roadstead. It exports copper and copper ore, and imports supplies for the mining population of this portion of the province of Atacama.

Coquimbo.—The business of this port is the same as Huasco. There is good shelter for vessels. A railway is in course of construction from the port to Serena, 8 or 9 miles in length; it is intended to extend this to a rich copper district, and terminate it at 30 or 40 miles from Coquimbo. Large quantities of rich copper ores are found in this region.

Tongoy, a small port for coasting trade, 30 miles south of Coquimbo. A railway has been surveyed from this port to the rich copper mines of Tamaya, and thence to Ovalle, a town in the interior, about 40 miles from the sea-coast. If built, this road will assist in developing one of the richest copper districts in the world. Señor Don Jose V. de Urmenita, of Chili, has a mine in this region which yields a net revenue of over $500,000 annually. The copper vein in this mine is about 15 feet thick, and yields ores from 30 to 70 percentum of pure metal.

Valparaiso.—This is the greatest port and city of the whole South Pacific coast. It is situated in latitude 33° 2'. The port is a semicircular bay about two miles in breadth, and open to the westward. Shelter is secure except in the winter months.

The great depth of water near the shore has thus far prevented the establishment of wharves for loading and discharging cargoes, and these operations are safely accomplished by means of launches, to and from which all packages are carried through the surf on men's shoulders. The harbor is well defended by several forts.

The city stands upon a steep declivity and in the ravines along its bay to the northward. It is mostly constructed of adobe or sun-dried bricks. It is well paved, but has few remarkable edifices. There is an English church, where the Episcopal service is performed every Sabbath; also a free Protestant chapel has been permitted. The hotels are numerous, but indifferent. There are two clubs, conducted after the English fashion. There is also one large theatre. The city is lighted with gas, and is supplied with good water from basins built on the eminences back of the town, and conveyed throughout the city in iron pipes; both these improvements are due to Mr. William Wheelwright, an American gentleman, whose name is identified with almost every important internal improvement which has been established in Chili for the last twenty years. Valparaiso monopolizes most of the foreign trade of Chili. Its direct imports in 1850 were $11,110,844, against the entire imports of the republic for that year, amounting to $11,500,968, or over $\frac{23}{24}$ths of its entire importing trade. There is a magnetic telegraph line connecting Valparaiso with Santiago, the capital and seat of government of the republic, 100 miles in the interior. There is also a railway in process of construction from Valparaiso to Santiago. Forty miles of this road (with the exception of one tunnel) has been completed and opened for travel; the remainder has progressed but slowly of late, on account of the difficulties attending its construction and the disturbed political state of the country. It is now in the hands of the government, and they propose to complete the whole line in three years, but this is very doubtful. The population of Valparaiso is about 45,000.

Constitucion, at the mouth of the River Maule, is the outlet of a rich and productive agricultural district. Population of the city between 4000 and 5000.

Tomé, a small port, with a business similar to Constitucion.

Talcahuano possesses a fine harbor, and is the entrepôt for the trade of a large and fertile surrounding district. The town is well built and flourishing. Population 5000. Extensive coal deposits exist in the vicinity of Talcahuano. It is proposed to connect Talcahuano with Concepcion, a city of considerable importance about 12 miles in the interior. Its business will be in passengers and general merchandise.

Coronel and *Lota*.—At these ports extensive deposits of coal exist, and form a large item of export. At Lota is a coaling depôt for the steam-ships of the Pacific Steam Navigation Company.

Valdivia is a secure harbor, formed by the estuary at the mouth of the river of the same name. The export trade here is in the agricultural products of the rich surrounding country. Lumber is largely exported. The city of Valdivia is 8 miles from the mouth of the river, which is navigable for large vessels to this point, and navigable for boats for 12 leagues farther. A colony of Germans have settled in this vicinity.

Ancud and Albuco, ports of the island and province of Chiloe, and Puerto Montt—these three are all small ports of export for lumber and provisions.

The ships of the Pacific Steam Navigation Company touch at all the above-mentioned ports (see Itinerary, page 152, et seq.).

The imports of Chili consist chiefly of distilled spirits, ale and porter, alpaca goods, baizes, bedsteads, books, buttons, cabinet-ware, calicoes, candles, canvas, carpets, carriages, cassimeres, cigars, clothing, cotton and woolen goods, crape shawls, drugs, earthen and glass ware, gloves, gold in bars and coin, gunpowder, horned cattle and horses, household furniture, indigo, iron and iron goods, jewelry and cutlery, leather, linen goods, machinery, matches, maté, merino cloths, muslins, molasses, oils, paints, paper, perfumery, pianos, quicksilver, raisins, rice, rigging, salt, satin goods, shoes and boots, silks, silver coin and bars, soap, steel, straw goods, sugar, tea, tobacco, umbrellas and parasols, velvets, watches, wax, wines, and wool shawls. Among the countries furnishing these goods, England holds commercially the first rank, France the second, United States the third. Germany, Switzerland, Belgium, Spain, Central America, Peru, and Bolivia also export to Chili certain of their manufactures and productions. Previous to the establishment of the Panama Railway the European trade with Peru was all carried on around Cape Horn, but since the completion of that road in 1855 large amounts of the most valuable goods have been sent by the direct route to the port of Aspinwall, and across the Isthmus by the Panama Railway, and from thence, by the steamers of the Pacific Steam Navigation Company, to the ports of Peru. The transportation by this route to South America for European goods, as well as American, is steadily and rapidly increasing.

Tariff of Chili on Articles received from the United States.

Denomination of Merchandise.	Number, Weight, or Measure.	Rate of Duty.	Percentage, Duty on fixed Value.
Beef..........................	quintal (101 lbs.)	$7 00	free.
Beer, ale, porter, in bottles	dozen, specific duty,	1 00	
" " in casks..	gallon, "	0 25	
Brandy in bottles	dozen, "	3 00	
" in casks............	gallon, "	1 00	
Cables and cordage..........	valuation,		$0 25
Candles, wax................	1.014 lb.	$0 50	0 25
" tallow................	101 lbs.	16 00	0 25
" spermaceti..........	1.014 lb.	0 40	0 25
Cheese of all kinds	"	0 18¾	0 25
Cider in bottles	same as beer.		
" in casks................	"		
Codfish.......................	101 lbs.	6 00	0 25
Copper, manufactures of..	1.014 lb.	0 40	0 25
" in bars	101 lbs.	13 00	0 25
Cotton, raw	101 lbs., picked,	8 00	0 25
" manufactures of...	1 lb.	0 37½	0 25
Flour, wheat.................	quintal, if price is under $4,		0 25

Denomination of Merchandise.	Number, Weight, or Measure.	Rate of Duty.	Percentage, Duty on fixed Value.
Glass, window	100 superficial feet,	$3.00	$0 25
Hams and bacon	1.014 lb.	0 14	0 25
Hats, straw		valuation,	0 25
Household furniture		"	0 25
Indian corn	fanega, if price is under $3,		0 25
" "	" " over $3,		free.
Lard	1.014 lb.	$0 12½	0 25
Lead in bars and sheets			free.
" manufactures of	101 lbs.	6 00	
Nails, iron	1.014 lb.	8 to 12½c.	
Paints	101 lbs.	$6 00	0 25
Paper, writing		valuation,	0 25
" printing		"	0 25
Pitch	101 lbs.	$2 00	free.
Pork	"	8 00	"
Rice	Carolina, 101 lbs.	5 50	0 25
Rosin	101 lbs.	2 00	free.
Shoes, boots, and leather.	dozen, for men, calf-skin,	18 00	0 15
Soap, common	101 lbs.	6 00	0 25
" perfumed	1.014 lb.	0 40	0 25
Sugar, refined	arroba of 25 lbs. 7 oz.	2 00	0 25
Tallow	101 lbs. (raw)	7 00	0 06
Tar	"	2 00	free.
Teas	pound, specific duty,	0 25	
Tobacco, unmanufactured	monopoly.		
" cigars	per pound,	0 75	
Umbrellas, silk	each,	2 50	0 25
" cotton	dozen,	6 50	0 25
Wax, raw, white	101 lbs.	0 50	0 25
" yellow	"	0 50	0 25
Wines, red	gallon, specific duty,	0 25	
" white	" "	0 37½	
Wood, boards, pine	1000 feet,	35 00	free.

PORT CHARGES.

The port charges of Chili are as follows: Tonnage dues, 25 cents per ton; light dues (where light-houses exist), 3⅛ cents per ton; captain of the port's fees, $4; harbor-master's fees, $8. National or foreign vessels of war, national or foreign steamers, whale-ships, vessels in distress or in ballast, or discharging under twenty packages, are exempt from tonnage and light dues. When tonnage dues have been paid at one port, they are not levied in another.

MEXICO.

THE chief and almost the sole communication between the Pacific coast of this country and the Panama Railroad is by the vessels of the Pacific Mail Steam-ship Company and the steamers of Flint and Holliday's Oregon and California Line.* Occasional British men-of-war, however, bring shipments of silver from the Mexican Pacific coast to Panama for transportation over the railroad for English ports.

Acapulco, the first Mexican port of entry of the Pacific Mail Steam-ship Company's steamers on their upward voyage, is situated in latitude 16° 55' north, 1440 miles from Panama. Its harbor is one of the finest on the whole Pacific coast. The Pacific Mail Steam-ship Company have established an agency there, and a depôt for coals, from which their vessels are supplied on their upward and downward voyages; they also take in occasional supplies of fresh provisions at that port.

Although the State of Guerrero, in which the port of Acapulco is situated, is rich in mineral resources, possessing extensive deposits of silver, gold, and copper, and a soil and climate capable of raising the tropical staples in abundance, its commerce has for many years been very small. Its exports of silver for the year 1860, by the Pacific Mail Steam-ship Company's steamers, amounted to a little more than $200,000, chiefly the returns from foreign

* The offices of this Company are at No. 88 Wall Street, New York, and corner of Liedsdorf and Sacramento Streets, San Francisco.

goods for Acapulco and the interior. In 1856 the legal returns of specie exported from the port of Acapulco amounted only to $32,485. Recently, however, the government roads from Acapulco to the city of Mexico have been reopened, and regular weekly communication established with the city of Mexico, which has given a fresh impetus to trade at this port. Population of Acapulco about 4000.

About 325 miles to the northeast from Acapulco is the port of Manzanilla, situated in the State of Colima, and is the port of export and import for a wide extent of rich mining country in the interior. The city of Colima, the capital of the state, 28 leagues in the interior, is a flourishing city, containing about 32,000 inhabitants. The exportation of silver from Manzanilla previous to the year 1860, according to the custom-house records of that port, amounted to about $500,000 per annum; but recently, on account of the difficulty and danger attending transportation of goods and treasure to the Gulf ports, *via* the capital, from the adjoining states Jalisco and Michoacan, a large portion of their trade has been carried on through the port of Manzanilla, and the exports of silver have increased to over four millions of dollars for the year 1860, with a prospect of much greater increase for the present year, 1861. Silver, the chief export of the Pacific ports of Mexico, is the only export at Manzanilla; this is shipped on the vessels of the Pacific Mail Steam-ship Company, which touch there on their downward voyages, for Panama. From Panama it goes to Aspinwall by the Panama Railroad, and from thence to England by the British West India Mail Line.

The remaining Pacific ports of Mexico—San Blas, in the State of Jalisco, 228 miles northeast from Manzanilla; Mazatlan, in the State of Sinaloa, 140 miles northeast from San Blas; Guaymas, in the State of Sonora, 400 miles northeast of Mazatlan; and Cape St. Lucas, 220 miles southwest from Guaymas, and 1066 miles from San Francisco, are touched at by the steamers of the San Francisco and Oregon Line, and will connect with the Pacific Mail Company's steamers at Manzanilla. Correct commercial data of these ports are not at present attainable. The British government keeps constantly on the coast of Mexico a ship of war, which receives from mercantile houses at the various ports above mentioned (brought from the mining districts of the interior) silver in coin and bars, varying in amount from three to six millions of dollars per annum, which is taken to the port of Panama for transportation over the Panama Railroad to Aspinwall, and from thence to England by the ships of the British West India Mail Line. All this treasure is consigned to the Bank of England. So soon as the recently organized line from San Francisco to these Mexican ports shall have become thoroughly established, it is expected that a large portion, if not the entire amount, of this treasure will find its way to the port of Manzanilla for reshipment to Panama by the Pacific Mail Steam-ship Company's steamers.

The merchandise for the Pacific Mexican ports has, until very recently, reached them chiefly from England *via* Cape Horn; but large amounts of goods have, during the past year, been received at the port of Aspinwall by the Panama Railroad's line of sailing vessels from New York, and by Holt's propeller line from England, and transported over the road for shipment by the Pacific Mail Steam-ship Company's steamers, and this trade is rapidly increasing.

Through bills of lading are now issued at the office of the Panama Railroad Company in New York for goods from thence to the Mexican ports of Acapulco and Manzanilla at rates varying from $50 to $60 per ton of forty feet.

The Pacific Mail Steam-ship Company's steamers now stop at the port of Manzanilla monthly, on their upward and downward voyages, leaving New York and San Francisco on the 11th, and arriving at Manzanilla about the 28th of each month.

PASSENGER REGULATIONS AT THE MEXICAN PORTS.

"Every passenger arriving at the ports of the republic shall be free to land without passport or letter of security, and shall be at liberty to take ashore a small bundle of wearing apparel.

"Every passenger can enter free of duty ten pounds of cigars or cigarettes, one bottle of snuff, two bottles of wine or liqueur, two watches, with their chains and seals, one pair of pistols, one sword, one rifle, musket, or carbine, and a pair of musical instruments, except pianos or organs.

"Passengers are prohibited the introduction with their luggage of goods by the piece, jewelry, gold or silver wrought, unless of personal wear, or of any other commercial commodity specified in this ordinance; but should they, through ignorance or as presents, bring in small quantities of any of these articles, by making, before the commencement of the examination, a declaration on oath of the fact, the officer of the customs shall appraise the articles, and collect corresponding duties.

"The dispatch of private apparel and jewelry is at the discrimination of the custom-house officers, with due regard for the character and personality of travelers.

"Operatic or comic artists shall be permitted, besides the exemptions already conceded to passengers, to introduce free of duty their scenic costumes and ornaments, provided the same make a part of their luggage and be not excessive. Should the officers consider the amount in excess, they shall collect 30 per cent. ad valorem, or by appraisement, to be practiced in the manner prescribed for goods entered under appraisement. The supreme government will ordain what is convenient as regards the privileges and exemptions to be extended to emigrants or colonists."

MEXICO.

Currency of Mexico.

1 onza	gold	=$16 00
1 peso	silver	= 1 00
1 real	"	= 0 12½
1 medio real	"	= 0 06¼
1 quartillo	copper	= 0 03⅛
1 tlaco	"	= 0 01 $\frac{9}{16}$

Weights.

1 onza	=	1 ounce.
1 marco	=	½ lb.
1 libra	=	1 lb.
1 arroba	=	25 lbs.
1 quintal	=100 lbs.
1 carga	=300 lbs.
1 fanega	=	2 bushels.

Measures.

1 foot	=0.928 feet English.
1 vara	=2.784 "
1 legua=5000 varas	=2.636 miles.

CALIFORNIA, OREGON, VANCOUVER, WASHINGTON TERRITORY, ETC.

The port of San Francisco, California, the great commercial entrepôt of the United States possessions on the Pacific, is situated in the Bay of San Francisco, in latitude 37° 47′ 35″ north, and 122° 26′ 15″ west longitude. Its harbor is one of the best of the Pacific Ocean. Through the port of San Francisco nearly all the foreign trade of California, Oregon, Washington Territory, and the British possessions is carried on.

The city of San Francisco, situated on the eastern slope of the ridge which divides the Bay of San Francisco from the Pacific Ocean, is handsomely laid out and well built, containing many fine public edifices and private dwellings of brick and stone, and is the centre of the wealth and commerce of the Northern Pacific coast. Population 80,000.

The great mineral resources of the State of California, the fertility and productiveness of its soil, its varied and delightful climate, are so familiar to the world that it is not thought worth while to give in this place more than such a brief summary of its commercial transactions as will enable the reader to form an estimate of their influence upon the great channels of steam communication between the Pacific coast and the United States, the resources of which it is the particular object of this volume to set forth.

EXPORTS.*

The great staple product of California is gold; but the recent discoveries of vast deposits of silver on the eastern slope of the Sierra Nevada Mountains at Washoe it is thought will, in time, make the exports of this metal rival the gold in commercial importance.

Quicksilver is also largely exported.

Next in importance among the exportable commodities of the state are hides, wool, and grain. The entire product of hides and wool go to the New York market. The grain, consisting of wheat, barley, and oats, have for the last five years found a market in New York, the west coast of South America, the East Indies, China, Australia, and the Pacific Islands.

Wool is a large and growing article of export. The exports of this article in 1856 amounted to 600,000 pounds; in 1860 the amount was 2,981,000 pounds.

The exports of gold from the port of San Francisco since its discovery in 1848, according to Custom-house manifests, were as follows:

Year.	Shipments to all Quarters.	Shipments to New York.	Rec'ts at U. S. Mint and its Branches.	Estimated Yield of California Mines.
1848	....	....	....	$ 60,000
1849	$ 4,921,250	....	$ 5,232,249	8,000,000
1850	27,676,346	....	28,206,226	33,000,000
1851	45,582,695	....	57,138,980	55,000,000
1852	46,586,134	....	51,470,675	57,000,000
1853	57,331,024	$47,916,448	62,838,395	69,000,000
1854	51,328,653	46,289,649	46,719,083	64,000,000
1855	43,080,211	38,730,564	47,419,945	65,000,000
1856	48,887,543	39,765,294	56,379,901	70,000,000
1857	48,592,743	35,287,778	55,217,843	70,000,000
1858	47,548,025	35,578,236	51,494,311	70,000,000
1859	47,640,463	39,831,937	52,000,000	70,000,000
1860	42,325,916	35,661,500	27,037,919	70,000,000

* The commercial statistics of California are taken, by permission, from advance sheets of the Annual Report of the New York Chamber of Commerce for 1861. See Table of Contents, p. 264.

Statement of Amounts and Destination of Treasure exported from San Francisco during the Year 1860.

To New York.		Exported to	
In January	$3,360,296 25	New York	$35,661,500 37
" February	3,126,183 77	New Orleans	57,795 93
" March	2,177,395 67	England	2,672,936 20
" April	2,692,728 88	China	3,374,680 27
" May	2,905,028 40	Japan	94,200 00
" June	3,709,755 01	Manilla	75,659 94
" July	1,969,435 05	Panama	300,819 00
" August	2,502,070 47	Sandwich Islands	40,679 57
" September	3,157,303 59	Mexico	19,400 00
" October	2,958,784 19	Costa Rica	3,145 00
" November	2,982,704 78	Vancouver Island	25,100 00
" December	4,119,814 31	Total	$42,325,916 28
	$35,661,500 37		

Exports of Silver.—The exports of silver ore during the year 1860, according to the San Francisco Custom-house records, were of the value of $416,613. This is, however, no guide as to what the ores yielded. In addition to the ores exported, several hundred tons were smelted at two establishments in San Francisco, yielding about $150,000. When it is considered that the Washoe mining district was a howling wilderness at the commencement of 1860, and that every necessary of life, even the material for habitations, had to be transported across the Sierra Nevada on the backs of mules, it must be conceded that vast progress has been made in opening the mines, and, without doubt, their product this year (1861) will ascend to millions.

Exports of Quicksilver.

Years.	To New York. Flasks.	To other Countries. Flasks.	Years.	To New York. Flasks.	To other Countries. Flasks.
1853	......	18,800	1857	8,374	18,888
1854	......	20,963	1858	3,559	20,573
1855	......	27,165	1859	250	3,149
1856	1,500	22,240	1860	400	8,948
Total				14,083	140,726

From the above it appears that the total amount of quicksilver exported from the state during the past eight years was 154,809 flasks; there was consumed within the state, during the same period, 16,000 flasks, making a total production (almost entirely from the New Almaden mine) of 170,809 flasks of 75 pounds each. The price ranged from 1853 to 1860 from 75 to 50 cents per pound.

Table of Exports of leading Articles of California Produce to New York for the last five Years.

Articles.	1856.	1857.	1858.	1859.	1860.
Barley, 84-lb. sacks.......	....	97,675	51,103	97,947	16,510
Hides, number	132,032	170,447	142,399	151,364	200,116
Quicksilver, flasks	2,414	8,374	3,559	250	400
Skins, bales................	1,506	798	876	975	939
" number	9,313	26,363	3,812	....	2,874
Salmon, barrels............	256	212	906	250	1,112
Tallow, packages	3	826	194	888	518
Wool, lbs...................	600,000	1,100,000	1,428,351	2,378,250	2,981,000
Wheat, 100-lb. sacks	....	....	....	12,054	203,528

Exhibit of the Exports of a few leading Articles of California Produce to all Countries in 1860.

Barley, 84-lb. sacks	136,916	Oats, 55-lb. bags................	76,590
Beans, 50-lb. "	1,397	Potatoes, 110-lb. bags........	34,161
Flour, barrels....................	121,688	Skins, packages	580
Hides, number	200,116	Tallow, packages	2,181
Hay, bales........................	9,637	Wheat, 100-lb. sacks.........	1,135,098
Lumber, M. feet................	3,976	Wool, lbs.........................	3,060,000

The value of the exports of California, other than treasure, during the last five years, has been as follows:

1856..........................	$4,270,260		1859..........................	$5,533,411
1857..........................	4,369,758		1860..........................	8,532,489
1858..........................	4,770,163			

IMPORTS.

The following statement of the tonnage arriving at San Francisco from Atlantic ports, from 1856 to 1861, will show the extent of the imports from that quarter for a series of years. The statement exhibits, 1st, the number of vessels; 2d, the aggregate registered tonnage; 3d, estimated tons of cargo at sixty per cent. over register; 4th, total amount of freight moneys paid in each year:

Where from.	No. of Vessels.	Registered Tonnage.	Tons of Cargo.	Amount of Freight paid.
1856: New York	79	103,532	165,652	$2,167,045
Boston	37	42,200	64,320	924,957
Other ports	7	5,602	8,963	144,867
Total for 1856	123	151,334	238,935	$3,236,869
1857: New York	61	74,402	119,043	$1,309,244
Boston	28	33,802	54,083	469,798
Philadelphia	1	1,219	1,950	22,390
Total for 1857	90	109,423	175,076	$1,801,432
1858: New York	66	77,882	124,611	$1,503,955
Boston	34	32,166	51,370	607,329
Other ports	5	4,345	6,952	68,919
Total for 1858	105	114,393	182,933	$2,180,203
1859: New York	90	107,276	171,641	$2,107,924
Boston	43	44,799	71,678	892,704
Other ports	8	5,001	8,002	92,582
Total for 1859	141	157,076	251,321	$3,093,210
1860: New York	76	93,240	149,184	$1,777,802
Boston	30	30,661	49,057	624,396
Other ports	9	6,341	10,145	82,988
Total for 1860	115	130,242	208,386	$2,485,186

The bulk of the imports of California come from the United States in sailing vessels *via* Cape Horn, but large quantities of light goods and provisions are sent *via* the Isthmus of Panama. The total value of shipments per steamers, and *via* the Panama Railroad, in 1860, according to Custom-house records, was but little short of eight millions of dollars.

The following figures exhibit the passenger movement of the port of San Francisco since 1856:

Arrivals.	1857.	1858.	1859.	1860.
From Panama	17,637	....	26,907	20,092
" other countries	6,963	40,739	11,276	10,619
Total arrivals	24,600	40,739	38,183	30,711
Departures.				
For Panama	12,367	27,994	19,030	10,084
" other countries	4,584	....	5,751	4,492
Total departures	16,951	27,994	24,781	14,576

On the 5th of March, 1860, the rates of fare were reduced, and a tri-monthly communication *via* Panama was established, instead of the previous semi-monthly trips, which accounts for the great increase of the inward passenger traffic for the year 1860.

OREGON, WASHINGTON TERRITORY, VANCOUVER ISLAND, AND BRITISH COLUMBIA.

THE commerce of this region, which is almost entirely carried on through the port of San Francisco, California, is yet in its infancy. Oregon, with an area of about 80,000 square miles, and possessing on its Pacific coast broad and fertile valley-lands, rich in agricultural resources, has as yet but about 50,000 inhabitants; the tide of emigration from the Western United States is, however, going on with vigor, and the time is probably not far distant when its population will be sufficient to develop an important exporting trade. Already large quantities of grain, lumber, etc., are exported to California. Cattle, fresh and dried fruits, salmon, eggs, butter, lard, hams, etc., are also becoming noticeable articles of export. Deposits of coal, iron, copper, and gold have been found in Oregon. Washington Territory, joining Oregon on the north, has an area of 113,821 square miles. Its white population in 1854 was only about 5000. Since that time it has been slowly but steadily increasing. It possesses much land well adapted to agriculture and grazing. It abounds with fine timber, and its rivers with excellent fish, which at present form its chief exports. Joining it on the north, at the parallel of 49°, is British Columbia, covering an area of about 200,000 square miles. This is also a country of great agricultural promise, and possesses a vast wealth in its salmon fisheries, its forests of fine timber, and its rich deposits of coal and gold; the latter, mined from the vicinity of Frazer River, has been exported to a considerable extent since its discovery in 1856.

SEA-PORTS.

The sea-ports of Oregon, Washington Territory, and the British possessions which have direct communication with San Francisco by the California and Oregon Line of Steamships are as follows, viz.: in Oregon,

Eureka, the most southern port of entry in Oregon, distant 238 miles northeast from San Francisco, is situated in Humboldt Bay, a deep and narrow indentation of the coast, with a dangerous shifting sand-bar at its entrance. The town of Eureka is about four miles to the north side of the entrance of the bay. There is a United States government fortification here, and an Indian reservation in the vicinity. It is a thriving town, and has a large lumber-trade with San Francisco.

Trinidad, 28 miles north from Eureka, is situated in a small bay protected only from the northeast winds. The town contains but few inhabitants. The chief export is lumber. The land in this vicinity is rich, and well adapted to agriculture. There is gold in the neighborhood.

Crescent City, 43 miles northward from Trinidad, on Crescent City Bay, is one of the most dangerous roadsteads on the whole coast. The town of Crescent City is the depôt for the supplies of miners working the gold diggings on the Kalmath, Trinity, and Salmon Rivers, in the interior; it is also the centre of a large and rich agricultural district. It contains about 1500 inhabitants.

Port Orford, 70 miles from Crescent City, is a good roadstead. A large lumber-trade is carried on here. A much-esteemed variety of the white cedar abounds in this vicinity, and is exported in considerable quantities under the name of the Port Orford cedar.

Gardiner City, 75 miles to the northward from Port Orford, is on the Umpqua River, five miles from its mouth.

A United States custom-house is located here, besides which there is only a small wharf and one house. A steam-boat runs from Gardiner City to Scottsburg, a town of 1000 inhabitants, fifteen miles farther up the river.

Astoria, 83 miles from Gardiner City, is the most northern port of Oregon. It is situated on the Columbia River (which separates Oregon from Washington Territory), nine miles from its mouth. The river at Astoria is between three and four miles in width. Population of Astoria 800. There is a dangerous bar at the mouth of the Columbia River which interferes greatly with its commercial growth.

Portland, the chief sea-port and chief town of Oregon, is situated on the Willamette River, a branch of the Columbia, 100 miles from Astoria. Population 2700. It is the centre of a rich and well-cultivated agricultural region. Large numbers of cattle are exported from Portland to Vancouver's Island. About forty miles south of Portland, on the Willamette, is Salem, the capital of Oregon. Population 1500.

The next port of entry northward is *Esquimault,* on the British island of Vancouver, 270 miles from Portland. Here is said to be one of the finest harbors on the Pacific coast. The neighboring country is very fertile. The fisheries in this section are extensive. Lumber is of excellent quality and abundant. There is a British naval station at Esquimault, and it is the rendezvous for the small steamers running on Frazer River.

Port Townsend, 35 miles from Esquimault, the most southern port of entry in Washington Territory, is favorably situated at the termination of the Straits of Fuca, at the outlet of the waters of Admiralty Inlet, Puget's Sound. The town contains about 500 inhabitants. A military post has been established two and a half miles from this place. In the vicinity of the town are some good farms. The principal export is lumber.

Olympia, 80 miles from Port Townsend, is situated at the head of a deep inlet six miles long by three quarters of a mile wide. It is a thriving town, and the capital of Washington Territory. Its principal business is in agricultural products and lumber. The total distance made by the vessels of the California and Oregon Steam-ship Company on their route from San Francisco to Olympia, the northern terminus of the route, is 1022 miles.

For rates of freight, passage, etc., see Appendix D, page 148.

BUSINESS BY EXPRESS BETWEEN THE UNITED STATES, EUROPE, AND THE PACIFIC COASTS.

The "Express System," which had long been an indispensable necessity in the Atlantic United States, became, on the discovery of gold in California, an equally valuable medium of transportation between the Atlantic and Pacific coasts. Prompt, reliable, and responsible, the Express Company occupies the middle ground between the shipper and the Steam-ship and Railroad Companies. Issuing "through receipts," and giving its careful personal supervision to the business, insure to their customers the most speedy delivery of their consignments, and, in case of loss or damage, prompt and liberal adjustment.

The express of Wells, Fargo, and Company is now, and has for several years been engaged in the Atlantic and Pacific express business, making the transit across the Isthmus of Panama, *via* the Panama Railroad, and giving no inconsiderable contribution to its business. This Company forwards an express by each steamer (on the 1st, 11th, and 21st of the month), and provides on the Isthmus for the prompt transmission of their consignments so as to go forward by connecting steamers. The charges upon small packages vary according to size and value. Upon bullion and gold dust the freight and insurance from San Francisco to New York is at present three per cent. Upon merchandise they charge a small percentage advance upon steamer rates, for which they give to the shipper the convenience of collecting his property at his place of business, attending to the Custom-house requirements, prepaying freight, and delivering in good order at the door of the consignee at San Francisco.

A prominent feature in their express business is the "Collection and General Agency" department: collecting and paying over money, attending to the execution and delivery of valuable papers and documents, receiving and transmitting property subject to charges to be paid on arrival at destination, called in express vocabulary C. O. D. (collect on delivery), and, in fine, executing almost every conceivable commission.

The house of Wells, Fargo, and Company has been engaged in this business for the past eight years. They are a joint-stock association, organized under the laws of the State of New York, with a capital of $1,000,000, having their principal office in the city of New York. They have also the only express to ports on the North Pacific Coast, Oregon, Vancouver's Island, and British Columbia, and now contemplate establishing agencies on the South Pacific Coast.

They also have the sole express in the interior of California, transporting from the mines to San Francisco an average of $60,000,000 in value of gold dust and silver ore per annum. They have over 100 offices in California, and sell exchange upon all the principal cities and towns in the United States and Canada, and on the principal cities of Great Britain and the Continent. They also have an agency at Honolulu, Sandwich Islands.

This Company is the agent and general consignee at Aspinwall, New Granada, for all shipments for San Francisco, Vancouver, etc., by the Royal Mail Steam Packet Company, running steamers semi-monthly between Havre, and Southampton, and Aspinwall, *via* St. Thomas. They receive at that point all the goods and merchandise brought by that line from Europe and the West Indies destined for all points north of Panama on the Pacific Coast, and also for the Sandwich Islands. The present rates from Havre and Southampton to Aspinwall are £6 per ton, and 5 per cent. primage, and from Aspinwall to San Francisco $80 per ton and 5 per cent. primage. To Victoria and northern ports on the Pacific, $20 per ton extra.

The present rates by express from New York to Aspinwall are $1 per cubic foot; from New York to Panama, $1 50 per cubic foot; from New York to San Francisco, $5 per cubic foot, or 25 cents per pound; from San Francisco to Victoria and other northern ports, $20 to $30 per ton.

The above rates to San Francisco are for "fast freight," or that which goes through by connecting steamer. For "slow freight" from New York to San Francisco, and going forward from Panama by next succeeding steamer, $2 per cubic foot, or $12\frac{1}{2}$ cents per pound only is charged.

The principal offices and agencies of Wells, Fargo, and Company are, at New York, 84 Broadway; at Boston, 39 and 40 Court Square; at Philadelphia, corner of Fourth and Chestnut Streets; at Havre, France, Davidson and Co., Agents; at London, England, Eives and Macey, Agents; at Havana, Cuba, E. Ramirez and Co., Agents; at Aspinwall, New Granada, Panama Railroad Company, Agents; at Panama, N. G., Panama Railroad Company, Agents; at San Francisco, Cal., corner of California and Montgomery Streets, Louis M'Lane, Agent; and at Honolulu, Sandwich Islands, at which offices all information in detail will be cheerfully given.

The following are the Subjects contained in the Third Annual Report of the Chamber of Commerce of the State of New York for the Year 1860–1861.

Proceedings of the Chamber of Commerce for the Year 1860; List of Members of the Chamber of Commerce, December 31st, 1860; Officers of the Chamber of Commerce from its Organization, 1768 to 1860; List of Donations to the Library of the Chamber of Commerce for the Year 1860; Imports of the Port of New York and of the United States for the Year 1860; Foreign Exports of the Port of New York and of the United States for the Year 1860; Imports and Exports of each State from 1856 to 1860; Annual Report on the Coffee Trade of New York and of the United States; Annual Report on the Sugar Trade of New York and of the United States; Annual Report on the Molasses Trade of New York and of the United States; Annual Report on the Cotton Crop of the United States; Annual Report on Naval Stores; Annual Report on the New York Leather Market for 1860; Annual Report on the Imports of Hides at the Port of New York and of the United States for the Year 1860; Annual Report on the New York Boot and Shoe Market for 1860; Annual Report on the New York Hide Market for 1860; Annual Report on the Wine and Liquor Trade for 1860; Annual Report on the Hemp Market for 1860; Annual Report on the Tobacco Market for 1860; Annual Report on the Currant Trade for 1860; Annual Report on the California Trade for 1860; Annual Report on the Dry Goods Trade of New York for 1860; Report on the Foreign Dry Goods entered for Consumption at the Port of New York during the Years 1857, 1858, 1859, and 1860; Tabular Statement of Real and Personal Property in the City of New York, with the Population as per Census of 1860; Tabular Statement of the Population of the State of New York, and of each County, from the Year 1790 to 1860 inclusive; Report of the Superintendent of the United States Coast Survey on the Harbor of New York; Report of the Superintendent of the United States Coast Survey on the Harbors and Rivers of the United States; Tabular Statement of Ship-building and Tonnage of New York; Commercial Treaties with Foreign Nations of the Year 1860: I. Treaty with Japan; II. Convention with Paraguay; III. Treaty with Paraguay; the Tariff Act of the United States, approved February 28, 1861, with the comparative Rates of Duty according to the Tariffs of 1842, 1846, and 1857; Rates of Toll on the New York Canals, as revised 1861; Comparative Prices of leading Articles in the New York Market for each Year, 1849–1861; Tabular Statement of the Progress of Banking in the State of New York; Report on the Banks of the City of New York; List of Savings Banks of New York, and Amount of Deposits of each; Tabular Statement of the Immigration of the Port of New York; Annual Report on the Salt Trade of the United States for the Year 1860; Annual Report on Drugs for the Year 1860; Tabular Statement of the Railroads of New York; Tabular Statement of the Life Insurance Companies; Annual Statement of the Marine Insurance Companies of New York for the Year 1860; Annual Statement of the Fire Insurance Companies of New York for the Year 1860; Annual Report on Breadstuffs and Provisions — Exhibit of the aggregate Value of Breadstuffs exported to Foreign Countries from the United States for each year from 1828 to 1st July, 1860; also the export Value of Provisions for the same Period; Annual Report on the Rates of Freight for the Year 1860; Annual Report on the Tea Trade for the Year 1860; Operations of the New York Assay Office; Transactions of the New York Clearing-house; Review of the Year 1860; Alphabetical Index of Subjects.

Copies of this volume and of the two preceding volumes may be had of the Secretary of the Chamber of Commerce, 63 William Street, New York.

CARRINGTON & CO.,

78 BROADWAY,

Commissionaires, or General Purchasing Agents.

Personal Orders, small or large, and for articles of every description, promptly and carefully attended to.

Who wants any thing from New York?

THIS AGENCY

Enables Non-Residents to make purchases in this City without troubling busy friends or mere acquaintances.

IF YOU WANT

Books, Clothing, Instruments, Music, Tools, Weapons, Sporting Implements, Jewelry, Silver or Plated Ware, Fine Groceries, Furniture, in short, ANY article, large or small, singly or in quantity, for Ladies' or Gentlemen's use or wear, or FOR DEALERS' SUPPLIES, from a seal-ring to a steam-engine; a cameo or a cashmere; lace or leather,

SEND ON YOUR ORDERS.

We can fill them on BETTER TERMS than you could obtain if here, while our commission, even on large orders, is much less than the expense of visiting the city in person.

Orders should be remitted for, either direct, or through some city friend, to be paid when filled. Every order should be as clearly worded as possible.

☞ *Orders may be given in French, Spanish, or German.*

Commission Charge, Five per Cent.

JOHN W. CARRINGTON.
GORDON M. NEWTON.

Special Correspondents.

F. L. HANKS, Honolulu, S. I.	L. G. DUCKWORTH, Aspinwall, N. G.
T. J. DE SABLA, Panama.	FREEMAN & CO., San Francisco, Cal.
S. H. HILL, Columbus, Ga.	ROBT. STRUTHERS, Valparaiso.
E. RAMIREZ & CO., Havana.	F. W. RAMSDEN, St. Jago de Cuba.

References.

DAVID HOADLEY, President Panama R. R. Co., New York.	Rev. DAVID TRUMBULL, Valparaiso.
ALSOP & CO., Lima and Valparaiso.	Hon. W. GOODALE, Honolulu, S. I.
C. M'CLELLAN, Rio de Janeiro.	HURTADO & HERMANOS, Panama.
E. ESCOBAR (Ossa & E.), Copiapo.	J. L. BRAVO, Panama.
J. P. ESCOBAR (Ruden & Co., Paita.	A. B. CORWINE, U. S. Consul, Panama.
	D. A. ROBINSON, Jr., U. S. Consul, Aspinwall.

THE NEW AMERICAN CYCLOPÆDIA.

A Popular Dictionary of General Knowledge.

EDITED BY
GEO. RIPLEY and C. A. DANA,

ASSISTED BY A NUMEROUS BUT SELECT CORPS OF WRITERS.

The design of THE NEW AMERICAN CYCLOPÆDIA is to furnish the great body of intelligent readers in this country with a popular Dictionary of General Knowledge.

THE NEW AMERICAN CYCLOPÆDIA is not founded on any European model; in its plan and elaboration it is strictly original, and strictly American. Many of the writers employed on the work have enriched it with their personal researches, observations and discoveries; and every article has been written, or re-written, expressly for its pages.

It is intended that the work shall bear such a character of practical utility as to make it indispensable to every American library.

Throughout its successive volumes THE NEW AMERICAN CYCLOPÆDIA will present a fund of accurate and copious information on SCIENCE, ART, AGRICULTURE, COMMERCE, MANUFACTURES, LAW, MEDICINE, LITERATURE, PHILOSOPHY, MATHEMATICS, ASTRONOMY, HISTORY, BIOGRAPHY, GEOGRAPHY, RELIGION, POLITICS, TRAVELS, CHEMISTRY, MECHANICS, INVENTIONS, and TRADES.

Abstaining from all doctrinal discussions, from all sectional and sectarian arguments, it will maintain the position of absolute impartiality on the great controverted questions which have divided opinions in every age.

PRICE.

This work is published exclusively by subscription, to be completed in sixteen large octavo volumes, each containing 750 two-column pages. Vols. I. to XII. are now ready. Price per volume, cloth, $3; library style, leather, $3 50; half morocco, $4; half Russia, extra, $4 50.

HOW TO OBTAIN THE CYCLOPÆDIA.

1. By applying to the nearest regularly-constituted agent in a city or town.
2. By remitting to the publishers the amount for one volume or more. Immediately upon receipt of the money, the book will be sent by mail, *postage paid* in strong wrappers, to any address, within 3,000 miles, in the United States.

IMPORTANT NOTICE.

Any one procuring four subscribers to the Cyclopædia, and sending the amount, $3 per volume, to the publishers, will be entitled to a copy of the work *gratis*, to be sent at the remitter's expense for carriage, or if ten subscribers are obtained, eleven copies will be sent at our expense, for carriage.

₊ Agents wanted in almost all sections of the United States. Liberal terms and exclusive territory given.

Works on Drawing.

Coe's New Drawing-Cards.

DESIGNED FOR CHILDREN. ACCOMPANIED WITH FULL INSTRUCTION.

In Ten Parts, each 25 cents.

Coe and Shell's Elementary Drawing-Cards.

CONTAINING STUDIES FROM OBJECTS, AND INSTRUCTIONS FOR DRAWING THEM IN PERSPECTIVE.

In Three Parts, each 19 cents.

Otis' Easy Lessons in Landscape Drawing.

In 6 Parts. Parts I., II., and III., each 25 cents; IV., V., and VI., 37 cents.

THE SIX PARTS, BOUND IN ONE VOLUME, $2 25.

These books are executed in a most beautiful and pleasing manner. The author has presented a series of lessons which will guide the learner in an easy, systematic, and intelligent manner, from simple lines through the intricacies of foliage, light, shade, and perspective, to the lessons which nature presents to her loving students. The peculiarities of different kinds of foliage, and the most approved methods of presenting them, are fully dwelt upon.

The subject of Perspective, together with its practical appplication, is treated in a manner which cannot fail of being comprehended by all who will give them a proper degree of attention. The size of each book being about that of an ordinary sheet of foolscap paper, the author has been able to exhibit the peculiarities of every surface represented, enabling the pupil to see the effect, and the method by which that effect is produced.

Otis' Drawing-Books of Animals.

In 5 Parts. I. and II., each 25 cents; III., 38 cents; IV. and V., 50 cents.

THE FIVE PARTS, BOUND IN ONE VOLUME, $2 25.

These books are of the same size as the "Landscape Drawing," and as beautifully executed. They are designed to present to the learner the easiest and most instructive progression, from the simple to the more difficult exercises.

HARPER'S WEEKLY.

Terms $2 50 a year.

It has been the aim of the Proprietors to render HARPER'S WEEKLY, before any thing else, A FIRST-CLASS NEWSPAPER — a Pictorial History of Current Events, equal to the daily press in fullness of description, and superior to the daily press as combining illustrations with text. How far they have attained their aim the Volumes now published will show. The arrangements for the present year are more complete than they have been heretofore. HARPER'S WEEKLY has regular artist-correspondents in almost every quarter of the globe, and is sure of promptly obtaining sketches of every leading event in which our countrymen are concerned. It commands the pencil of the first artists at home, and can render its readers eye-witnesses of striking scenes wherever they occur. In a word, the Subscriber to HARPER'S WEEKLY may rely on finding in its pages this year an accurate, well-drawn, well-engraved, and well-printed picture of every memorable event which occurs, and a portrait of every man who attracts the general attention of the people of this country.

HARPER'S MAGAZINE.

Terms $3 00 a year.

THE Publishers have endeavored, by a well-directed use of the abundant resources at their command, to render it not only the cheapest, but the most attractive and most useful Magazine for popular reading in the world; and the extent to which their efforts have been successful is indicated by the fact that it has attained a greater circulation than any similar periodical ever issued.

Special efforts will be made to render it still more interesting and valuable during the present year. The New Volume commenced with the Number for JUNE. No labor or expense will be spared to render it in every way, and in all its departments, still more worthy of the unparalleled favor with which it has been received.

HARPER'S NEW MONTHLY MAGAZINE owes its success to the fact that *it presents* MORE *reading matter, of a* BETTER *quality, in a* MORE ELEGANT *style, and at a* CHEAPER *rate, than any other publication.*

Published by HARPER & BROTHERS,
Franklin Square, New York.

www.ingramcontent.com/pod-product-compliance
Lightning Source LLC
Chambersburg PA
CBHW032007230426
43672CB00010B/2281